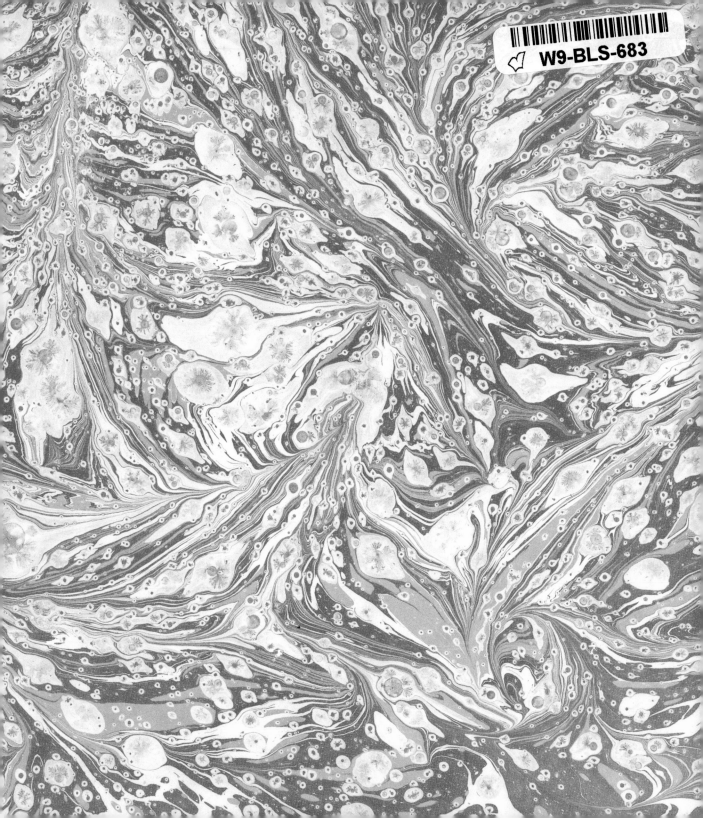

For GOODNESS TASTE

THE JUNIOR LEAGUE OF ROCHESTER

*Bring out the best in food and
the best in you…*

For
GOODNESS
TASTE

*In the tradition of our original
bestselling cookbook Applehood & Motherpie*

JUNIOR LEAGUE OF ROCHESTER
PUBLICATIONS, INC.

The Junior League of Rochester reaches out to women of all races, religions and national origins, who demonstrate an interest in and commitment to voluntarism. Since 1929, the League has been committed to improving the Rochester community through effective volunteer efforts. They have provided the womanpower and financial aid to programs which address child welfare, substance abuse, women's issues, aging, voluntarism and community development.

Proceeds from the sale of FOR GOODNESS TASTE will be returned to the community through the League's support of these and other volunteer projects.

Additional copies of FOR GOODNESS TASTE may be obtained by writing:

FOR GOODNESS TASTE
Junior League of Rochester Publications, Inc.
110 Linden Oaks, Suite A
Rochester, NY 14625
(716) 385-8590

Suggested retail price $18.95. Please include $3.50 postage and handling charge. New York residents add sales tax.

Copies of our original best seller, APPLEHOOD AND MOTHERPIE, may also be obtained at the above address.

Suggested retail price for APPLEHOOD AND MOTHERPIE is $16.95. Please include $3.50 postage and handling charge. New York residents add sales tax.

Adele Kent, The Marble Room, Cover Border
Tucker Printers, Inc.
Mary Mullard Young, Illustrator

First Printing: 25,000 copies, September 1991
Second Printing: 30,000 copies, March 1992

ISBN 0-9605612-1-8
Library of Congress Card Catalogue 91-61726

FOR GOODNESS TASTE IS THE RESULT OF OVER THREE YEARS
DEDICATION OF THE FOLLOWING COMMITTEE MEMBERS AND THEIR FAMILIES:

Linda Dehler Burns
Chairperson

Peggi Martin Godwin
Sustaining Advisor

Deborah Wanzer Eisenberg
Recipes

Kirsten Olson Koenig
Public Relations

Diane Love Okel
Editor

Dorothy Ostrander Johnson
Distribution

Marilyn Echter Lewis
Chairperson

Margaret M. Futran
Secretary

Amanda Acker Rice
Elizabeth Brisbin Mullard
Marketing

Cheryl Leisner
Computer

Mary Kay Roth Mullin
Design

THE FOR GOODNESS TASTE COMMITTEE WISHES TO
ACKNOWLEDGE THE EFFORTS AND SUPPORT OF THE COMMITTEE MEMBERS AND STAFF:

Judy Ackerman
Jaime Porter Armstrong
Suzanne Barbee
Ann Beckerman
Carolyn Brigham
Debbie Cain
Chris Culp
Elaine R. Davin
Elizabeth DeBruyne
Jane Fassett
Barbara Fulford
Lindsay Garrett
Julia Garver
Becky Gilbert
Kam Glassburn
Marian Gutowski

Denise Hadley
Cindy Harper
Sue Henderson
Mary Anne Hoppe
Katherine Horoschak
Deena Banks Hucko
J.L.R. Publications Committee
Sandy Johnson
Abigail Kennedy
Jody Lehr
Amy Flatley Levine
Barbara Lipari
Karen Mack
Mary Elizabeth A. McCahill
Carroll Meyers
Gail Miller

Sue O'Toole
Diane Smith Scheible
Susan Schwind
Lucia Shaw
Kathy Shea
Mary Lisa Sisson
Alice Smith
Lisa Strasenburgh
Patricia Taylor
Sally Thomas
Melissa Thompson
Sherry Timms
Sharon Walker
Catherine Ward
Elizabeth White
Barb Whitney

TABLE OF CONTENTS

Introduction / 7

Menus / 8

Appetizers and Beverages / 19

Soups / 53

Salads / 69

Bread and Breakfast / 97
Bread, Muffins, Eggs, Cheese and Pancakes

Pasta Plus / 129
Pasta, Pizza and Enchiladas

Vegetables and Accompaniments / 145
Vegetables, Rice and Potatoes

Meats / 177
Beef, Pork, Veal and Lamb

Poultry / 209

Fish and Seafood / 229

Desserts / 247
Cakes, Pies, Cookies and Candy

Appendix / 319

Acknowledgements / 322

Index / 325

INTRODUCTION

For Goodness Taste is a unique collection of exciting recipes that reflect the rich flavor and cultural diversity of upstate New York life-styles, traditions, and geographic regions.

For Goodness Taste brings you more than 400 delicious recipes, with a tempting selection of ingredients ranging from garden fresh to processed fresh, accommodating today's contemporary trends and fast-paced schedules.

These wonderfully easy-to-prepare recipes are fresh and surprising, yet reliable and uncomplicated, following the tradition of our original best seller, **Applehood & Motherpie**.

For Goodness Taste offers many opportunities to experience the joy of your own special gatherings. Creative menus have been planned for a variety of occasions, ranging from intimate dinners for two—to tea parties for twenty-two. To help you set the stage, each menu is followed by ideas for those extra-special touches that will transform the event into a joyous occasion.

Throughout our cookbook, you'll find wonderful suggestions for serving many of the recipes. **For Goodness Taste** also provides recommendations for a number of delicious but reasonably-priced wines to enhance your meals. These are wines that are widely distributed throughout the country. This valuable resource is provided separately in the Appendix.

So, whether you're a down-home, cost-conscious cook or a flamboyant gourmet chef, **bring out the best in food, and the best in you...**

For Goodness Taste!

Special Note:

> If you are among the cooks who are concerned about bacterial problems with uncooked egg yolks and/or egg whites, particular recipes should be avoided or modified. Eaters at special risk may be infants, pregnant women, the elderly and anyone with an impaired immune system.

MENUS

AULD LANG SYNE

Create a dramatic New Year's buffet! Cover the buffet table with black-and-white sheets tied up at the corners with black and white gingham ribbon. For the centerpiece, fill a large white birdcage with curled metallic ribbon and black and white balloons. Sprinkle the table and the birdcage with colorful confetti and arrange noisemakers and party hats around the table.

Shape the *Marinated Broccoli* into a wreath on a round silver tray and dot with cherry tomatoes. Place the *Glazed Kielbasa* in a decorative chafing dish. Decorate the *Brie En Croute* using frosted red grapes. Serve the *Fancy Fudge* on a raised compote dish and other sweets on silver trays with doilies. Wrap things up by tying a wide satin ribbon around the *Tally Ho Trifle* bowl.

To keep up with all guest activity, hire two or three high school students to pass trays and pick up glasses, plates and napkins.

What a wonderful way to welcome your guests, and the New Year!

Male Chauvinist Punch

Wine Suggestion: Champagne

Herbed Brie En Croute

Hot Florentine Dip

Marinated Broccoli with Lime Dip

French Coconut-Battered Shrimp

Smoked Oyster Spread

Glazed Kielbasa

Polynesian Crabmeat Bites

Bacon-Cheese Toasties

Chicken Nips

Chilled Tenderloin with Blue Ribbon Marinade

Tally Ho Trifle

Catch-A-Husband Squares

Holiday Jewels

Fancy Fudge

TEA FOR TWENTY-TWO

A LILAC TIME MOTHER-AND-DAUGHTER TEA PARTY

Lemon Tea Punch

Raisin Scones

Strawberry Créme with Fresh Fruits

Pizza Primavera

White Satin

Butterhorns

Chinese Sweet Sesames

Pucker-Up Lemon Kisses

Chocolate Intrigues

Old-Fashioned Currant Tarts

Gateau Au Chocolat

Celebrate lilac time, the coming of spring and the shared bond between mothers and daughters. Both generations will enjoy the graceful and timeless tradition of afternoon tea. A delicate lace tablecloth will set off a cherished silver tea service, crystal punch bowl and assortment of china teacups. Arrange a generous and fragrant bouquet of lilacs in a large china, porcelain or pewter bowl. Use silver tongs for sugar cubes and candied violets for garnish. Enhance your cookies and other sweets by placing them on tiered silver dishes or crystal serving pieces. For that extra-special touch, use calligraphy to write out your tea menu, and place it in a silver frame for the tea table.

As the afternoon shadows lengthen and another pot of tea is steeping, your tea party will leave everyone feeling warm and lovely.

MEXICAN HAT DANCE

Use a brightly colored serape for a tablecloth, set off by a large sombrero centerpiece filled with calla lilies. Round up some small cacti, votive candles in small green candle holders and colorful piñatas to enhance this Mexican motif. Serve the *Chalupa* in a large hollowed-out red cabbage and the *Mandarin Romaine* in a colorful Mexican pottery bowl. Brightly colored napkins, terra cotta serving pieces and Fiesta Ware dishes would be convincing final touches for this south-of-the-border feast. Ole!

Lemon Sangria

Chalupa

Tortilla Tucks with Firecracker Salsa

Fiesta Corn Flan

Mandarin Romaine

Limelight Pie

BABY, IT'S COLD OUTSIDE

Elegant Artichoke Canapés

Hail, Caesar!

Wine Suggestions: California Chardonnay
Australia Chardonnay
White Burgundy

Kennebunkport Lobster

Elegant Wild Rice

Wine Suggestions: Sauvignon Blanc
White Bordeaux

Mocha Cloud

Truffles for Your Valentine

Wine Suggestions: Asti
Dry Sherry

Dinner in front of a glowing fireplace is a must, even if you have to rearrange the furniture to create a romantic setting. Pull comfortable chairs with soft pillows up to the table. Lay a white lace tablecloth over red satin and arrange velvety red roses in a vase for the centerpiece. Take advantage of the romantic effect of candlelight everywhere. And as a fait accompli, play Mozart!

Use a heart-shaped cookie cutter when making the *Elegant Artichoke Canapés*. In fact, use heart-shaped bowls and trays for all your serving pieces. Create your *Hail, Caesar!* right at the table and serve the *Kennebunkport Lobster* in scallop shells. End your romantic dinner by offering *Truffles for Your Valentine* in a small, delicately decorated box.

Your Valentine is sure to be smitten, again!

HOME, HOME ON THE RANGE

Here's a picnic that will remind everyone of "down home cookin." The table could be set with a red-and-white checked tablecloth, bandana napkins and a cowboy hat filled with Queen Anne's lace, zinnias, dill flowers and black-eyed susans. Use baskets lined with plaid tea towels and crocks for serving pieces. Fresh garden vegetables will make this a real outdoor meal. In fact, why not have it outdoors for a "lazy-days-of-summer" feel! Then invite your guests to go western by wearing blue jeans and cowboy boots!

Bourbon Slush

Rochester Wings

Gone-in-a-Flash Taco Dip

Back Country Cookout
(Kielbasa, Shrimp, Corn & Zucchini Brewed in Beer)

Wine Suggestion: Riesling

Sweet and Sour Beans

Crunchy Cracked Wheat Bread

Carolina Cole Slaw

Fresh Apple Cake with Caramel Glaze

P.B.O. Collosals

NIGHTS IN WHITE SATIN

Snowlight Egg Nog or Berry Wassail

Elegant Caviar Pie

Shrimp in Dill Cream

Wine Suggestions: Champagne
Muscadet
Chardonnay

Stuffed Tenderloin of Beef with Bordelaise Sauce

Carmelized Carrots with Grand Marnier

Calico Peas

Wine Suggestions: Pinot Noir
Beaujolais
Red Burgundy

Eastman House Rolls

Chocolate Raspberry Torte

Wine Suggestions: Champagne
Chambord

Send out formal invitations suggesting black tie for the gentlemen and white for the ladies. The evening of the party, line your entrance walk with luminarias to welcome your guests from a frosty night. Your tablecloth might be antique lace over white satin with sparkling white china and shiny crystal. White candles in a silver candelabra and a large bouquet of white roses in a silver bowl are exquisite touches. Decorate your *Elegant Caviar Pie* by shaping black caviar into a tree shape, dotted with red caviar ornaments. Serve the *Shrimp in Dill Cream* as the first course before delighting your guests with the remainder of this exquisite meal. For your finalé, serve a pot of freshly brewed gourmet coffee.

AUTUMN LEAVES

Cranberry Bow Daiquiri

Hazelnut Mushroom Bisque

Florentine Roll with Shrimp Sauce

Wine Suggestions: Chardonnay
White Burgundy

Raspberry Endive Salad

Lemon Bubble Bread

Lemon Charlotte

When the children are back in school and you are settled into your fall routine, invite some friends over for a relaxing fall luncheon. Set your table by starting with a salmon-colored tablecloth and natural woven placements to enhance the rich fall colors of this autumn luncheon. For a centerpiece, hollow-out a pumpkin or squash to hold an arrangement of silver pennies, bittersweet and leafy autumn-colored branches. Lay a few bright orange, red and yellow leaves on the table as well. Use clear glass serving pieces to show off the beautiful ruby color of the *Cranberry Bow Daiquiri*, the rich texture of the *Hazelnut Mushroom Bisque* and the pearly coral color of the *Shrimp Sauce* on the dark green *Florentine Roll*.

Place a small bouquet garni at each place setting. This useful favor will stimulate conversation and put everyone in the mood for cooking autumn soups and stews.

RAINY DAYS AND SUNDAYS

A TWO-FAMILY SUPPER

Addicting Munchies

Pop-A-Cheese Stacks

Ol' South Gumbo

Wine Suggestions: Alsace Riesling
Alsace Gewürztraminer

Bella's Special Chicken

Superlative Spinach Salad

Graham Glories

Babe Ruth Bars

Invite another family over for Sunday night supper. Set your kitchen table with a colorful quilt. Use your favorite tureen, stoneware soup bowls and wooden serving pieces for salad and dessert. The delicious aroma of *Ol' South Gumbo* will welcome your guests and comfort their tummies on a chilly Sunday night. Serving this with a crusty French bread completes the meal. The choice of two entrees will suit even the youngest guest.

Fill brown paper bags with *Addicting Munchies* for the children to eat, while the adults enjoy their zesty appetizers from a large wooden bowl.

Plan some after-dinner games that include everyone and make this two-family gathering a complete success.

TIPTOE THROUGH THE TULIPS

Forget breakfast in bed! Here's a meal that any mother would love, and the guests will too. For a lovely setting, use a soft, flowered chintz or a light fluff of pastel chiffon to adorn the buffet table. A white wicker basket filled with tulips, daffodils, hyacinths and crocuses will make a centerpiece worthy of this delicious brunch.

Another symbol of spring is pastel-dyed eggs. Place them in a wire basket on the buffet or dining table. Wrap each guest's silverware in a pastel napkin and tie with a contrasting satin ribbon. Use white wicker baskets of varying shapes to display muffins and rolls. Complete this feminine, spring-like setting by serving this special luncheon on old-fashioned, light-colored glassware or delicate china. Mom will love it!

A MOTHER'S DAY BRUNCH

Apricot Daiquiri Blush or Tex's Bloody Mary

Morning Glory Salad

Skewered Fruit with Fantastic Fruit Dip

French Pockets

Ham Strudel

Breakfast Extraordinaire

An Excuse to Eat Carrot Cake for Breakfast

Cinnamon Apple Treasures

Strawberry Ginger Bliss

APPETIZERS & BEVERAGES

Appetizers & Beverages / Index

Cold Appetizers

Addicting Munchies / 30
Crispy Broccoli with Zesty Lime Dip / 29
Les Petits Choux / 29
Pizza Primavera / 31
Tortilla Tucks / 30

Dips and Spreads

Caviar Pâté / 24
Cheese Royale / 23
Creamy Bacon Combo / 25
Devilicious Cheese / 24
Elegant Caviar Pie / 22
Firecracker Salsa / 27
Gone-in-a-Flash Taco Dip / 26
Hot Fiesta Dip / 26
Hot Florentine Dip / 21
Irresistible Pisa Dip / 25
Party Poulet / 21
Pesto Cheesecake / 22
Sloppy Joe Dip / 27
Velvet Fruit Dip / 28
White Satin / 28

Hot Appetizers

Artichokes Dijon / 32
Bacon-Cheese Toasties / 33
Chalupa / 34
Chicken Nips / 35
Elegant Artichoke Canapés / 33
The Emperor's Wontons / 36
Glazed Kielbasa / 38
Herbed Brie en Croûte / 34
Nachos Supreme / 36

Pop-A-Cheese Stack / 32
Pot Stickers / 37
Rochester Wings / 39
Windemere Mushrooms / 38

Seafood

Apres-Ski Shrimp / 43
Clams Rock / 41
For Sardine Lovers Only / 45
French Coconut-Battered Shrimp / 42
Naples Mussels / 44
Polynesian Crabmeat Bites / 39
Scallops Jezebel / 40
Shrimp in Dill Cream / 40
Shrimp Orleans / 41
Smoked Oyster Spread / 45
Spicy Baked Shrimp / 42

Beverages

Apricot Daiquiri Blush / 47
Berry Wassail / 52
Bourbon Slush / 49
Bristol Mulled Wine / 52
Cranberry Bow Daiquiri / 48
Lemon Sangria / 46
Lemon Tea Punch / 47
Male Chauvinist Punch / 50
Open House Golden Punch / 49
Park Avenue Punch / 48
Second Helping Tea / 51
Snowlight Eggnog* / 50
Sun-sational Slush / 51
Tex's Bloody Mary Mix / 46

Hot Florentine Dip

A DELIGHTFUL SPINACH DIP PREPARED EASILY IN THE MICROWAVE!

- Microwave cream cheese in 1 quart casserole on High 30 to 60 seconds to soften.
- Add milk, onions and seasoning; mix well.
- Place frozen spinach package on plate and microwave on High 5 to 6 minutes or until defrosted and partially cooked. Drain well; squeeze dry.
- Stir ham and spinach into cheese mixture.
- Microwave on High 4 minutes, stirring after 2 minutes.
- Fold in sour cream and pecans. Microwave on Medium High 2 to 4 minutes, or until hot.
- Serve with crackers or firm chips.

3 cups

INGREDIENTS

1 package (8 ounces) cream cheese

2 tablespoons milk

2 tablespoons finely chopped green onion

½ teaspoon garlic powder

¼ teaspoon salt

¼ teaspoon pepper

1 package (10 ounces) frozen chopped spinach

1 can (6¾ ounces) chunk ham, drained

1 cup sour cream

¾ cup chopped pecans

Party Poulet

- Beat together cream cheese, steak sauce, curry powder and garlic.
- Blend in chicken, celery and 2 tablespoons parsley. Shape mixture into 9 inch log (or mold in bowl).
- Wrap in plastic wrap; chill 4 hours or overnight.
- Toss together remaining parsley and nuts; coat log or bowl.
- Serve with crackers.

3 cups

Hint: For stunning presentation, add various crudites (cherry tomatoes, cauliflower, colorful peppers) to this party platter.

INGREDIENTS

2 packages (8 ounces each) cream cheese, softened

1 tablespoon bottled steak sauce

½ teaspoon curry powder

1-2 garlic cloves, minced

1½ cups cooked chicken, finely chopped

⅓ cup chopped celery

¼ cup minced fresh parsley, divided

¼ cup toasted, chopped almonds, pecans, or walnuts

Party crackers

ELEGANT CAVIAR PIE

INGREDIENTS

6 hard-cooked eggs, finely chopped

2 green onions, finely chopped

1 teaspoon curry powder

1 teaspoon dry mustard

⅛ teaspoon onion salt

White pepper to taste

½ cup mayonnaise, divided

8 ounces whipped cream cheese

2 teaspoons snipped fresh chives

2 to 3 ounces red or black caviar

Parsley

Melba toasts

CAVIAR GILDS A FLAVORFUL CURRIED EGG SALAD BASE, ADDING AFFORDABLE ELEGANCE — WITHOUT EXCESSIVE EXTRAVAGANCE — TO THIS PARTY FAVORITE

- Combine eggs, onions, curry, mustard, onion salt and pepper. Add enough mayonnaise to form a spreadable consistency.
- Spread egg salad into a circle in a shallow dish.
- In a small bowl, combine cream cheese, 2 tablespoons mayonnaise and chives. Spread over egg salad.
- Before serving, gently rinse caviar; drain thoroughly. Sprinkle caviar over topping. Garnish with parsley sprigs. Serve with melba toasts.

10 to 12 servings

PESTO CHEESECAKE

PESTO

3 cups fresh basil leaves, washed and dried

6 large cloves garlic, peeled and chopped

1 cup pine nuts or walnuts

1 cup extra virgin olive oil

1 cup freshly grated Parmesan cheese

- Combine basil, garlic and nuts in food processor or blender. Chop roughly. (If using blender, divide into two batches).
- While chopping, add olive oil in a steady stream. Add cheese and blend.

- Combine breadcrumbs, Parmesan cheese and margarine. Toss to blend; press into bottom of 9-inch springform pan. Bake 5 to 10 minutes.
- Beat cream cheese until smooth. Beat in eggs, cream and 2 cups of pesto. Pour into pan and bake for one hour or until set. Chill.
- Before serving, run a knife around edge of pan; remove sides of pan. Garnish with sun-dried tomatoes. Serve with crackers or thin slices of french bread.

Note: The pesto freezes well.

Temperature: 325°

Time: 5 to 10 minutes
        1 hour

15 to 30 servings

CHEESECAKE

1 cup breadcrumbs made from toast (approximately 6 slices)

½ cup grated Parmesan cheese

½ cup margarine, melted

4 packages (8 ounces each) cream cheese

4 eggs

½ cup heavy cream

Oil-packed sun-dried tomatoes, drained and chopped

Crackers or French bread

CHEESE ROYALE

- Combine cheeses, bacon, sherry and chives; form into a ball.
- Mix together pecans, parsley, and paprika. Roll ball in mixture until completely covered.
- Chill. Serve with crackers.

10 servings

INGREDIENTS

1 package (8 ounces) cream cheese, softened

1 container (4 ounces) Old English Cheese spread

4 slices of bacon, cooked and crumbled.

1 ounce sweet sherry

¼ cup chopped chives

¾ cup chopped pecans

½ cup minced fresh parsley

¾ teaspoon paprika

Crackers

INGREDIENTS

3 hard-cooked eggs, halved

¾ cup sour cream

¼ cup chopped onion

3 tablespoons mayonnaise

2 tablespoons lemon juice

½ teaspoon salt

½ teaspoon Worcestershire sauce

¼ teaspoon white pepper

2 to 3 drops hot pepper sauce

1½ teaspoons unflavored gelatin

2 tablespoons cold water

3 ounces salmon caviar

½ cup minced fresh parsley

1 tablespoon snipped fresh dill

Additional caviar

Thinly sliced pumpernickel

CAVIAR PÂTÉ

<small>A LOVELY PRESENTATION, ESPECIALLY FOR THE HOLIDAYS</small>

- Mix first 9 ingredients in food processor until well blended. Refrigerate.

- Sprinkle gelatin over cold water in a small bowl. Set in pan of simmering water; stir until dissolved.

- Add gelatin to sour cream mixture; stir. Fold in caviar, parsley and dill.

- Pack into 2-cup loaf pan or decorative mold. Cover and refrigerate at least 3 hours.

- Remove from mold; garnish with additional caviar. Serve with pumpernickel.

8 servings

Hint: This recipe can be prepared 2 days in advance.

INGREDIENTS

4 ounces cheddar cheese, shredded

1 package (8 ounces) cream cheese, softened

1 can (4¼ ounces) deviled ham

3 green onions, thinly sliced

1 can (4 ounces) green chiles

⅛ teaspoon garlic powder

Finely chopped almonds

DEVILICIOUS CHEESE

- In medium bowl, mix together all ingredients except almonds.

- Shape into disk or ball; roll in nuts. May be chilled if too soft to handle.

- Chill. Leave at room temperature briefly to soften before serving with crackers.

12 servings

CREAMY BACON COMBO

INGREDIENTS

- Mix together all ingredients except crackers in a large ovenproof bowl.
- Bake for 45 minutes. Keep warm in a chafing dish or crockpot on low. Serve with crackers.

Note: The dip may ooze oil if the heat of the chafing dish or crockpot is too high. Remedy by reducing heat, blotting off oil and stirring.

Temperature: 350°

Time: 45 minutes

15 servings

1 pound cheddar cheese, shredded

1 pound Swiss cheese, shredded

1 pound mushrooms, coarsely chopped

1½ pounds bacon, cooked, drained and crumbled

⅔ cup mayonnaise

½ teaspoon garlic powder

1 tablespoon Worcestershire sauce

Crackers

IRRESISTIBLE PISA DIP

INGREDIENTS

- Mix together all ingredients except bread.
- Pour into ovenproof dish; bake 30 minutes.
- Use bread cubes as dippers.

Temperature: 350°

Time: 30 minutes

4 to 5 cups

¾ cup mayonnaise

12 ounces pepperoni, chopped

1 pound Mozzarella cheese, shredded

1 tomato, diced

10 water-packed hot pepper rings, finely chopped

8 black olives, sliced or chopped

1 loaf Italian bread, cubed

INGREDIENTS

4 slices bacon, cut into ½-inch strips

⅓ cup chopped green onion

1 large tomato, chopped

1 can (4 ounces) chopped green chiles, drained

½ teaspoon ground cumin

½ teaspoon dried oregano

1 pound sharp cheddar cheese, shredded

½ to 1 cup tomato juice, optional

Tortilla chips

HOT FIESTA DIP

- In a large skillet, fry bacon over medium heat until crisp. Discard half of the drippings.

- Add onion and tomato; cooking about 4 minutes, until onion is translucent.

- Stir in chiles, cumin and oregano. Cook 3 to 4 minutes more, stirring frequently. Reduce heat to low; gradually add cheese, stirring until melted. Thin with tomato juice, if desired.

- Remove skillet from heat; transfer dip to a chafing dish. Serve with tortilla chips.

12 servings

INGREDIENTS

4 ounces cream cheese, softened

1 cup sour cream

1½ tablespoons taco seasoning

½ cup bottled taco sauce

¼ cup finely chopped onions

1½ cups shredded lettuce

1 cup diced tomato

½ cup diced green pepper

½ cup sliced black olives

½ pound cheddar cheese, shredded

Tortilla chips

GONE-IN-A-FLASH TACO DIP

- Mix cream cheese and sour cream. Add taco seasoning; mix thoroughly. Spread evenly on large round platter.

- Top cream cheese layer with taco sauce.

- Layer onions, lettuce, tomato, pepper, olives and cheese.

- Use sturdy tortilla chips for dippers.

4-6 servings

Firecracker Salsa

Customize this zesty salsa to fit your own tastes. Serve with tortilla chips or fresh vegetables.

- In a large bowl, combine all ingredients; mix well.
- Refrigerate, covered, 2 to 3 hours to blend flavors. Adjust ingredients and seasonings to taste.

INGREDIENTS

1 can (28 ounces) crushed tomatoes, drained

1 jar (about 15 ounces) prepared salsa

2 cans (4 ounces each) chopped jalapeños, drained

2 cans (6 ounces each) black olives, drained and sliced

3 to 4 tomatoes, chopped

1 to 2 hot fresh chiles, chopped

2 to 3 bunches green onions, sliced

1 clove garlic, minced

1 to 2 tablespoons wine vinegar

Sloppy Joe Dip

- Brown ground beef. Add remaining ingredients; mix well.
- Heat through and serve with corn chips.

8 servings

Hint: For more zest, add diced hot chiles or hot pepper sauce.

INGREDIENTS

1 pound ground beef

1 can (6 ounces) tomato paste

1 envelope sloppy joe mix

1 cup sour cream

Corn chips

INGREDIENTS

2 lemons

*1½ packages (8 ounces each)
cream cheese, softened*

½ cup butter, softened

½ cup sour cream

½ cup sugar

1 envelope plain gelatin

¼ cup cold water

½ cup golden raisins

1 cup slivered almonds, toasted

Crackers

WHITE SATIN

- Grate lemon rinds, then squeeze for juice.

- In a large mixing bowl, combine cream cheese, butter and sour cream. Add sugar gradually.

- Dissolve gelatin in water. Heat until water simmers; add gelatin to the cream cheese mixture.

- Stir in raisins, almonds, lemon rind and lemon juice.

- Pack into an oiled 1½-quart mold; refrigerate overnight.

- Unmold and serve with crackers.

24 servings

INGREDIENTS

*1 package (8 ounces) cream cheese,
softened*

*1 jar (7 ounces) marshmallow
cream*

3 tablespoons orange juice

½ teaspoon fresh orange peel

1 teaspoon ground ginger

Fresh fruits

VELVET FRUIT DIP

- Beat together all ingredients until smooth. May be refrigerated 1 to 2 days before serving.

- Serve in a bowl surrounded with fresh fruits such as pineapple, bananas, and mandarin oranges.

Variation: Substitute 3 crushed fresh strawberries for orange juice.

2½ cups

LES PETITS CHOUX

MUNCHING THESE CRISPY, BRIGHT BRUSSELS SPROUTS
IS A DELICIOUS WAY TO FOLLOW
THE HEALTHFUL ADVICE TO EAT MORE VEGGIES

- Cook Brussels sprouts just until tender-crisp. Halve large sprouts, if desired.
- Combine remaining ingredients, pour over sprouts and marinate, refrigerated, for several hours.
- Drain and serve with cocktail picks.

6 servings

INGREDIENTS

2 cups Brussels sprouts [or 1 package (10 ounces) frozen sprouts]

½ cup low-calorie Italian dressing

1 clove garlic, minced

2 tablespoons finely chopped onion

2 teaspoons minced fresh parsley

1 teaspoon snipped fresh dill (or ½ teaspoon dried dillweed)

CRISPY BROCCOLI WITH ZESTY LIME DIP

- Cut broccoli into florets. Blanch in boiling water 3 minutes to brighten color; cool immediately with cold water.
- In nonreactive bowl or zip-top plastic bag, marinate broccoli in Italian dressing. Refrigerate 2 to 3 hours or overnight.
- Remove zest from lime and squeeze juice. Combine with remaining dip ingredients and refrigerate.
- On round platter, center bowl of dip and encircle with broccoli.

10 servings

Hint: For Christmas, garnish with red pepper strips.

INGREDIENTS

2 bunches broccoli

1 bottle (8 ounces) Italian dressing

DIP

1 cup mayonnaise

1 cup sour cream

1 fresh lime

2 to 3 tablespoons prepared horseradish

2 tablespoons Dijon mustard

1 teaspoon salt

TORTILLA TUCKS

INGREDIENTS

10 6-inch flour tortillas

2 packages (8 ounces each) cream cheese, softened

9 ounces cheddar cheese, shredded

2 cups bottled salsa

5 to 6 green onions, chopped

1 can (16 ounces) black olives, chopped

1 ripe avocado, sliced thinly

- Spread each tortilla with a layer of cream cheese.
- Sprinkle with cheddar cheese, salsa, green onions and olives. Layer avocado.
- Roll up as tightly as possible and place seam side down in flat dish. Cover with plastic wrap; refrigerate 8 to 24 hours.
- To serve, slice into 1-inch rounds.

6 to 8 servings

Hint: May be prepared 2 days in advance.

ADDICTING MUNCHIES

INGREDIENTS

⅔ cup oil

2 teaspoons dill weed

¼ teaspoon garlic salt

1 package (1 ounce) dry "original" ranch salad dressing

9 cups snack items (salted peanuts, mini crackers, corn snacks, thin pretzels, cereal and/or oyster crackers)

- Mix together oil, dill, garlic salt and dry dressing.
- Place snacks in large roasting pan. Add oil mixture; toss thoroughly.
- Bake 1½ hours, uncovered, stirring every ½ hour. Drain on paper towels until cool. Store in glass or plastic containers.

Temperature: 200°

Time: 1½ hours

9 cups

Pizza Primavera

INGREDIENTS

- Unroll crescent rolls and shape (pat) to fit baking sheet.

- Bake at 375° for 10 to 12 minutes, or until golden brown. Cool.

- Combine softened cream cheese, mayonnaise and onion, and spread on cooled pastry, leaving narrow border on all sides.

- Randomly cover "pizza" with tomatoes, carrots, and pepper.

- Sprinkle Parmesan cheese over entire surface. Refrigerate.

- Cut into squares to serve.

Hint: These are best if made and refrigerated overnight.

Variation: Substitute your favorite vegetables or other items such as broccoli, black olives, hot peppers, cheese and shrimp.

Temperature: 375°

Time: 10 to 12 minutes

10 to 20 servings

2 packages refrigerated crescent rolls

1½ packages (8 ounces each) cream cheese, softened

¾ cup mayonnaise

1 onion, finely chopped

2 to 3 tomatoes, thinly sliced

2 to 3 carrots, pared and finely chopped

1 green pepper, finely chopped

½ cup grated Parmesan cheese

4 jars (5 ounces each) Old English cheese

1 tablespoon dill weed

1 tablespoon onion powder

Dash hot pepper sauce

1 pound butter, softened

3 loaves very thin white bread

POP-A-CHEESE STACK

- Mix cheese, dill, onion powder, pepper sauce and butter thoroughly.
- Remove crusts from bread.
- Spread cheese mixture on bread slices. Stack 3 slices high. Spread on top layer also.
- Use bread knife to cut bread stacks into 9 squares. Place on baking sheets; freeze.
- When frozen, store in freezer bag.
- To serve, bake frozen stacks on baking sheet for 15 minutes.

Temperature: 350°

Time: 15 minutes

INGREDIENTS

2 fresh artichokes, halved lengthwise

2 tablespoons lemon juice

2 tablespoons butter

4 tablespoons Dijon mustard

¼ pound pork sausage, cooked, drained and crumbled

2 cloves garlic, minced

1 package (10 ounces) frozen chopped spinach thawed, well drained

½ cup fresh breadcrumbs

Grated Parmesan cheese

ARTICHOKES DIJON

- Place artichokes and lemon juice in large saucepan of boiling water. Cook 25-30 minutes or until tender; drain.
- Arrange artichokes in shallow baking pan. Mix butter with 1 tablespoon mustard; drizzle over artichokes.
- Combine remaining ingredients except cheese. Spoon on artichokes.
- Sprinkle with cheese. Broil until cheese melts.

4 servings

ELEGANT ARTICHOKE CANAPÉS

INGREDIENTS

1 loaf firm bread

1 can (14 ounces) artichoke hearts, cut in 4 pieces

½ cup mayonnaise

½ cup shredded Provolone or grated Parmesan cheese

Dash Worcestershire sauce

Dash hot pepper sauce (optional)

Paprika

- Use round biscuit cutter to cut 35 to 40 circles from bread. Toast one side under broiler; set aside.

- In small mixing bowl, combine mayonnaise, cheese, Worcestershire and hot pepper sauce.

- Place bread rounds, toasted side down, on foil-lined baking sheets. Top each bread round with artichoke and a dollop of mayo-cheese mixture. Sprinkle with paprika.

- Broil until bubbly and lightly browned (approximately 3 minutes).

Temperature: Broil

Time: 3 minutes

35 to 40 canapés

BACON-CHEESE TOASTIES

INGREDIENTS

1 loaf firm white bread

1 pound bacon, cut into one-inch pieces

1 pound cheddar or Gruyère cheese, cubed

- Remove bread crusts.

- In food processor with steel blade, process bacon and cheese until almost smooth.

- Spread on bread; cut into triangles.

- Place on baking sheet. Broil at least 6 inches from heat source for 5 to 6 minutes.

Temperature: Broil

Time: 5 to 6 minutes

20 servings

INGREDIENTS

1 sheet of frozen puff pastry, defrosted

1 small wheel of Brie

8 ounces garlic-and-herb cheese

1 egg

1 tablespoon water

HERBED BRIE EN CROÛTE

- Roll pastry thin enough to encase Brie.

- Spread herb-and-garlic cheese on top of Brie; wrap Brie in pastry. Trim excess; seal well. Place seam side down on baking sheet.

- Blend egg and water, brush over top. Form pastry decorations from pastry scraps. Affix to egg-coated pastry.

- Bake for 30 to 35 minutes. Let stand 10 minutes before serving.

Temperature: 375°

Time: 30 to 35 minutes

12 to 14 servings

Wine Suggestions: California Cabernet
Red Bordeaux
Pinot Noir
Red Burgundy

INGREDIENTS

1 pound pinto beans, rinsed, soaked overnight and drained

3 pounds pork roast

7 cups water

½ cup chopped onion

2 cloves garlic, minced

1 teaspoon salt

2 tablespoons chili powder

1 tablespoon ground cumin

CHALUPA

A DISTINCTIVE MEXICAN APPETIZER —
GREAT FOR THE HEARTY APPETITE!

- Put all ingredients except corn chips into a Dutch oven or crockpot. Cover and simmer approximately 5 hours until roast falls apart and beans are done.

- Uncover and cook about 30 minutes more until mixture is desired thickness.

- Serve over corn chips with assorted toppings.

Hint: Can be prepared 2 days in advance and reheated.

8 servings

1 teaspoon dried oregano

1 can (4 ounces) chopped green chiles

Tortilla or corn chips

Toppings: chopped tomatoes, chopped avocado, chopped green onion, shredded lettuce, grated cheese, taco sauce, etc.

CHICKEN NIPS

- Cut chicken into bite-sized pieces. Dip each piece into melted butter.
- Combine Crispy Coating ingredients. Roll chicken in coating, placing pieces on foil-lined baking sheets. Bake for 20 minutes.
- For dip, combine mustard and sour cream.

Temperature: 400°

Time: 20 minutes

60 pieces

INGREDIENTS

4 whole boneless chicken breasts

½ cup melted butter

CRISPY COATING

1 cup crushed Champagne cracker

½ cup grated Parmesan cheese

¼ cup finely chopped walnuts

1 teaspoon dried thyme

1 teaspoon dried basil

½ teaspoon salt

¼ teaspoon pepper

ZESTY DIP

½ cup Dijon mustard

¼ cup sour cream

NACHOS SUPREME

1 bag (7½ ounces) taco-flavored tortilla chips

1½ cups minced green pepper

1½ cups chopped tomatoes

1½ cups finely chopped mushrooms

¾ cup chopped celery

¾ cup finely chopped onion

1 cup shredded cheddar cheese

1 cup shredded Monterey Jack cheese

Salsa, guacamole and/or sour cream

- Place layer of chips on well-oiled cookie sheet.
- Top with layers of peppers, tomatoes, and mushrooms.
- Combine celery and onion; sprinkle over other ingredients. Top with cheese.
- Broil 3 to 5 minutes until cheese melts.
- Serve hot with salsa, guacamole and/or sour cream.

Temperature: Broil

Time: 3 to 5 minutes

THE EMPEROR'S WONTONS

MUSTARD SAUCE

¼ cup Dijon mustard

1 cup sour cream

1 teaspoon lemon juice

WONTONS

1 package (10½ ounces) frozen chopped spinach, thawed

½ pound Ricotta cheese

4 green onions, chopped

2 cups cooked chicken, finely diced

1 can (8 ounces) water chestnuts, chopped

- For sauce, combine all ingredients and refrigerate until ready to serve.
- Squeeze thawed spinach to drain well. In a bowl, combine spinach, cheese, green onions, chicken, water chestnuts, salt and pepper.
- Place ½ teaspoon of mixture on each wonton wrapper. Moisten edge with beaten egg. Fold wonton diagonally to form a triangle. Fold again. Bring opposite corners up to the center. Use egg mixture to seal.
- In wok or skillet, add oil to a 3-inch depth. When hot, fry

3 to 4 wontons at a time until golden, turning frequently.

- Drain cooked wontons on paper towel. Serve with mustard sauce or other oriental sauces.

40 wontons

POT STICKERS

In China, pot stickers are served at morning tea, but we suggest you serve them at your next cocktail party.

- Place all filling ingredients into bowl of food processor fitted with steel blade. Process 8 to 10 seconds or until mixture is well blended.

- Place a piece of waxed paper on work area. Place single wonton skin onto paper; top with a tablespoon of mixture.

- In a small bowl, combine flour and water to make a smooth paste. Use your finger to place flour paste around edges of pastry. Bring all four sides together at the top of the mixture; pinch to seal.*

- In non-stick frying pan, heat peanut oil over medium heat. Place pot stickers, flat side down, in oil; fry until they are medium brown, but not burned on bottom.

- Add water to pan. Cover pan and steam until water evaporates. Serve with Mustard Street Sauce or your favorite Chinese dip.

Hint: May be made ahead to this point and frozen. Do not thaw before frying. Result will be more moist than freshly made.

3 dozen

Salt and pepper to taste

1 package wonton wrappers

1 egg, beaten

Peanut oil

INGREDIENTS

½ pound ground pork

1 package (10 ounces) chopped spinach, thawed and well-drained

1 tablespoon minced fresh ginger

1 tablespoon soy sauce

1 tablespoon sherry

1 tablespoon oriental sesame oil

1 package (16 ounces) wonton skins

2 tablespoons flour

2 tablespoons water

2 tablespoons peanut oil

½ cup water

24 mushrooms (1½ to 2 inch
diameter)

2 tablespoons butter

2 tablespoons olive oil

5 garlic cloves, minced

Dash hot pepper sauce

¾ cup dry sherry, divided

½ teaspoon salt

1 teaspoon pepper

2 tablespoons minced fresh parsley

¼ teaspoon paprika

1 tablespoon basil

5 to 7 artichoke hearts, chopped
and drained

1 cup breadcrumbs

Grated Parmesan cheese

WINDEMERE MUSHROOMS

- Remove mushroom stems; chop. Reserve caps.

- Sauté stems in butter and oil. Add garlic and hot pepper
sauce; simmer 1 minute.

- Add ¼ cup sherry to deglaze pan.

- Add salt, pepper, parsley, paprika, basil, artichokes,
breadcrumbs and ½ cup Parmesan cheese.

- Fill caps with mixture, mounding the stuffing.

- Brush with olive oil and sprinkle with additional Parmesan.
May be made ahead to this point and refrigerated.

- Place caps in 9 x 13-inch pan; add ½ cup sherry.

- Bake for 30 minutes or until golden brown.

Temperature: 375°

Time: 30 minutes

6 servings

¾ pound kielbasa

¾ cup white wine

1 tablespoon sugar

2 tablespoons Dijon mustard

1 tablespoon minced fresh parsley

GLAZED KIELBASA

- Halve kielbasa lengthwise, then cut into 1-inch chunks.

- Add kielbasa and wine to large skillet. Boil rapidly until
wine is syrupy and almost evaporated.

- Add sugar and mustard; remove from heat.

- Transfer to serving dish; sprinkle with parsley. Serve with
toothpicks.

6 servings

Rochester Wings

INGREDIENTS

- Mix together all ingredients except chicken.
- Add chicken and marinate 8 hours or overnight.
- Bake uncovered for 1 hour, basting often with extra sauce.

Hint: Use sauce to marinate pork chops or steaks before grilling.

Temperature: 325°

Time: 1 hour

6 servings

3 pounds chicken wings

⅓ cup soy sauce

2 tablespoons salad oil

2 tablespoons chili sauce

¼ cup honey

1 teaspoon salt

½ teaspoon ground ginger

¼ teaspoon garlic powder

¼ teaspoon cayenne pepper

Polynesian Crabmeat Bites

INGREDIENTS

- In a medium bowl, combine crabmeat, cream cheese and seasonings. Mix well.
- Place heaping teaspoon of crab mixture on each wonton. Gather 4 corners of wonton together at top; moisten edges with egg yolk; pinch to seal.
- Heat oil in wok or electric fry pan to 375°. Fry 5 or 6 wontons at a time until golden brown. Drain on paper towels.
- Serve hot with mustard and/or sweet and sour sauce.

2½ to 3 dozen

½ pound fresh or thawed crabmeat, drained and chopped

1 package (8 ounces) cream cheese, softened

½ teaspoon steak sauce

¼ teaspoon garlic powder

½ teaspoon dried chopped chives

2½ to 3 dozen wonton wrappers

1 egg yolk, well-beaten

Peanut oil

Chinese mustard

Sweet and sour sauce

INGREDIENTS

*1 pint bay scallops or sea scallops,
halved*

¾ pound bacon slices, halved

JEZEBEL SAUCE

*1 jar (12 ounces) apple jelly,
melted*

*1 jar (6 to 8 ounces) pineapple
preserves, melted*

¾ cup prepared horseradish

2 tablespoons Dijon mustard

2 tablespoons fresh lemon juice

SCALLOPS JEZEBEL

THIS SUPERB JEZEBEL SAUCE IS A WINNER!

- Combine all sauce ingredients; refrigerate several hours to blend flavors before using.

- Rinse scallops and pat dry. Wrap each scallop in ½ slice of bacon; secure with toothpick.

- Broil until bacon is crispy.

- Serve hot with Jezebel sauce for dipping.

6 to 8 servings

INGREDIENTS

1 cup mayonnaise

¼ cup lemon juice

¼ cup sugar

½ cup sour cream

1 large red onion, thinly sliced

2 tablespoons dill weed

⅛ teaspoon salt

2 pounds medium shrimp, cooked

SHRIMP IN DILL CREAM

A TASTER'S CHOICE RECIPE

- Mix all ingredients, except shrimp.

- Stir in shrimp; cover and refrigerate several hours.

- Serve with wooden picks.

8 to 10 servings

Shrimp Orleans

A Cajun first course guaranteed
to liven everyone's palate!

- In a large mixing bowl, combine mustard, paprika, cayenne pepper and salt; mix well.

- Using a wire whisk, beat in vinegar then gradually add oil in slow stream. Whisk until thick and smooth.

- Stir in green onions, celery and parsley.

- Cover tightly; let stand at room temperature for approximately 4 hours to blend flavors.

- Place shredded lettuce in a mound on individual serving plates. Arrange chilled shrimp on lettuce. Spoon sauce over shrimp and serve.

8 servings

INGREDIENTS

¼ cup prepared brown mustard

2 tablespoons paprika

1 teaspoon cayenne pepper

2 teaspoons salt

½ cup tarragon vinegar

1 cup olive oil

1 cup coarsely chopped
green onions

½ cup finely chopped celery

¼ cup coarsely chopped fresh
parsley

1 head iceberg lettuce, shredded

3 pounds medium shrimp, cooked
and chilled

Clams Rock

- Thaw spinach; squeeze dry.

- Combine remaining ingredients (except shells), using 2 tablespoons cheese.

- Spoon onto well-oiled shells. Sprinkle with additional cheese. Bake for 20 minutes.

Temperature: 350°

Time: 20 minutes

4 servings

INGREDIENTS

1 package (10 ounces) frozen
chopped spinach

½ cup mayonnaise

⅓ cup seasoned dry breadcrumbs

2 cans (6½ ounces each) chopped
or minced clams, drained

1 tablespoon lemon juice

¼ teaspoon salt

Grated Parmesan cheese

8 clam shells

INGREDIENTS

1½ pounds medium shrimp,
shelled and deveined

2 cups peanut oil

BATTER

1 egg

¼ cup milk

¼ cup water

½ cup flour

⅛ teaspoon salt

1 tablespoon melted butter

1 package (7 ounces) grated
coconut

DIP

½ cup orange marmalade

2 tablespoons sherry

1 tablespoon prepared horseradish

Dash hot pepper sauce

FRENCH COCONUT-BATTERED SHRIMP

NOT YOUR ORDINARY SHRIMP COCKTAIL! WORTH EVERY MINUTE
TO WOW YOUR GUESTS WITH THIS SPECIALTY!

- Beat all batter ingredients, except coconut, until smooth.
  Stir in coconut and refrigerate for 2 hours.

- Just before serving, combine dip ingredients in small
  saucepan and heat gently.

- In deep fryer or deep saucepan, heat oil. Coat shrimp with
  batter and fry a few at a time for 2 to 3 minutes or until
  shrimp are done. Drain on paper towels and keep warm.
  Serve with warm dip.

8 servings

INGREDIENTS

1 pound shrimp (approximately
30), peeled and cleaned

3 tablespoons unsalted butter

1 teaspoon chili powder

½ teaspoon freshly ground
black peppercorns

SPICY BAKED SHRIMP

- Arrange shrimp in pinwheel design in glass pie plate large
  enough to hold them in one layer.

- In a small saucepan, combine butter, chili powder, black
  pepper, white pepper, cayenne, hot pepper sauce, garlic,
  Worcestershire, wine and salt. Bring mixture to a boil; pour
  over shrimp.

- Bake shrimp 8 to 10 minutes or until done.
- Serve with a crusty Italian or sourdough bread.

Temperature: 400°

Time: 8 to 10 minutes

4 servings

⅛ teaspoon freshly ground white peppercorns

⅛ teaspoon cayenne pepper

Dash hot pepper sauce

1 teaspoon minced garlic

2 teaspoons Worcestershire sauce

2 tablespoons dry red wine

¼ teaspoon salt

Italian or sourdough bread

APRÉS-SKI SHRIMP

IN THE SOUTH, IT'S A TRADITION TO TAKE
"PICKLED SHRIMP" TO THE SHORE. UP NORTH, THESE
TAKE "TO THE SLOPES" WITH EQUAL APLOMB.

- Peel oranges; dice into bite-sized segments.
- In nonreactive bowl, combine shrimp, oranges, onions and tomato.
- Combine marinade ingredients; pour over shrimp and marinate, refrigerated, overnight.
- Serve with toothpicks or on plates with small forks.

Hint: Crusty French baguette slices are the perfect accompaniment.

INGREDIENTS

1½ pounds shell-off cooked shrimp

2 navel oranges

1 cup frozen pearl onions, thawed

1 tomato, diced into bite-sized pieces

MARINADE

¾ cup white or cider vinegar

⅓ cup oil

⅓ cup freshly squeezed lemon juice

¼ cup ketchup

1 tablespoon capers

1 tablespoon freshly minced parsley

1 clove garlic, minced

1 teaspoon sugar

1 teaspoon mustard seeds

½ teaspoon celery seeds

¼ teaspoon pepper

INGREDIENTS

48 mussels, cleaned

2 tablespoons finely chopped green onions

1 tablespoon minced fresh parsley

1 teaspoon curry powder

⅛ teaspoon salt

⅛ teaspoon pepper

2 teaspoons lemon juice

2 tablespoons chili sauce

1 tablespoon mussel broth (strained through cheesecloth)

1 cup mayonnaise

Parsley for garnish

NAPLES MUSSELS

- Steam mussels in 1½ cups water until shells open, approximately 8 minutes.

- Remove mussels from shells; chill. Reserve shells and broth.

- Combine remaining ingredients; chill.

- To serve, place mussel in shell and spoon sauce over each mussel. Garnish with fresh parsley sprigs.

6 servings

For Sardine Lovers Only

An extra special treat for sardine lovers!

- In a blender, combine sardines, lemon juice, egg, mayonnaise, and hot pepper; process until smooth. Chill.
- Before serving, garnish with lemon slices and parsley. Serve with crackers.

6 servings

INGREDIENTS

1 can (4½ ounces) sardines in mustard or tomato sauce

1 tablespoon lemon juice

1 hard-cooked egg, quartered

2 tablespoons mayonnaise

1 drop hot pepper sauce

½ lemon, cut into paper-thin slices

⅓ cup minced fresh parsley

Whole wheat crackers

Smoked Oyster Spread

- Combine all ingredients. Chill until ready to serve.
- Serve with crackers or melba toast.

Hint: May be prepared 2 days ahead.

1 cup

INGREDIENTS

1 package (3 ounces) cream cheese, softened

2 tablespoons mayonnaise

2 tablespoons milk

1 tablespoon chopped onion

2 teaspoons chopped pimiento

1 can (3 ounces) smoked oysters, drained and chopped

Dash hot pepper sauce

1 teaspoon lime juice

1 garlic clove, minced

Crackers or melba toast

INGREDIENTS

1 can (46 ounces) tomato juice

Juice of 1 lemon

¼ teaspoon seasoned salt

2 tablespoons horseradish

½ teaspoon hot pepper sauce

4½ teaspoons sugar

⅛ teaspoon ground black pepper

1½ teaspoons Worcestershire sauce

Vodka

1 lemon or lime, sliced

Celery sticks

TEX'S BLOODY MARY MIX

- Mix all ingredients, except vodka, lemon and celery. Refrigerate, covered, overnight.
- To serve, shake well and add vodka to taste. Garnish with lemon or lime slice and celery stick swizzle.

8 servings

INGREDIENTS

3½ cups Chablis

3 lemons, sliced

1 orange, sliced

1 green apple, peeled and sliced

½ cup cognac

¼ cup sugar

10 ounces club soda or seltzer

LEMON SANGRIA

EVEN THE FRUIT IS REFRESHING ON A HOT SUMMER DAY!

- In a 2 quart pitcher, combine the Chablis, sliced fruit, cognac and sugar. Mix well.
- Cover; refrigerate 6 to 8 hours (or overnight).
- Before serving, add club soda; stir gently.

8 servings

Lemon Tea Punch

ROSEMARY IS THE SECRET INGREDIENT
IN THIS DELIGHTFUL BEVERAGE!

- Place tea bags and rosemary in large saucepan. Add boiling water; steep 5 minutes. Remove tea bags.

- Stir in sugar until dissolved. Strain and cool. Chill mixture until ready to serve.

- Pour into punch bowl. Add soda and lemon juice; stir gently. Garnish with fresh lemon slices and float an ice ring on top.

30 ½ cup servings

INGREDIENTS

12 tea bags

4 teaspoons dried rosemary leaves

2 quarts boiling water

2 cups sugar

2 quarts lemon-lime soda, chilled

1 cup fresh lemon juice, strained

Fresh lemon slices

Ice ring

Apricot Daiquiri Blush

- Put all ingredients in blender. Blend on high speed until slushy. Pour into individual glasses; serve immediately.

6 to 8 servings

INGREDIENTS

1 can (6 ounces) frozen lemonade concentrate

6 ounces apricot nectar

6 ounces apricot brandy

3 ounces vodka

1 cup ice cubes

INGREDIENTS

*1 can (12 ounces) frozen
cranberry juice concentrate*

6 ounces white rum

2½ tablespoons sugar

1 ounce Rose's Lime Juice

1 ounce fresh lime juice

CRANBERRY BOW DAIQUIRI

A RUBY-RED TASTE SENSATION

- Put all ingredients in blender and blend until very smooth.
- Add ice and blend to a slush.

4 servings

Hint: The color of this drink lends itself to holiday entertaining.

INGREDIENTS

2 cups sugar

2½ cups water

*1 cup lemon juice (about 6
lemons)*

*1 cup orange juice (about 3
oranges)*

*1 can (6 ounces) frozen pineapple
juice concentrate, thawed*

2 quarts ginger ale

1 quart whiskey, optional

Fresh mint, optional

PARK AVENUE PUNCH

THE PERFECT "PICK", WHETHER YOUR PARTY PLANS CALL FOR
NON-ALCOHOLIC OR ALCOHOLIC PUNCH — OR BOTH

- In nonreactive pan, make a simple syrup by boiling sugar and water for 10 minutes.
- Remove from heat and stir in juices. Leave at room temperature for 1 hour, then refrigerate.
- To serve as a punch, combine chilled juices, ginger ale and whiskey, if desired, in punchbowl. Garnish with mint.

16 servings

Hint: To serve by the glass, combine equal parts fruit base and ginger ale, with or without a shot of whiskey.

OPEN HOUSE GOLDEN PUNCH

INGREDIENTS

2 cups sugar

3 cups freshly squeezed lemon juice

2 bottles (750 ml each) American-made sauterne wine

1 bottle (750 ml) brandy

Fresh mint

THIS IS A SOPHISTICATED UPDATE OF
AN OLD-FASHIONED WHISKEY SOUR

- In a gallon jar with lid, shake sugar and lemon juice until sugar dissolves.
- Add remaining ingredients, except mint, and chill.
- To serve, pour over ice in punchbowl and garnish with mint.

40 "punch-cup size" servings

BOURBON SLUSH

INGREDIENTS

1 can (12 ounces) frozen lemonade concentrate, thawed

1 can (6 ounces) frozen orange juice concentrate, thawed

12 ounces unsweetened tea

12 ounces bourbon

48 ounces water

½ cup sugar

EVEN WHEN FROZEN, THIS STAYS SLUSHY

- In a large jar or freezer container, combine all ingredients. Freeze.
- Scoop slush from container and serve.

16 servings

Hint: Use lemonade can to measure water and bourbon.

INGREDIENTS

5 large eggs

⅓ cup sugar

1 quart whole milk

1 teaspoon vanilla

¾ cup whiskey

3 tablespoons dark rum

SNOWLIGHT EGGNOG*

- In blender, place eggs, sugar, vanilla, 2 cups milk, whiskey and rum; blend until smooth. Transfer to serving container.

- Add remaining 2 cups milk to blender to "rinse" blender. Stir milk into eggnog; serve.

1½ quarts

* This recipe contains uncooked egg yolks/whites. See SPECIAL NOTE page 7.

INGREDIENTS

1 quart blended whiskey or bourbon

1 pint orange juice

Juice of 2 lemons

¾ cup pure maple syrup

10 to 12 ounces maraschino cherries, undrained

32 shakes of aromatic bitters

1½ quarts club soda or seltzer water

1 lemon, sliced

1 orange, sliced

MALE CHAUVINIST PUNCH

A REAL ICE-BREAKER!

- Combine whiskey, orange juice, syrup, cherries and bitters. Cover and refrigerate 2 to 3 hours or overnight.

- Before serving, transfer to punch bowl, add soda or seltzer. Garnish with citrus slices.

3 quarts

Sun-sational Slush

- Dissolve gelatin in warm water. Add all other ingredients, except soda and garnish. Freeze at least 24 hours.

- To serve, fill tall glasses ⅓ full with frozen mixture. Add soda to fill glass to the top and mix to a slush consistency. Garnish with mint leaf or orange slice.

10 Servings

Hint: For a low calorie recipe, substitute diet gelatin and diet soda. Use 8 packets of artificial sweetener instead of sugar.

INGREDIENTS

1 package (3-ounce) strawberry gelatin

7 cups very warm water

1 can (12 ounces) frozen lemonade

1 can (12 ounces) frozen orange juice

2 cups strong tea (5 tea bags)

1 cup sugar

2½ cups vodka

Lemon-lime soda or club soda

Mint leaves or orange slices

Second Helping Tea

- In large pot, heat all ingredients, except citrus slices, to boiling. Reduce heat and simmer gently for 30 minutes or longer.

- Serve hot in heatproof mugs; float a citrus slice on each serving.

16-20 servings

INGREDIENTS

1 quart strong hot tea

1 quart pineapple or cranberry juice

1 quart apple cider

1 quart orange juice

¾ cup lemon juice

4 cinnamon sticks

12 whole cloves

½ cup sugar (optional)

Lemon or orange slices

BERRY WASSAIL

INGREDIENTS

2 quarts cider or apple juice

1 pint cranberry juice

¾ cup sugar

1 teaspoon aromatic bitters

2 cinnamon sticks

1 teaspoon whole allspice

1 small orange, studded with whole cloves

1 cup rum (optional)

- Place all ingredients in large pan, cover and cook on medium high heat for 1 hour.

- Reduce temperature to low; simmer 4 hours. Serve warm.

12 servings

BRISTOL MULLED WINE

INGREDIENTS

5 cups burgundy

5 cups cranberry juice

5 cups pineapple juice

1 cup brown sugar

1 tablespoon whole cloves

6 cinnamon sticks

Dash of salt

Lemon slices or zest

THE ALCOHOL SIMMERS OFF, LEAVING BEHIND A TOE-WARMING HOT PUNCH GREAT FOR APRÉS-ANYTHING

- In a large nonreactive pot, simmer all ingredients except lemon for 45 minutes or longer.

- Serve garnished with lemon slices or zest.

20 servings

Hint: May be prepared ahead and reheated in large coffee percolator.

SOUPS

Soups / Index

Bistro Tomato Soup / 64

Cajun Cream of Tomato Soup / 57

Carrot Vichyssoise / 56

Cheesy Cheddar Cauliflower Soup / 58

Cottage Celery Soup / 58

Cream of Vidalia Onion Soup / 61

Creamy Salmon Soup / 64

Curried Tomato Bisque / 60

Fresh Cream of Broccoli Soup / 63

Gazpacho / 56

Harvest Soup with Brandy Cream / 55

Hazelnut Mushroom Bisque / 59

Hearty Sicilian Soup / 68

Mom's Lentil Soup / 57

Roquefort Soup / 60

Sausage Tortellini Soup / 62

Scallop Chowder / 62

Seafarer's Pantry / 65

Swiss Potato Soup / 67

Tavern Beef Soup / 66

Harvest Soup with Brandy Cream

INGREDIENTS

1 large white onion, coarsely chopped

2 medium butternut squash, peeled, quartered, seeded

2 "20-Ounce" apples, peeled, cored, quartered

4 to 5 cups chicken broth, divided

1 tablespoon honey

½ teaspoon dried thyme

½ teaspoon dried basil

¼ teaspoon dried sage

Freshly ground pepper to taste

4 ounces sour cream

1 to 2 teaspoons brandy

Minced fresh parsley

- In large stockpot, "sweat" onions, covered, over low heat until translucent but not burned.

- Stir in squash, apples and about 2 cups broth. Cook, covered, over low heat until squash and apple pieces are soft.

- Remove from heat. Purée ⅓ of the mixture at a time in food processor fitted with a steel blade. Return soup to pan and add additional chicken broth to achieve consistency of thick cream soup.

- Season with honey, thyme, basil, sage and pepper. Simmer but do not boil.

- In a small bowl, combine sour cream with enough brandy to achieve a thick consistency.

- Serve in individual bowls garnished with brandy cream and parsley.

8 to 10 servings

Hint: For elegance, fill plastic squeeze bottle with brandy cream, then apply 3 concentric circles to each serving. Use toothpick to "feather" the rings.

INGREDIENTS

3 cups fresh tomatoes, peeled,
seeded and chopped

½ cup finely chopped onion

½ cup finely chopped green pepper

1 cucumber, peeled, seeded and diced

3 tablespoons minced fresh parsley

2 tablespoons snipped fresh chives

2 cups tomato juice

¼ teaspoon cayenne pepper

⅓ cup red wine vinegar

¼ cup olive oil

Salt to taste

4 slices French bread, cubed

GAZPACHO

- Combine all ingredients except bread.
- Stir in bread.
- Refrigerate, covered, at least 6 hours before serving. Serve chilled.

4 to 5 servings

INGREDIENTS

½ cup butter

1 medium onion, chopped

4 leeks, thinly sliced

4 cups chicken broth

2 chicken bouillon cubes

5 medium potatoes, cubed

4 carrots, thinly sliced

2 cups half-and-half

Hot pepper sauce

Salt and pepper to taste

Chives

CARROT VICHYSSOISE

- Sauté onions and leeks in butter over medium heat until soft.
- Add chicken broth, bouillon, potatoes and carrots. Simmer on low heat until vegetables are tender.
- Cool, then process small amounts at a time in blender until smooth.
- Chill, then add half and half, hot pepper sauce, salt and pepper.
- Before serving, garnish with chopped chives.

Variation: Equally good served hot.

10 servings

Cajun Cream of Tomato Soup

- In large stockpot, combine tomatoes, juices and sugar. Simmer gently.
- In large skillet, melt 3 tablespoons butter and sauté onions with garlic powder, salt, basil and cajun spice.
- When onions are browned, stir in flour and 1 tablespoon butter.
- Add onions to tomatoes, mixing well.
- Gradually add half and half. Heat, but do not boil.
- Serve immediately.

8 to 10 servings

INGREDIENTS

1 can (32 ounces) crushed tomatoes

1 can (32 ounces) tomato juice

2 cans (12 ounces each) spiced tomato vegetable juice

3 tablespoons sugar

4 tablespoons butter, divided

2 cups chopped onions

1 teaspoon garlic powder

1 teaspoon salt

2 tablespoons dried basil

Cajun spice to taste

3 tablespoons flour

2 cups half-and-half

Mom's Lentil Soup

- In skillet, fry bacon and onion until bacon is brown and onion is limp. Discard drippings.
- In large stockpot, combine bacon, onions, stock, lentils, carrot, bay leaf, thyme and 1½ pounds kielbasa.
- Bring to boil, reduce heat and simmer for 1 hour.
- Add remaining ½ pound kielbasa and cook 5 minutes more.
- Season to taste with salt and pepper.

4 to 6 servings

INGREDIENTS

2 slices bacon, chopped

3 medium onions, chopped

1½ quarts beef stock or bouillon

2 cups (1 pound) dried lentils

1 cup shredded carrots

1 bay leaf

Pinch thyme

2 pounds kielbasa, sliced thinly, divided

Salt and pepper

½ cup butter or margarine

½ cup chopped onion

5 cups chopped celery

2 cloves garlic, minced

2 medium potatoes, peeled and chopped

⅓ cup minced fresh parsley, divided

5 cups chicken broth

½ teaspoon Beau Monde seasoning

¼ to ½ teaspoon white pepper

COTTAGE CELERY SOUP

- In stockpot over medium heat, melt butter or margarine and sauté onion and celery for 5 minutes or until tender. Add garlic and sauté an additional minute.

- Stir in potatoes, ¼ cup parsley and broth. Bring to boil, cover, reduce heat and simmer 20 minutes or until potatoes are tender.

- Remove soup from heat; cool slightly. Season with Beau Monde and white pepper.

- In food processor fitted with steel blade, process soup (in 3 to 4 batches) until smooth, about 5 seconds.

- Reheat. Before serving garnish with reserved parsley.

6 to 8 servings

INGREDIENTS

3 tablespoons vegetable oil

2 medium sized leeks (white part only), washed and chopped

1½ pounds cauliflower florets

1 teaspoon dried oregano

⅛ teaspoon white pepper

Dash cayenne or hot pepper sauce (more to taste if desired)

7 cups chicken broth

2 tablespoons butter

¼ cup flour

CHEESY CHEDDAR CAULIFLOWER SOUP

- In large stockpot, heat oil and sauté leeks and cauliflower.

- Stir in oregano, pepper, cayenne and broth. Simmer until cauliflower is tender, approximately 10 minutes.

- Using a slotted spoon, transfer cauliflower from stock to food processor or blender. Chop to fine bits (but not pulverized). Return to stock.

- In small pot over medium heat, melt butter. Stir in flour and mix well. Add to stock mixture and whisk until it simmers.

- Gradually add cheese, stirring until melted.

- In small bowl, beat egg yolks then add half and half and beat again. Stir ½ cup of hot soup into egg/cream mixture before adding eggs to soup.

- Simmer soup, stirring occasionally.

- Just prior to serving, add wine and sprinkle each bowl with nutmeg.

8 servings

2 cups shredded cheddar cheese

2 medium egg yolks

1 cup half-and-half

¼ cup dry white wine

Freshly ground nutmeg

HAZELNUT MUSHROOM BISQUE

THIS SAVORY BISQUE IS A GENUINE COMFORT ON A COLD WINTER EVENING

- Spread hazelnuts on cookie sheet and toast at 275° for 20 minutes.

- Remove shells and coarsely chop hazelnuts.

- In a large stockpot, combine half-and-half, mushrooms, garlic, shallots, and all except ¼ cup of the nuts.

- Cook over medium-high heat, stirring often, until mixture is reduced by one half, approximately 1 hour. Cool then pureé in food processor.

- While mushrooms are cooking, in separate pan, combine stock and sherry. Boil until reduced by one-half, approximately 20 minutes.

- Combine both mixtures in stockpot and reheat. Season to taste.

- Serve hot, garnished with reserved nuts, chives or parsley.

8 to 10 servings

INGREDIENTS

1 pound hazelnuts in shell, divided

1½ quarts half-and-half

1½ pounds mushrooms, chopped

8 garlic cloves, quartered

3 shallots, quartered

3 cups chicken stock

1 cup sherry

Salt and pepper to taste

Fresh chives or parsley

½ cup butter

1 cup chopped celery

1 cup chopped onion

½ cup chopped carrots

⅓ cup flour

*2 cans (28 ounces each)
crushed tomatoes*

2 teaspoons sugar

2 teaspoons dried basil

1 teaspoon dried marjoram

4 cups chicken broth

2 cups heavy cream

½ teaspoon paprika

½ teaspoon curry powder

¼ teaspoon white pepper

Salt to taste

CURRIED TOMATO BISQUE

- In large stockpot, melt butter and sauté celery, onion and carrots.

- Stir in flour, cook 2 minutes, stirring constantly.

- Add tomatoes, sugar, basil, marjoram and broth. Cover and simmer 30 minutes, stirring occasionally.

- Purée ⅓ of the mixture at a time in a blender or food processor and return the mixture to the stockpot.

- Stir in cream, paprika, curry and pepper. Heat through but do not boil.

- Before serving, salt to taste.

8 to 10 servings

INGREDIENTS

5 tablespoons butter, divided

1 medium onion, thinly sliced

2 tablespoons brandy

2½ cups low-salt chicken broth

3 ounces Roquefort cheese

*2 cups fresh spinach leaves, cut in
julienne strips*

*2 tomatoes, peeled, seeded and
diced*

ROQUEFORT SOUP

- In medium saucepan, melt 2 tablespoons butter and sauté onion until golden, stirring frequently.

- Remove pan from heat, add brandy and ignite.

- When flames subside, return pan to heat and stir in broth and cheese. When mixture starts to boil, remove from heat. Cool slightly then purée in blender or food processor fitted with steel blade.

- In large saucepan, melt 1 tablespoon butter and sauté spinach, tomatoes and thyme approximately 2 minutes or until spinach wilts.

- Cool slightly then pureé this mixture also. Return it to pan, along with half-and-half and broth mixture. Season with pepper.

- When soup simmers, stir in remaining 2 tablespoons butter.
- To serve, garnish with additional crumbled cheese.

4 servings

CREAM OF VIDALIA ONION SOUP

ALTHOUGH THE SWEET VIDALIA ONIONS ARE ONLY AVAILABLE A FEW MONTHS OF THE YEAR, THIS EXTRA SPECIAL SOUP IS WORTH THE WAIT!

- In large stockpot, fry bacon until crisp. Remove bacon, leaving drippings in pot.
- Add butter, onions and garlic to drippings. Cover and cook over low heat until onions are translucent and lightly caramelized, approximately 30 minutes.
- Stir in wine, stock, bay leaf and thyme. Bring to a boil, then reduce heat and simmer, covered, 20 minutes.
- Discard bay leaf. With slotted spoon, transfer solids to a food processor fitted with steel blade. Process until smooth then return to stockpot.
- Whisk in heavy cream and sour cream. Season with lemon juice, salt, pepper, hot pepper sauce and nutmeg.
- Chill to serve cold or heat slowly to serve hot.
- Garnish with bacon and green onions before serving.

8 servings

Hint: For a winter treat, make extra to freeze (through Step 4).

Wine Suggestions: Chardonnay
White Burgundy
Vouvray

¼ teaspoon dried thyme

½ cup half-and-half

Freshly ground pepper

Additional Roquefort cheese

INGREDIENTS

¼ pound bacon, chopped

½ cup unsalted butter

3 pounds Vidalia onions, peeled and thinly sliced

8 cloves garlic

2 cups white wine

4 cups chicken stock

1 bay leaf

1 teaspoon dried thyme

1 cup heavy cream

1 cup sour cream

3 tablespoons lemon juice

½ teaspoon salt

Freshly ground pepper

Hot pepper sauce to taste

Freshly ground nutmeg

Chopped green onions

INGREDIENTS

1 pound bulk Italian sausage, cut into small pieces

1 medium onion, chopped

4 medium tomatoes, peeled and chopped [or 1 can (16 ounces) tomatoes, cut-up]

1 can (8 ounces) tomato sauce

5 cups beef broth

½ cup water

½ cup red wine

½ teaspoon dried basil

½ teaspoon dried oregano

1 medium zucchini, peeled and chopped

3 to 4 carrots, sliced thinly

1 green pepper, diced

8 to 12 ounces uncooked tortellini

SAUSAGE TORTELLINI SOUP

- In large stockpot, cook sausage with onion until well done. Drain fat.

- Add remaining ingredients, except tortellini, to the pot and simmer 30 minutes.

- Stir in tortellini and simmer an additional 30 minutes.

- Before serving, skim off any melted fat that has risen to top of soup.

4 to 6 servings

Wine Suggestions: Italian Red
                                   Italian White

INGREDIENTS

4 cups bottled clam juice

¼ cup dry white wine

1 bay leaf

4 tablespoons butter

¾ cup finely chopped onion

¼ cup flour

SCALLOP CHOWDER

- In saucepan over medium heat, simmer clam juice, wine, and bay leaf, uncovered, for 10 minutes.

- Remove from heat; discard bay leaf.

- In large saucepan or Dutch oven over medium heat, melt butter and sauté onion until soft, but not browned, approximately 5 minutes.

- Stir in flour, then gradually add half-and-half. Cook, stirring constantly, until sauce is thickened.
- Reduce heat to low and slowly add hot broth to thickened sauce. Stir in scallops and corn. Cook 4 to 5 minutes, just until scallops are cooked.
- Ladle into warmed soup bowls and sprinkle with parsley. Serve immediately.

7 servings

2 cups half-and-half

8 ounces bay scallops

1 cup fresh corn kernels

Fresh minced parsley

FRESH CREAM OF BROCCOLI SOUP

INGREDIENTS

1 bunch fresh broccoli

2 tablespoons butter or margarine

1 medium onion, chopped

1 potato, pared and diced (1 cup)

2 cans (14½ ounces each) chicken broth

½ teaspoon salt

Dash cayenne pepper

1 cup half-and-half

⅛ teaspoon ground nutmeg

- Trim outer leaves and discard tough ends from broccoli, cut stalks into 2 to 3-inch lengths.
- Parboil broccoli for 5 minutes; drain well.
- In large saucepan, add butter and sauté onion until soft, but not brown.
- Add potato, chicken broth, salt and pepper. Heat until boiling, lower heat and simmer 15 minutes.
- Stir in broccoli, reserving a few florets for garnish. Simmer 5 minutes longer or until vegetables are tender.
- Pour mixture, half at a time, in blender or food processor fitted with steel blade. Process until smooth, then return mixture to saucepan.
- Add cream and nutmeg and heat but do not boil. (If soup is too thick, thin with additional cream.)
- Before serving, garnish with reserved florets.

6 servings

1 packet (1.9 ounces) of imported powdered mushroom soup mix

2 tablespoons vegetable oil

1 meaty beef bone

1 can (16 ounces) stewed tomatoes

2 beef bouillon cubes

1 small onion, minced

1 leek, chopped

1 bay leaf

¼ to ½ teaspoon each of the following: basil, minced fresh parsley, oregano, marjoram, thyme, garlic salt

Salt and pepper to taste

½ to 1 cup water

¼ to ½ cup red wine

BISTRO TOMATO SOUP

- In a small bowl, combine mushroom soup mix with 2 cups hot water. Stir to blend.

- In a skillet over high heat, heat vegetable oil and brown bone on all sides.

- Reduce skillet heat. Add mushroom soup, tomatoes, bouillon, onion, leek, bay leaf and spices. Cover and simmer 2 hours, stirring occasionally. Add additional water if necessary.

- After 30 minutes, add red wine and adjust seasonings. Discard bay leaf before serving.

- Remove meat from bone and add to soup.

4 to 5 servings

Hint: For a heartier mushroom flavor, add 1 cup sliced fresh mushrooms to the simmering soup.

2 cans (16 ounces each) pink or red salmon

¼ cup butter or margarine

¾ cup sliced green onions

¼ cup flour

2 cups half-and-half

¼ teaspoon dried marjoram

¾ teaspoon paprika

CREAMY SALMON SOUP

- Drain salmon and flake, reserving liquid. Discard bones. Add water to reserved liquid to make 2 cups.

- In a large saucepan, melt butter and sauté onions until soft.

- Stir in flour and cook 1 minute. Slowly add salmon liquid and cook over low heat, stirring until thick and smooth.

- Gradually stir in half-and-half, marjoram, paprika, Worchestershire sauce, salt and pepper.

- Add salmon and mushrooms and simmer, covered, 15 minutes.
- Before serving, stir in sour cream and parsley. Do not boil.

6 servings

1½ teaspoons Worcestershire sauce (or ½ teaspoon hot pepper sauce)

Salt and pepper to taste

1 pound fresh mushrooms, sliced

2 cups sour cream

2 tablespoons minced fresh parsley

SEAFARER'S PANTRY

- In a 4-quart pot over medium heat, melt butter and sauté carrot, celery and onion until tender.
- Stir in soups, milk, cayenne pepper, Worcestershire sauce, parsley, pepper and salt. Heat over medium high heat, but do not boil.
- Stir in scallops, shrimp, and clams with juice. Reduce heat to low and simmer 20 minutes.
- Serve garnished with bacon.

6 servings

INGREDIENTS

2 tablespoons butter

1 carrot, chopped

1 stalk celery, chopped

1 small onion, chopped

1 can (10¾ ounces) cream of potato soup

1 can (10¾ ounces) shrimp soup

1 can (10¾ ounces) celery soup

1 can (10¾ ounces) vichyssoise soup

1½ soup cans of milk

¼ teaspoon cayenne pepper

1½ teaspoons Worcestershire sauce

1 teaspoon dried parsley

½ teaspoon fresh ground pepper

½ teaspoon seasoning salt

¼ pound fresh small bay scallops

¼ pound fresh small shrimp

1 can (7½ ounces) whole clams with juice

4 strips bacon, cooked and crumbled (optional)

INGREDIENTS

1 pound lean ground beef

1 large onion, finely chopped

10 ounces ketchup

6 cups water

1 can (10½ ounces) beef gravy

2 teaspoons Worcestershire sauce

½ cup flour

¾ cup cold water

3 beef bouillon cubes

2 teaspoons salt

¼ teaspoon freshly ground black pepper

1 tablespoon brown sugar

1 tablespoon cider vinegar

2 whole cloves

10 whole allspice

1 bay leaf

¼ cup medium dry sherry

1 lemon, sliced thin

2 to 3 hard-cooked eggs, chopped

TAVERN BEEF SOUP

IT'S TIME THE REST OF THE WORLD DISCOVERED THE GREAT FLAVOR OF THIS CINCINNATI FAVORITE

- In a large pot, brown beef over medium heat. Add onion and cook until tender. Drain excess fat.

- Add ketchup, water, gravy and Worcestershire sauce. Bring to a boil, reduce heat and simmer approximately 30 minutes.

- Meanwhile, place flour in dry frying pan over medium heat and cook until flour is light brown, stirring constantly. Remove from heat.

- In a small bowl, mix flour and water to make a smooth paste. Stir paste into soup mixture, along with bouillon, salt, pepper, brown sugar and vinegar.

- Tie cloves, allspice and bay leaf in a cheesecloth bag and put into soup.

- Simmer, covered, for 2 hours, stirring occasionally. Discard spice bag.

- Add sherry, lemon slices and eggs, and simmer 5 minutes before serving.

6 to 8 servings

SWISS POTATO SOUP

½ pound bacon

6 green onions, chopped

2 cups chopped onions

6 to 8 medium potatoes, pared and cut in half

6 cups chicken stock or bouillon mixture

2 cups heavy cream

A HEARTY, SOOTHING SOUP FOR A COLD WINTER'S DAY

- In skillet, fry bacon until crisp. Drain bacon on paper towel, reserving 2 tablespoons drippings in skillet. Crumble bacon.

- In same skillet, sauté green onions and onions, reserving a few green onions for garnish.

- In stockpot, cook potatoes in stock. When potatoes are tender, stir in sautéed mixture.

- In blender or food processor fitted with steel blade, pureé soup in several batches.

- Return soup to stockpot and add cream and bacon, reserving a few pieces for garnish. Reheat slowly, but do not boil.

- Before serving, garnish with reserved green onions and bacon.

4 to 6 servings

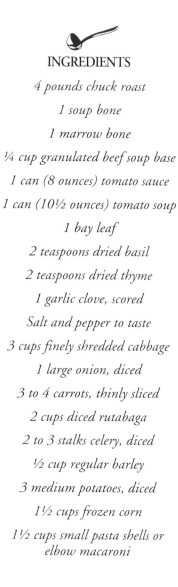

INGREDIENTS

4 pounds chuck roast

1 soup bone

1 marrow bone

¼ cup granulated beef soup base

1 can (8 ounces) tomato sauce

1 can (10½ ounces) tomato soup

1 bay leaf

2 teaspoons dried basil

2 teaspoons dried thyme

1 garlic clove, scored

Salt and pepper to taste

3 cups finely shredded cabbage

1 large onion, diced

3 to 4 carrots, thinly sliced

2 cups diced rutabaga

2 to 3 stalks celery, diced

½ cup regular barley

3 medium potatoes, diced

1½ cups frozen corn

1½ cups small pasta shells or
elbow macaroni

HEARTY SICILIAN SOUP

THIS SOUP IS A WONDERFULLY DELICIOUS,
NUTRITIOUS ONE-DISH MEAL

- In 12-quart stockpot, cover meat and bones with about 6 quarts of water. Cover and simmer 30 minutes.

- Stir in beef soup base. Reduce heat to low and simmer, covered, 2 hours.

- Stir in tomato sauce, soup, bay leaf, basil, thyme, garlic, salt, pepper, cabbage, onion, carrots, rutabaga and celery. Simmer, covered, 30 minutes.

- Remove beef and bones. Shred or cut lean beef into small pieces and return to pot.

- Add barley, potatoes, and corn. Cover and simmer 45 minutes.

- Add pasta and cook 15 minutes longer. Serve immediately.

8 to 10 quarts

SALADS

Salads / Index

Main Dish

Adirondack Chicken Salad / 73
Chicken Salad Oriental / 72
Clubhouse Chicken Salad / 74
Grab-bag Tortellini Salad / 71
Roast Beef Niçoise / 77
Shrimp Salad with Raspberry Dressing / 72
Summer Night Chicken Salad / 75
Vineyard Chicken Salad / 74
Wonton Chicken Salad / 76

Vegetable

Antipasto Medley / 76
Carolina Coleslaw / 79
Couscous Marrakesh / 81
Coye Point Salad / 80
Fennel Salad with Sesame Dressing / 88
Festival of Greens / 84
Greek Tomato Salad / 85
Hail, Caesar!* / 82
Lentil Antipasto / 79
Mandarin Romaine / 82
Morning Glory Salad / 85
Popeye's Spinach Salad / 78
Potatoes El Greco / 87

Raspberry Endive Salad / 83
Red, White and Green Salad / 81
Spring Potato Salad / 87
Summer Rice Salad / 78
Sunny Broccoli Salad / 80
Superlative Spinach Salad / 86
Vegetable Vinaigrette / 90
Winter Sunshine Salad / 89

Molded

Cranberry Molded Salad / 91
Lemon Refresher / 92
What's-the-Secret Salad / 91

Dressings

Buttermilk Blue Dressing / 95
Citrus Dressing / 93
Creamy Mustard Dressing* / 94
Creamy Tarragon Dressing / 92
Tangy Dijon Dressing / 94
Vermont Salad Dressing / 93

Condiments

Fruity Cranberry Relish / 95
Marvelous Mustard Mousse / 96

Grab-bag Tortellini Salad

- Combine first ten ingredients.
- Whisk together all dressing ingredients.
- Pour dressing over salad. Toss, cover and refrigerate at least 3 hours.
- Toss again before serving.

10 to 12 servings

INGREDIENTS

2 medium zucchini, cut into ¼-inch strips

1 green pepper, cut into slivers

1 sweet red pepper, cut into slivers

3 cups cauliflower florets, steamed crisp

3 cups broccoli florets, steamed crisp

2 carrots, cut into diagonal strips

1 medium red onion, sliced in thin rings

½ to 1 cup frozen peas, thawed

1 pound tortellini, cooked

1 to 2 cups cooked beef, chicken, or ham, cubed

DRESSING

¼ cup minced fresh parsley

⅛ cup minced fresh basil leaves

¼ teaspoon garlic salt

¼ cup vegetable oil

¼ cup chicken broth

¼ cup red wine vinegar

4 teaspoons Dijon mustard

2 teaspoons sugar

Freshly ground pepper

2 teaspoons oregano

INGREDIENTS

1½ pounds large shrimp, peeled and deveined

2 tablespoons vegetable oil

1 box (6 to 6.25 ounces) long-grain and wild rice

1 head Bibb lettuce or endive

½ cup sliced almonds

DRESSING

⅓ cup vegetable oil

2 tablespoons sugar

2 tablespoons raspberry vinegar

1 tablespoon sour cream

1½ teaspoons Dijon mustard

SHRIMP SALAD WITH RASPBERRY DRESSING

- Whisk together all dressing ingredients.

- In a large skillet over medium heat, heat 2 tablespoons oil and sauté shrimp 3 to 4 minutes until pink and cooked through. Remove from heat; refrigerate until needed.

- Cook rice according to package directions and transfer to a large bowl. Add shrimp and dressing. Gently fold to combine thoroughly. Refrigerate 2 to 3 hours before serving.

- To serve, arrange salad on bed of lettuce. Sprinkle with sliced almonds.

4 servings

INGREDIENTS

4 whole chicken breasts

1 sweet red pepper, seeded and cut into julienne strips

1 can (8 ounces) whole water chestnuts, drained and halved

5 green onions, trimmed and cut into julienne strips

4 dozen snow peas, blanched

¾ cup toasted cashews

2 tablespoons toasted sesame seeds

CHICKEN SALAD ORIENTAL

- Poach chicken breasts. When cool enough to handle, cut meat into julienne strips.

- Combine chicken with red pepper, water chestnuts, green onions, snow peas, and cashews. Refrigerate.

- In the bowl of a food processor, mince together parsley and garlic. Add remaining dressing ingredients; process until smooth.

- Fold dressing into the salad. Refrigerate, covered, 4 to 6 hours before serving.

- Prior to serving, transfer salad to a large platter or a glass bowl. Sprinkle with the sesame seeds and serve immediately.

8 servings

Hint: Add a few drops of prepared hot pepper sauce to the dressing for some zing!

DRESSING

2 tablespoons parsley

2 cloves garlic

½ cup prepared teriyaki sauce

¼ cup oriental sesame oil

¼ cup olive or vegetable oil

2 tablespoons rice vinegar

2 tablespoons dry sherry

1 tablespoon brown sugar

2 teaspoons ground coriander

ADIRONDACK CHICKEN SALAD

A PERENNIAL FAVORITE FROM THE ADIRONDACKS

- In large serving bowl, combine chicken, bacon, tomatoes, lettuce and avocado.
- Whisk dressing ingredients together.
- Pour over salad. Toss and serve.

4 servings

INGREDIENTS

4 cups chicken, cooked and shredded

¾ pound bacon, cooked and crumbled

2 large tomatoes, peeled (if desired) and chopped

½ head lettuce, torn into bite-sized pieces

1 avocado, peeled and sliced

DRESSING

½ cup vegetable oil

¼ cup white wine vinegar

1 teaspoon salt

2 teaspoons sugar

¾ teaspoon pepper

1¼ teaspoon dry mustard

1 clove garlic, minced

⅓ cup minced fresh parsley

INGREDIENTS

1 package (6 ounces) rice pilaf

3 cups cubed cooked chicken

3 cups cubed crisp tart apples

½ cup raisins

1 head curly or leaf lettuce, torn

1 cup toasted slivered almonds

DRESSING

¾ cup mayonnaise

½ cup orange marmalade

¼ cup sour cream

2 to 3 tablespoons lemon juice

½ to 1 teaspoon curry powder

CLUBHOUSE CHICKEN SALAD

- In a small bowl, combine dressing ingredients. Refrigerate, covered, at least 2 hours.

- Prepare rice pilaf according to package directions, then refrigerate at least 1 hour.

- Combine chilled rice with chicken, apples and raisins. Add dressing and mix well.

- Place lettuce on individual serving plates. Top with ¾ to 1 cup salad. Garnish each serving with almonds. Serve immediately.

8 servings

INGREDIENTS

3 whole chicken breasts, split and skinned

2 cups mayonnaise

3 tablespoons lemon juice

¼ cup soy sauce

3 to 4 teaspoons curry powder

2 tablespoons minced onion

3 tablespoons chutney, chopped

VINEYARD CHICKEN SALAD

- Poach chicken breasts. When cool enough to handle, cut into cubes and refrigerate.

- In a medium bowl, combine the mayonnaise, lemon juice, soy sauce, curry, onion and chutney.

- Add celery, water chestnuts, grapes and pineapple to the chicken and mix well. Fold in the mayonnaise mixture and blend thoroughly.

- Refrigerate for at least 4 hours or overnight. Before serving, toss with nuts.

6 to 8 servings

Hint: Serve on marinated artichoke hearts, lettuce leaves, in orange cups, or stuff tomatoes.

1½ cups chopped celery

1 can (8 ounces) water chestnuts, drained and sliced

2 cups seedless green grapes, stemmed and halved

1 can (20 ounces) pineapple chunks, drained and chilled

¾ cup toasted slivered almonds

SUMMER NIGHT CHICKEN SALAD

- In a small mixing bowl, blend dressing ingredients. Refrigerate until ready to use.
- Slice green beans into 1½-inch lengths. Add chicken, water chestnuts, egg and pickle. Toss.
- Add dressing to salad and toss. Refrigerate 3 to 4 hours before serving.

4 servings

INGREDIENTS

2 cups crisply cooked green beans, chilled

1 cup cubed cooked chicken

1 can (8 ounces) water chestnuts, drained and sliced

1 hard-cooked egg, diced

⅓ cup coarsely chopped sweet pickles, drained

DRESSING

¼ cup mayonnaise

1 tablespoon finely chopped onion

1 teaspoon prepared mustard

1 teaspoon sweet pickle juice

1 teaspoon salt

INGREDIENTS

*1 pound mushrooms, sliced ¼
inch thick*

*1 can (8½ ounces) artichoke
hearts, halved lengthwise*

*1 package (10 ounces) frozen baby
carrots, cooked and drained*

¼ cup coarsely chopped pimientos

1 cup pitted black olives, sliced

DRESSING

⅔ cup vinegar

⅔ cup olive oil

¼ cup finely chopped onion

2 cloves garlic, crushed

1 teaspoon salt

1 teaspoon sugar

1 teaspoon dried basil leaves

1 teaspoon dried oregano leaves

INGREDIENTS

4 ounces wonton skins

2 to 3 cups vegetable oil

1 whole chicken breast

*1 head iceberg lettuce, coarsely
shredded*

4 green onions, thinly sliced

2 tablespoons sliced almonds

ANTIPASTO MEDLEY

THIS VERSATILE CLASSIC ALSO MAKES A
GREAT APPETIZER OR MEAT ACCOMPANIMENT

- In small saucepan, combine dressing ingredients. Bring to a boil, reduce heat, and cook 5 minutes, stirring occasionally. Cool 10 minutes.

- In medium serving bowl, layer mushrooms, artichoke hearts, carrots, pimientos and olives.

- Pour dressing over vegetables. Cover and refrigerate several hours or overnight.

- Toss gently before serving.

1 quart

WONTON CHICKEN SALAD

- In a small saucepan over medium-high heat, combine all dressing ingredients. Bring mixture to a boil, stirring constantly. Reduce heat, cover, and simmer 3 to 4 minutes.

- Cool slightly, then refrigerate at least 4 hours.

- Separate wonton skins and cut into strips ½-inch wide. In a large skillet on medium-high, heat oil and cook wonton skins until golden brown. Remove from skillet and drain on paper towel.

- Poach chicken. When cool enough to handle, remove skin and pull chicken into shreds.

- In large bowl, combine chicken, lettuce, green onions and almonds. Add fried wonton strips and dressing. Toss and serve.

6 servings

DRESSING

¼ cup vinegar

¼ cup ketchup

¼ cup water

3 tablespoons sugar

1 tablespoon soy sauce

ROAST BEEF NIÇOISE

- Whisk together all dressing ingredients.

- In a medium bowl, toss green beans with ½ cup of dressing. Refrigerate.

- In a large bowl, combine potatoes and shallots.

- Heat broth and pour over potatoes.

- Add ½ cup dressing; toss.

- In a shallow salad bowl or large serving platter, arrange from the outside in: onion rings, green beans, potatoes and roast beef.

- Decorate center with a rosette of onions rings. Sprinkle with chopped parsley and chives.

- Serve at room temperature accompanied with Mustard Dressing.

8 servings

INGREDIENTS

2 pounds cooked roast beef, cut into slices and 2-inch squares

1 pound green beans, cooked tender-crisp

2 pounds potatoes, cooked, thinly sliced

¼ cup minced shallots

¼ cup beef broth

2 red onions, sliced and separated into rings

Freshly minced parsley

Chives

MUSTARD DRESSING

¼ cup vinegar

2 tablespoons Dijon mustard

1 teaspoon salt

Pepper to taste

1 cup olive oil

INGREDIENTS

*1 box (6¼ ounces) long grain
wild rice*

1 cup chopped celery

1 cup chopped tomatoes

1 cup chopped cucumber

½ cup mayonnaise

¼ cup plain yogurt

1½ cups peanuts

SUMMER RICE SALAD

A GREAT HIT AT BARBECUES!

- Cook rice according to package directions. Cool and refrigerate.

- Add celery, tomatoes, cucumber, mayonnaise and yogurt; refrigerate.

- Before serving, sprinkle peanuts over salad.

6 servings

*Hint: Perk up any leftover salad by adding extra peanuts
for crunch.*

INGREDIENTS

1 pound fresh spinach

1 tablespoon vegetable oil

1 tablespoon flour

1 tablespoon sugar

2 tablespoons minced onion

¼ cup mayonnaise

3 tablespoons vinegar

½ cup water

Homemade croutons

Hot crispy bacon, crumbled

POPEYE'S SPINACH SALAD

- Wash spinach, remove coarse stems and pat dry. Cut roughly and arrange in large salad bowl.

- In skillet, heat oil and stir in flour, sugar, and onion. Blend in mayonnaise.

- Combine vinegar and water. Add slowly to skillet, stirring constantly, and bring sauce to boil. Cook 3 minutes.

- Pour hot sauce over spinach, tossing until every leaf is coated. Sprinkle with croutons and crisp bacon. Serve immediately.

4 to 6 servings

Carolina Coleslaw

THIS SPECIAL COLESLAW VARIATION MUST BE
MADE IN ADVANCE FOR BEST RESULTS!

- In a large bowl, toss vegetables together.

- In a small saucepan, mix together sugar, salt, mustard, and celery seed. Add vinegar and oil. Bring to boil over medium heat, stirring until sugar dissolves.

- Pour hot dressing over salad; toss well.

- Cover and refrigerate for 1 to 2 days before serving.

8 servings

INGREDIENTS

1 head cabbage (red, green or mix), shredded

½ red pepper, chopped

½ green pepper, chopped

1 medium sweet onion, finely chopped

2 carrots, grated

DRESSING

1 cup sugar

1 teaspoon salt

1 teaspoon dry mustard

1 teaspoon celery seed

1 cup cider vinegar

⅔ cup vegetable oil

Lentil Antipasto

- Cook lentils according to package directions; drain and cool.

- Cook pepper strips in small amount of water for about 6 minutes. Drain and cool.

- Cut salami into thin strips.

- In a small bowl, whisk together vinegar, oil, mustard, salt and pepper.

- In a large salad bowl, toss lentils, peppers, salami, and artichokes with dressing.

- Garnish with fresh parsley.

6 servings

INGREDIENTS

1⅓ cup dry lentils

2 sweet red peppers, cut into strips

½ pound lean cooked salami

1 can (8½ ounces) artichoke hearts

3 tablespoons white wine vinegar

¼ cup oil

1½ teaspoons Dijon mustard

Salt and pepper

Fresh parsley

COYE POINT SALAD

INGREDIENTS

*1 bag (10 ounces) spinach,
washed and torn*

1 cup cantaloupe balls

1 cup sliced zucchini

4 green onions, chopped

VINAIGRETTE

⅔ cup olive oil

¼ cup fresh lemon juice

¼ cup Parmesan cheese

2 cloves garlic, crushed

1 teaspoon salt

Freshly ground pepper

- Whisk together vinaigrette ingredients at least one hour before serving.

- Arrange spinach, melon, zucchini and onions on salad plates or in small salad bowls.

- Just before serving, spoon 2 to 3 tablespoons vinaigrette on each salad. Sprinkle with freshly ground pepper.

6 servings

SUNNY BROCCOLI SALAD

INGREDIENTS

*1 large bunch fresh broccoli
(approximately 5 cups)*

1 cup raisins

¼ cup diced red onion

*10 strips bacon, fried and
crumbled*

1 cup sunflower seeds

3 tablespoons sugar

½ cup mayonnaise

1 tablespoon red wine vinegar

- Chop broccoli into small florets.
- Combine broccoli, raisins, onion, bacon and sunflower seeds.
- Mix together sugar, mayonnaise and vinegar.
- Pour dressing over salad and toss. Refrigerate for several hours before serving.

6 servings

Hint: Add cheddar cheese, mushrooms or golden raisins.

Couscous Marrakesh

TAKE THIS HEARTY, HEALTHY SALAD TO YOUR NEXT PICNIC

- Whisk together vinaigrette ingredients. Refrigerate until ready to serve.
- In a large mixing bowl, combine couscous, green onions, tomatoes, cucumber, baked beans and parsley. Gently stir to blend.
- Just before serving, add vinaigrette and mix well.

6 servings

INGREDIENTS

2 cups cooked couscous

6 green onions, sliced and chopped

½ pint cherry tomatoes, stemmed and halved

1 medium cucumber, peeled, seeded and chopped

1 can (16 ounces) baked beans, drained

½ cup minced fresh parsley

VINAIGRETTE

½ cup white vinegar

2 cloves garlic, minced

1 teaspoon Dijon mustard

1 teaspoon salt

¾ cup olive oil

Red, White and Green Salad

- Rinse peas in hot water and drain.
- Combine vegetables, nuts, bacon and sour cream in serving dish.
- Combine dressing, mustard and garlic. Pour over vegetables.
- Toss and chill until serving.

8 servings

INGREDIENTS

1 package (10 ounces) frozen peas

1 cup chopped celery

1 cup chopped cauliflower

¼ cup chopped green onion

2 tablespoons pimiento

1 cup chopped cashews

¼ cup cooked, crumbled bacon

½ cup sour cream

1 cup prepared ranch-style dressing

½ teaspoon Dijon mustard

1 small clove garlic, minced

½ cup sliced almonds

4 teaspoons sugar

1 head romaine

2 stalks celery, chopped

2 green onions, including tops, sliced

1 can (11 ounces) mandarin orange sections, drained

VINAIGRETTE

¼ cup salad oil

2 tablespoons sugar

2 tablespoons white wine vinegar

1 tablespoon minced fresh parsley

½ teaspoon salt

MANDARIN ROMAINE

- In a small bowl, whisk together vinaigrette ingredients. Refrigerate until ready to use.

- In a small sauté pan, combine almonds and sugar. Using low heat, stir constantly until almonds are coated with melted sugar and slightly browned. Remove from heat. When cool, break almonds apart.

- Tear romaine into bite-sized pieces and place in a large salad bowl. Add celery, green onions and orange sections. Toss and refrigerate.

- Before serving, toss with almonds and dressing.

4 to 6 servings

INGREDIENTS

2 heads romaine lettuce

¾ cup garlic-flavored olive oil, divided

½ teaspoon salt

½ teaspoon freshly ground black pepper

1 clove garlic, minced

1 large lemon, juiced

HAIL, CAESAR!*

- Gently tear romaine and place in a large salad bowl. Pour ½ cup garlic-flavored oil over romaine; toss.

- Add salt, pepper and garlic; toss slightly.

- Add lemon juice and Worcestershire sauce.

- Break eggs over salad, add remaining ¼ cup oil and the cheese. Toss again until leaves are well-coated.

- Add croutons and anchovies, if desired, and serve immediately.

4 to 6 servings

Hint: To coddle an egg, bring a small pan of water to a boil. Add 2 eggs and take pan off heat. After 1 minute, remove eggs from water and set aside.

* This recipe contains uncooked egg yolks/whites. See SPECIAL NOTE page 7.

6 to 8 drops Worcestershire sauce

2 coddled eggs

¼ cup freshly grated Parmesan cheese

1 cup croutons

1 can (2 ounces) anchovies, drained (optional)

RASPBERRY ENDIVE SALAD

- Whisk together salad oil, sugar, vinegar, and lemon juice in small mixing bowl.
- Gradually add sour cream, poppy seeds and Dijon mustard.
- Add liqueur, and salt and pepper, if needed.
- Arrange plates with assorted greens. Sprinkle with walnuts and raspberries.

4 servings

INGREDIENTS

½ cup salad oil

3 tablespoons sugar

2 tablespoons raspberry vinegar

1 tablespoon fresh lemon juice

1 tablespoon sour cream

1 tablespoon poppy seeds

1 teaspoon Dijon mustard

1½ tablespoons Framboise liqueur (optional)

Salt and freshly ground pepper

Assorted greens (endive, Boston lettuce, and/or watercress)

Chopped walnuts

Whole raspberries (in season)

INGREDIENTS

*2 large bunches watercress, torn
into bite-sized pieces*

*1 small head romaine lettuce, torn
into bite-sized pieces*

*1 head Bibb lettuce, torn into
bite-sized pieces*

1 cup cold water

1 teaspoon lemon juice

*1 Crispin or "20-Ounce" apple,
cored and sliced*

⅔ cup toasted walnuts

VINAIGRETTE

2 tablespoons minced shallots

2 tablespoons apple cider vinegar

2 tablespoons fresh lemon juice

¾ teaspoon freshly ground pepper

½ teaspoon sugar

½ teaspoon salt

⅔ cup walnut oil

⅔ cup blue cheese, crumbled

FESTIVAL OF GREENS

- In a small mixing bowl, combine shallots, vinegar, lemon juice, pepper, sugar and salt. Slowly whisk in oil.

- Add cheese and set aside 30 minutes for flavors to blend.

- Place greens in large salad bowl; refrigerate.

- To prevent apple from turning brown, dip each slice into water mixed with lemon juice. Pat dry.

- Before serving, toss greens with vinaigrette. Add apples and nuts; toss again.

8 servings

MORNING GLORY SALAD

- Combine lettuce, banana, raisins, walnuts and apple in serving dish.
- Whisk together vinaigrette ingredients.
- Pour vinaigrette over salad; toss and serve immediately.

4 to 6 servings

INGREDIENTS

1 medium head lettuce, shredded

1 banana, sliced

¾ cup raisins

¾ cup chopped walnuts

1 large apple, chopped

VINAIGRETTE

½ 6-ounce can orange juice concentrate, undiluted

½ cup salad oil

2 tablespoons honey

2 tablespoons white vinegar

1 teaspoon poppy seeds

GREEK TOMATO SALAD

THIS OIL-FREE DRESSING IS EXTRA REFRESHING

- Place tomatoes, cheese, onions and olives in a 13 x 9-inch glass dish.
- In a small bowl, mix remaining ingredients. Blend thoroughly.
- Pour dressing over tomatoes, gently lifting top slices to coat evenly.
- Refrigerate, covered, at least 2 hours.
- Drain salad and serve on a platter lined with lettuce leaves.

8 servings

INGREDIENTS

6 medium tomatoes, sliced

¼ pound Feta cheese, crumbled

1 small Bermuda onion, thinly sliced

1 can (3½ ounces) pitted ripe olives, drained and sliced

⅓ cup red wine vinegar

2 teaspoons minced fresh parsley

4 teaspoons sugar

¼ teaspoon salt

½ teaspoon dried basil

¼ teaspoon freshly ground pepper

Lettuce leaves

INGREDIENTS

2 packages (10 ounces each)
spinach

1 pound cottage cheese

1 cup coarsely chopped pecans

1 cup drained mandarin oranges

DRESSING

½ cup sour cream

3 tablespoons red wine vinegar

½ cup sugar

¼ teaspoon dry mustard

1 tablespoon horseradish

1 small onion, grated

½ teaspoon salt

½ teaspoon pepper

SUPERLATIVE SPINACH SALAD

DON'T LET THIS INTERESTING COMBINATION
OF INGREDIENTS FOOL YOU!

- Wash spinach, discard tough stems and tear large leaves into bite-sized pieces.

- Combine spinach, cottage cheese, pecans and oranges.

- Blend dressing ingredients until smooth.

- Before serving salad, add dressing and toss.

6 servings

Potatoes El Greco

- Scrub potatoes; cut into ½-inch slices.
- Steam over medium heat until potatoes are just tender.
- Transfer potatoes to a large bowl. Toss with 2 tablespoons lemon juice.
- When potatoes are completely cool, add olives, green onions and cheese.
- In blender, combine remaining lemon juice, oregano, salt and olive oil. Mix at medium speed for 10 seconds. Pour over potatoes; toss gently. Serve immediately or refrigerate. If made ahead, remove from refrigerator 1 hour before serving.

6 servings

INGREDIENTS

2 pounds small red potatoes

⅓ cup fresh squeezed lemon juice, divided

½ cup pitted, sliced black olives

½ cup sliced green onions

¾ cup crumbled Feta cheese

1 teaspoon dried oregano

¼ teaspoon salt

½ cup olive oil

Spring Potato Salad

- Combine vinegar, sugar, chopped celery, fresh dill and dried dill.
- Pour marinade over potatoes. Refrigerate several hours or overnight.
- Add remaining vegetables to potatoes. Stir in mayonnaise.
- Before serving, line salad bowl with greens and fill center with salad.

6 to 8 servings

INGREDIENTS

4 cups tiny new potatoes, cooked and halved

¼ cup vinegar

¼ cup sugar

¼ cup chopped celery

1 tablespoon fresh dill

1 teaspoon dried dill weed

1½ cups very small cherry tomatoes

½ cup diced green pepper

6 green onions, thinly sliced

1 cup sliced celery

2 cups broccoli florets

1 cup mayonnaise

Greens for garnish

INGREDIENTS

1 head red leaf lettuce

1 fennel bulb

*1 to 2 tablespoons pine nuts,
toasted*

DRESSING

1 tablespoon Dijon mustard

½ teaspoon sugar

2 tablespoons red wine vinegar

*2 tablespoons sesame seeds, crushed
with a pinch of salt*

*1 tablespoon white wine
Worcestershire sauce*

2 cloves garlic, minced

Salt to taste

Freshly ground pepper

3 tablespoons olive oil

3 tablespoons vegetable oil

FENNEL SALAD
WITH SESAME DRESSING

- In a medium mixing bowl, combine mustard, sugar, vinegar, sesame seeds, Worcestershire sauce, garlic, salt and pepper. Slowly whisk in oils. Refrigerate until ready to use.

- Slice white portion of fennel bulb. Add to bite-size pieces of lettuce in large salad bowl.

- Pour dressing over salad. Add pine nuts and toss.

4 servings

Winter Sunshine Salad

PERK UP WINTER DOLDRUMS WITH THIS COLORFUL SALAD!

- Steam beans and peas, leaving them tender-crisp. Drain.

- In a salad bowl, combine vegetables.

- In a saucepan, bring dressing ingredients to a boil. Remove from heat; cool to room temperature.

- Pour dressing over salad. Refrigerate at least 4 hours before serving.

8 to 10 servings

INGREDIENTS

1 package (10 ounces) frozen French-style green beans

1 package (10 ounces) frozen peas

1 can (16 ounces) shoe peg or white corn, drained

1 cup diced onion

1 cup diced celery

1 cup diced green or red pepper

1 jar (2 ounces) diced pimiento, drained

DRESSING

¾ cup vinegar

½ cup salad oil

1 tablespoon water

½ teaspoon pepper

1 teaspoon salt

⅓ to ½ cup sugar

INGREDIENTS

1 pound asparagus

2 firm, ripe tomatoes

1 can (14-ounce) hearts of palm, drained

1 medium onion, thinly sliced

VINAIGRETTE

⅔ cup olive oil

1 tablespoon lemon juice

3 tablespoons wine vinegar

2 tablespoons Dijon mustard

1 clove garlic, minced

1 tablespoon fresh basil

1 tablespoon parsley

VEGETABLE VINAIGRETTE

- Clean asparagus and bias cut into 1½ to 2-inch segments.
- Cook asparagus until tender crisp.
- Cut tomatoes into 8 to 12 wedges.
- In a serving bowl combine the prepared vegetables.
- Combine the vinaigrette ingredients in a small bowl.
- Gently toss dressing with vegetables.

6 servings

Hint: When fresh asparagus is not in season, green beans may be substituted.

WHAT'S-THE-SECRET SALAD

INGREDIENTS

1½ cups cider, divided

3 tablespoons red cinnamon candies

1 package (3 ounces) lemon-flavored gelatin

1 envelope unflavored gelatin

2 cups applesauce

- In a saucepan over medium heat, boil 1 cup cider. Add candies and gelatin, stirring to dissolve. Remove from heat.
- Stir in applesauce and remaining cider.
- Pour into a lightly oiled 1½-quart mold or serving bowl. Refrigerate until firm.

6 servings

CRANBERRY MOLDED SALAD

INGREDIENTS

1 can (16 ounces) whole berry cranberry sauce

4 large seedless oranges

1 tablespoon lemon juice

1 package (3 ounces) orange-flavored gelatin

1 pint vanilla ice cream or frozen yogurt

2 teaspoons grated orange rind

Salad greens

- Place cranberry sauce in a strainer over a large measuring pitcher. Break sauce into small chunks, catching the syrup in the measurer.
- Peel oranges and dice sections, reserving juice.
- Combine cranberry syrup, orange and lemon juices. Add enough water to yield 1 cup liquid. Bring liquid to boil and and pour liquid over gelatin, stirring until dissolved.
- Add ice cream; mix well. Chill until partially jelled.
- Fold in orange rind, oranges and cranberry sauce.
- Pour into lightly-oiled 2-quart mold or individual molds. Chill until firm.
- Unmold to a serving platter or individual plates lined with salad greens.

6 to 8 servings

INGREDIENTS

*1 can (15 ounces) crushed
pineapple*

*1 package (3 ounces) lemon
gelatin*

½ cup sugar

¼ teaspoon salt

2 tablespoons lemon juice

1 cup finely grated carrots

1 cup heavy cream, whipped

LEMON REFRESHER

- Drain crushed pineapple, reserving juice.

- Add water to juice to measure 1½ cups. Heat to boiling and stir in gelatin until dissolved.

- Add sugar, salt and lemon juice.

- Refrigerate until slightly thickened, then add carrots and drained pineapple.

- Fold in whipped cream and pour into lightly-oiled mold. Refrigerate until firm.

10 servings

INGREDIENTS

2 shallots, minced

*2 tablespoons fresh minced
tarragon (or 1 tablespoon dried)*

1 teaspoon Dijon mustard

3 tablespoons lemon juice

½ cup plus 2 tablespoons oil

Salt and pepper

CREAMY TARRAGON DRESSING

THIS SILKY DRESSING IS REMINISCENT OF BEARNAISE SAUCE

- Blend or process all ingredients in a blender or food processor fitted with a metal blade. Adjust seasonings to taste.

¾ cup

Citrus Dressing

- In a small saucepan, beat egg with a whisk until foamy.

- Stir in juices and sugar. Boil one minute over medium heat, stirring constantly. Cool.

- Before serving, gently fold in whipped cream. Serve immediately over your favorite salad greens or fresh fruit.

2½ cups

INGREDIENTS

1 egg

Juice of 1 lemon

Juice of ½ orange

⅓ cup frozen orange juice concentrate, thawed

5 heaping tablespoons confectioners' sugar

2 cups heavy cream, whipped

Vermont Salad Dressing

- In a blender, combine vinegar and garlic. Blend at low speed until garlic is finely chopped.

- Strain the mixture through a fine sieve into a small mixing bowl. Discard garlic.

- Add salt, pepper, mustard and maple syrup. Whisk until well blended.

- Add oils in a slow stream, whisking until dressing is emulsified.

- Refrigerate dressing in a jar or airtight container. Before using, bring dressing to room temperature. Shake before using.

1½ cups

Hint: For zippier flavor, don't discard the garlic!

INGREDIENTS

¼ cup cider vinegar

1 garlic clove

¼ teaspoon salt

¼ teaspoon freshly ground pepper

1 teaspoon Dijon mustard

2 tablespoons maple syrup

⅔ cup olive oil

⅓ cup vegetable oil

INGREDIENTS

1 cup vegetable oil

½ cup cider vinegar

½ cup granulated sugar

⅓ cup grated Parmesan cheese

2 tablespoons Dijon mustard

TANGY DIJON DRESSING

A TANGY SWEET DRESSING WITH A ZESTY ACCENT

- Blend dressing ingredients in blender at high speed.
- Refrigerate until ready to serve.

2⅓ cups

INGREDIENTS

1 small egg yolk

1 teaspoon Dijon mustard

Dash hot pepper sauce

1 teaspoon white vinegar

½ cup olive oil

2 teaspoons lemon juice

¼ cup heavy cream

Salt and pepper

CREAMY MUSTARD DRESSING*

- Beat egg yolk, then add mustard, hot pepper sauce, and vinegar.
- Using a whisk, add oil until thick and smooth.
- Stir in lemon juice and cream; beat well.
- Season to taste. If not serving immediately, refrigerate. Shake well before using.

¾ cup

* This recipe contains uncooked egg yolks/whites. See SPECIAL NOTE page 7.

BUTTERMILK BLUE DRESSING

INGREDIENTS

1 cup buttermilk

3 to 4 ounces blue cheese, crumbled

1½ to 3 teaspoons garlic salt

1 cup mayonnaise

- Combine buttermilk, cheese and garlic salt in blender.
- Add mayonnaise and pulse blender. (Over mixing will break down the mayonnaise and make the dressing too thin.)
- Refrigerate until ready to serve.

1½ pints

FRUITY CRANBERRY RELISH

INGREDIENTS

12 ounces fresh cranberries, chopped

1½ cups sugar

2 unpeeled apples, cored and chopped

Juice of 2 oranges

Zest of one orange

1 can (8 ounces) crushed pine-apple, drained

- Combine all ingredients. Keep refrigerated.
- Serve as a side dish or as a topping.

6 servings

INGREDIENTS

¼ cup lemon juice

1 envelope unflavored gelatin

4 eggs, beaten

⅔ cup sugar

½ cup water

½ cup cider vinegar

3 tablespoons Dijon mustard

¼ teaspoon salt

1 cup heavy cream, whipped

2 tablespoons minced fresh parsley

MARVELOUS MUSTARD MOUSSE

A UNIQUE COMPLEMENT FOR PORK, HAM OR BEEF

- In a small bowl or cup, sprinkle gelatin over lemon juice. Let stand 5 minutes to soften.

- In a medium saucepan, combine eggs, sugar, water, vinegar, mustard and salt. Add gelatin mixture. Cook over medium heat, stirring constantly, until mixture begins to thicken; do not boil.

- Refrigerate until mixture is very thick and almost set (approximately 1 hour).

- Remove mixture from refrigerator. If lumpy, whisk until smooth. Fold in whipped cream and parsley. Pour mixture into a well-oiled 4-cup mold. Cover with plastic wrap; refrigerate several hours or overnight.

- To unmold, run the tip of table knife around edges of mold, dip bottom of mold in warm water and invert onto platter.

8 servings

Hint: If mold has a hollow center, fill it with fresh herbs or beets for a colorful garnish.

BREAD & BREAKFAST

Bread & Breakfast / Index

Bread & Muffins

An Excuse to Eat Carrot Cake
for Breakfast / 100

Angel Biscuits / 110

Apricot Nut Bread / 103

Banana Blueberry Bread / 100

Blueberry Hill Muffins / 101

Butterhorns / 109

Cherry Blossom Coffee Cake / 105

Cinnamon Apple Treasures / 99

Cinnamon Sensations / 104

Crunchy Cracked Wheat Bread / 112

Eastman House Rolls / 110

Family Swedish Rye / 113

Finger Lakes Grape Bread / 103

Hawaiian Bread / 102

Irish Soda Bread / 106

Lemon Bubble Bread / 108

Medieval Apple Fritters / 107

Poppy Seed Lemon Bread / 102

Raisin Scones / 106

Taster's Choice Zucchini Bread / 104

Eggs & Cheese

Blintz Soufflé / 114

Breakfast Extraordinaire / 115

Breakfast Pizza / 114

Eggs in Bacon Baskets / 116

Feather-light Cheese Soufflé / 117

Ham and Sauerkraut Puff / 116

Ham Strudel / 118

Matzo Kugel / 118

Onion Cheese Strata / 119

Strasbourg Quiche / 121

Sunday Night Frittata / 120

Swiss Brunch / 120

Pancakes

Baked Apple Pecan Pancake / 122

Batter-Up French Toast / 123

Fancy French Toast Pockets / 124

Marmalade Monte Cristo / 123

Orange Waffles / 125

Sour Cream Pancakes / 124

Side Dishes

A+ Apricots / 126

Baked Aloha / 127

Orange Noodle Pudding / 128

Pears Burgundy / 127

Spiced Peaches / 126

Strawberry Créme / 128

Cinnamon Apple Treasures

- In a large bowl, combine butter, sugar and egg. Stir in grated apple.
- In a medium bowl, combine flour, baking powder, salt and nutmeg. Gradually add dry ingredients and milk to the butter and apple mixture.
- Fill greased muffin tins ⅔ full.
- Bake for 20 to 25 minutes, or until golden.
- While muffins are baking, melt ½ cup butter. Set aside. In a small bowl, combine sugar and cinnamon. Set aside.
- Remove muffins from tins and roll tops and sides immediately in melted butter. Dip into mixture of sugar and cinnamon. Serve immediately.

Note: Can be made through step 4 and cooled. Reheat and complete recipe.

Temperature: 350°

Time: 20 to 25 minutes

12 muffins

INGREDIENTS

⅓ cup soft butter

½ cup sugar

1 egg

½ cup grated, pared apple

1½ cups flour

1½ teaspoons baking powder

½ teaspoon salt

¼ teaspoon nutmeg

½ cup milk

TOPPING

½ cup butter

½ cup sugar

1 teaspoon cinnamon

INGREDIENTS

2 cups flour

1¼ cups sugar

2 teaspoons baking soda

2 teaspoons cinnamon

½ teaspoon salt

2 cups grated carrots

½ cup nuts

½ cup raisins

½ cup coconut

1 apple, peeled, cored and grated

3 eggs

1 cup oil

2 teaspoons vanilla

An Excuse to Eat Carrot Cake for Breakfast

- In a large bowl, mix flour, sugar, baking soda, cinnamon and salt together.

- Stir in carrots, nuts, raisins, coconut and apple.

- In separate bowl, beat together eggs, oil and vanilla; add to the batter.

- Spoon batter into well-greased muffin tins, filling almost to the top.

- Bake for 20 minutes.

Temperature: 350°

Time: 20 minutes

14 to 18 muffins

INGREDIENTS

1¾ cups flour

2 teaspoons baking powder

¼ teaspoon baking soda

½ teaspoon salt

⅓ cup butter

⅔ cup sugar

Banana Blueberry Bread

An unusual but winning combination

- Sift together flour, baking powder, soda and salt. Set aside.

- In a large bowl, cream butter and sugar until light and fluffy.

- Beat in eggs one at a time.

- Alternately stir in dry ingredients and bananas, one third at a time.

- Gently stir in blueberries.

- Bake in a well-oiled 5 x 9-inch loaf pan for 50 minutes or until a toothpick inserted in center "comes clean".

- Cool in pan for 10 minutes, then remove from pan and finish cooling on a rack.

Temperature: 350°

Time: 50 minutes

1 loaf

2 eggs

1 cup mashed ripe bananas

1 cup fresh or frozen blueberries

BLUEBERRY HILL MUFFINS

INGREDIENTS

- In a medium bowl, combine all ingredients except blueberries. Mixture should remain lumpy.

- Fold in blueberries.

- Pour batter into muffin tins, filling ⅔ to ¾ full. Paper liners may be used, if desired.

- Bake for 25 to 35 minutes.

Temperature: 375°

Time: 25 to 35 minutes

12 muffins

1 cup sugar

¼ cup melted margarine

1⅓ cups flour

1 teaspoon cinnamon

1 teaspoon nutmeg

1 cup milk

1 egg

2 teaspoons baking powder

½ teaspoon vanilla

¼ teaspoon salt

¾ to 1 cup fresh blueberries, stemmed

INGREDIENTS

⅔ cup plus 1 tablespoon sugar

2 eggs

½ cup milk

½ cup butter, melted and cooled

1 tablespoon lemon extract

1½ cups flour

1 teaspoon baking soda

1 teaspoon baking powder

½ teaspoon salt

3½ tablespoons poppy seeds

POPPY SEED LEMON BREAD

- In large bowl, beat sugar and eggs until light and fluffy.
- Slowly add milk, butter and lemon extract, continuing to mix.
- Sift together flour, baking soda, baking powder and salt, then add to egg mixture. Add poppy seeds.
- Pour into greased and floured 4 x 7½-inch loaf pan. Bake for 55 minutes or until lightly browned.

Temperature: 325°

Time: 55 minutes

1 loaf

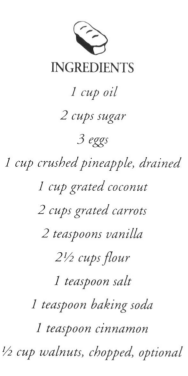

INGREDIENTS

1 cup oil

2 cups sugar

3 eggs

1 cup crushed pineapple, drained

1 cup grated coconut

2 cups grated carrots

2 teaspoons vanilla

2½ cups flour

1 teaspoon salt

1 teaspoon baking soda

1 teaspoon cinnamon

½ cup walnuts, chopped, optional

HAWAIIAN BREAD

- Combine oil, sugar and eggs.
- Add crushed pineapple, coconut, carrots, vanilla and nuts, if desired.
- Sift together dry ingredients. Stir into batter.
- Pour batter into 2 greased and floured 5 x 9-inch loaf pans.
- Bake for 1 hour. Cool before slicing.

Note: Letting batter sit in pans about 20 minutes before baking may minimize the tendency for the top to crack.

Temperature: 350°

Time: 1 hour

2 loaves

Finger Lakes Grape Bread

INGREDIENTS

- In large bowl, combine all ingredients, except grape skins.
- When well-blended, gently fold in grape skins.
- Pour batter into 2 well-oiled 5 x 9-inch loaf pans. Bake 1 hour or until tester comes out clean.
- Let stand 5 minutes before removing from pans.

Temperature: 325°

Time: 1 hour

2 loaves

Hint: If Concord grapes are not available, substitute a sweet blue grape used for juice making.

INGREDIENTS

3 large eggs, beaten

2 cups sugar

2 teaspoons vanilla

1 cup vegetable oil

3 cups flour

¾ teaspoon salt

1 teaspoon baking soda

1 teaspoon cinnamon

¾ to 1 cup chopped walnuts

3 cups Concord grape skins

Apricot Nut Bread

- Soak chopped apricots in hot water for 30 minutes.
- In separate bowl, mix sugar and egg; beat well.
- Add dry ingredients alternately with orange juice.
- Stir in butter, nuts and apricots.
- Pour batter into well-oiled 5 x 9-inch loaf pan.
- Bake for 50 minutes.

Temperature: 350°

Time: 50 minutes

1 loaf

INGREDIENTS

1 cup chopped dried apricots

¼ cup hot water

1 cup sugar

1 egg

2 cups flour

2 teaspoons baking powder

½ teaspoon baking soda

½ cup orange juice

2 tablespoons butter, melted

½ cup chopped walnuts or pecans

INGREDIENTS

2 cups sugar

1 cup vegetable oil

3 eggs, beaten

*2½ cups shredded, fresh zucchini
(approximately 1½ pounds)*

*1 medium orange, ground
with peel*

3 cups flour

1 teaspoon salt

1 teaspoon baking soda

¼ teaspoon baking powder

1 teaspoon cinnamon

3 teaspoons vanilla

1 cup coconut

½ cup pecans, chopped

½ cup raisins

TASTER'S CHOICE ZUCCHINI BREAD

ORANGE AND COCONUT MAKE THIS
ZUCCHINI BREAD THE TASTER'S CHOICE!

- Mix sugar, oil and eggs.
- Stir in all other ingredients.
- Grease and flour pans (either 2 large or 3 small). Pour dough into pans.
- Bake for 40 to 45 minutes for small pans, or 75 minutes for large pans.

Temperature: 325°

Baking time: 40 to 45 minutes, small pans
75 minutes, large pans

3 small or 2 large loaves

INGREDIENTS

1 large loaf thin-sliced bread

*2 packages (8 ounces each)
cream cheese*

2 egg yolks

½ cup sugar

CINNAMON SENSATIONS

- Trim bread crusts; roll each slice as thinly as possible.
- In medium bowl, cream together cream cheese, egg yolks and sugar. Spread on one side of each slice of bread.
- Roll up each slice and press edge to secure roll.
- Combine brown sugar and cinnamon in shallow bowl.

- Dip each roll into butter and then immediately coat each roll with sugar mixture. Place rolls on greased baking sheet and freeze at least 4 hours or overnight.

- Slice each roll into 3 or 4 sections and return to a greased cookie sheet.

- Bake 8 to 10 minutes, turning once while baking.

- Serve hot. May be served with sour cream for dipping.

Temperature: 375°

Time: 8 to 10 minutes

32 rolls

1 teaspoon cinnamon

1½ cups butter or margarine, melted

1½ cups brown sugar

Sour cream, optional

CHERRY BLOSSOM COFFEE CAKE

- Combine flour, sugar, baking soda, baking powder and salt.

- Cut in butter until fine crumbs form.

- In separate bowl, beat together buttermilk, eggs and vanilla.

- Add buttermilk mixture to dry ingredients and stir to moisten.

- Pour half of batter into an oiled 9 x 13-inch pan. Spread cherry filling over batter in pan. Spoon remaining batter in small mounds on top of filling.

- Combine topping ingredients until fine crumbs form; sprinkle over batter.

- Bake for 40 to 45 minutes.

Temperature: 350° (325° for glass pan)

Time: 40 to 45 minutes

10 to 15 servings

INGREDIENTS

3 cups flour

1 cup sugar

1 teaspoon baking soda

1 teaspoon baking powder

1 teaspoon salt

1 cup butter

1 cup buttermilk

2 eggs, slightly beaten

1 teaspoon vanilla

1 can (21 ounces) cherry pie filling

TOPPING

¾ cup sugar

½ cup flour

¼ cup butter

Raisin Scones

INGREDIENTS

2 cups all purpose flour

2 teaspoons baking powder

½ teaspoon baking soda

½ teaspoon salt

3 tablespoons sugar

½ teaspoon nutmeg

6 tablespoons chilled, unsalted butter, cut in pieces

1 cup golden raisins

6 ounces plain or lemon yogurt, or sour cream

1 egg, separated

¼ cup cinnamon sugar

- In large bowl, combine flour, baking powder, baking soda, salt, sugar and nutmeg.

- Cut in butter until mixture resembles coarse crumbs. Stir in raisins.

- In small bowl, blend yogurt or sour cream with egg yolk. Add to crumb mixture, stirring until dough clings together.

- On a generously floured surface, knead gently for 10 to 12 strokes.

- Pat the dough into a 9-inch circle, about ½-inch thick. Cut into 2 to 3-inch circles with a biscuit cutter.

- Brush top with egg white and sprinkle with cinnamon sugar.

- Bake 15 to 20 minutes or until scones are golden brown.

Temperature: 375°

Time: 15 to 20 minutes

6 to 8 servings

Irish Soda Bread

INGREDIENTS

4 cups flour

3 heaping teaspoons baking powder

¼ teaspoon baking soda

1½ teaspoons salt

4 teaspoons caraway seeds

- In a large bowl, combine flour, baking powder, baking soda, salt, caraway seeds and sugar. Mix well. Stir in raisins.

- In a small bowl, lightly beat egg. Add sour cream and milk; blend well.

- Add the egg mixture, a little at a time, to the dry ingredients, mixing well. The mixture will be a little sticky.

- Divide the bread mixture into two greased and floured 9-inch cake pans. Pat the mixture evenly in the pans.

- Bake for 1 hour until golden brown.

- Remove from pans and cool on a rack. Lightly brush with butter while hot.

Temperature: 350°

Time: 1 hour

2 loaves

½ cup sugar

1 cup raisins

1 egg

2 cups sour cream

½ cup milk

Butter

MEDIEVAL APPLE FRITTERS

- In a large bowl, combine flour, egg and salt. Pour in ale. Stir with a fork until the ingredients are just blended, custard-like and lumpy. Do not overbeat or batter will be tough.

- Add enough oil to measure 1½ to 2 inches deep in a large skillet. Heat on medium-high. When oil is hot, dip apple slices into batter and immediately fry in hot oil, until both sides are golden brown, turning once.

- Drain fritters on paper towels.

- Combine sugar and cinnamon. Use a sifter to sprinkle mixture over fritters. Serve hot.

Hint: If batter thickens, add an additional ¼ cup ale.

2½ dozen

INGREDIENTS

1 cup unbleached white flour

1 large egg, beaten

¼ teaspoon salt

1 cup ale

4 large firm apples, cored, peeled and sliced into ¼-inch slices

3 to 5 cups vegetable oil

TOPPING

½ cup confectioners' sugar

1 teaspoon cinnamon

INGREDIENTS

5½ cups all purpose flour, divided

1 cup sugar, divided

1 teaspoon salt

2 packages rapid-action active dry yeast

1 cup milk

½ cup water

¼ cup plus 2 tablespoons butter or margarine, divided

2 eggs

Grated peel of 2 lemons

¼ teaspoon ground mace

LEMON BUBBLE BREAD

- In a large bowl, combine 2 cups flour, ½ cup sugar, salt and yeast.

- In medium saucepan, over low heat, heat milk, water and ¼ cup butter or margarine until very warm. (Butter doesn't need to melt.)

- With mixer at low speed, gradually pour liquid into dry ingredients. Beat until just mixed. Increasing speed to medium, add eggs and beat 2 minutes.

- Beat in ½ cup flour or enough to make a thick batter. Continue beating 2 minutes with a spoon, stirring in enough flour (about 2 cups) to make soft dough.

- Turn dough onto lightly floured surface and knead until smooth and elastic (about 10 minutes).

- Shape into ball and place in greased bowl. Cover with towel and let rise until doubled (about 1 hour).

- Punch down dough. Turn onto lightly floured surface. Cut dough in half. Cover with bowl and let stand 15 minutes.

- Meanwhile in small bowl, combine ½ cup sugar, lemon peel and mace. Set aside.

- In saucepan, melt 2 tablespoons butter or margarine.

- Cut each dough half into 16 pieces. Shape each piece into a ball.

- Place 16 balls in well-oiled 10-inch tube pan. Brush with half the melted butter or margarine. Sprinkle with half the lemon mixture.

- Repeat with remaining balls, butter and lemon mixture.

- Cover with towel. Let rise in warm place 45 minutes.

- Bake for 35 minutes. Cool on wire rack.

Temperature: 350°

Time: 35 minutes

1 loaf

BUTTERHORNS

- In a saucepan over medium heat, combine milk and butter. Heat until milk is scalded. Cool slightly.

- Add yeast and ¼ teaspoon sugar to water.

- In a large bowl, mix sugar, salt and eggs. Stir in the milk-butter mixture and the yeast.

- Beat in 2 cups of flour, then remaining flour, gradually mixing by hand.

- Place dough in an oiled bowl, cover and let rise until doubled in volume.

- Transfer dough to a lightly floured board. Divide dough into 4 equal parts; and roll each piece into a 6 to 8-inch circle.

- Cut into 8 pie-shaped wedges. Roll starting at wider end. Put seam down on a lightly oiled cookie sheet.

- Cover and allow to rise about 1 hour.

- Bake for 12 to 15 minutes. Remove rolls to a rack to cool.

- For glaze, combine confectioners' sugar, vanilla and enough milk to achieve a spreading consistency. Spread over cool rolls.

Temperature: 350°

Time: 12 to 15 minutes

32 servings

INGREDIENTS

1 cup milk

1 cup butter

2 packages dry yeast

¼ cup warm water

¼ teaspoon sugar

½ cup sugar

1 teaspoon salt

2 eggs

4½ cups flour

1 cup confectioners' sugar

½ teaspoon vanilla or almond extract

1 to 2 tablespoons milk

INGREDIENTS

1 cake or package dry yeast

2 tablespoons warm water

5 cups flour

1 teaspoon baking soda

1 tablespoon baking powder

¼ cup sugar

1 teaspoon salt

1 cup shortening

2 cups buttermilk

ANGEL BISCUITS

- Dissolve yeast in warm water and set aside.
- Sift flour with other dry ingredients.
- Cut in shortening, using pastry blender or fork.
- Add buttermilk and yeast mixture to flour mixture. Stir until soft dough forms.
- Knead on floured board 2 minutes.
- Roll out to desired thickness and cut with biscuit cutter. Bake for 10 minutes. Serve warm with butter and honey.

Note: After kneading, dough can be put in covered plastic bowl and kept in refrigerator up to 7 days.

Temperature: 450°

Time: 10 minutes

45 biscuits

INGREDIENTS

6 to 6½ cups unbleached flour

½ cup sugar

2 teaspoons salt

2 packages rapid-action active dry yeast

1 cup butter

1 egg

EASTMAN HOUSE ROLLS

WORTH THE EFFORT!

About 3½ hours before serving:

- In a large bowl, combine 2¼ cups flour, sugar, salt and yeast. Add ½ cup butter.
- With mixer at slow speed, gradually pour 2 cups hot water into dry ingredients.
- Add egg. Increase speed to medium and beat 2 minutes.

- Beat in ¾ cup flour or enough to make thick batter; continue beating 2 minutes.

- With spoon stir in enough flour, about 2½ cups, to again make a thick dough.

- Turn dough onto lightly floured surface, knead until smooth and elastic, about 10 minutes.

- Shape dough into ball, place in bowl. Place in unheated oven in which you have placed a pan of hot water. Let rise until doubled in volume, about 1½ hours.

- Punch down dough. Turn onto floured surface and knead 1 minute. Cover with towel and let rest 15 minutes.

- In a 17½ x 11½-inch roasting pan, over low heat, melt remaining ½ cup butter. Tilt to cover bottom.

- Roll out dough to ½-inch thickness. With a floured 2¾-inch round biscuit cutter, cut dough into circles. Holding dough circle by edge, dip both sides into melted butter. Fold in half and pinch edges slightly. Arrange folded dough in rows in pan, spaced about ½-inch apart.

- Return pan to unheated oven and let dough rise for about 1 hour.

- Bake for 18 to 20 minutes. Serve warm.

Temperature: 425°

Time: 18 to 20 minutes

60 rolls

INGREDIENTS

2 cups boiling water

2 cups cracked wheat

½ cup brown sugar or honey

2 tablespoons butter or margarine

1 tablespoon salt

2 packages dry yeast

½ cup warm water

5 to 5½ cups white flour

CRUNCHY CRACKED WHEAT BREAD

THIS BREAD IS SO DELICIOUS IT
WILL NEVER HAVE A CHANCE TO GET COLD!

- In a large bowl, combine boiling water, wheat, sugar, butter, and salt.

- Stir yeast into warm water.

- When wheat mixture is slightly cooled, add yeast, then beat in 4 cups flour.

- Knead in remaining 1 to 1½ cups flour to obtain a nonsticky consistency. Knead for about 10 minutes, until dough is smooth.

- Place dough in a large oiled bowl; cover and let rise until double in volume (about 1½ hours).

- Shape dough into 2 large or 4 small loaves. Place on oiled baking sheets and let rise for 45 minutes.

- Bake small loaves for 20 minutes; large loaves for 30 minutes.

Temperature: 400°

Time: 20 to 30 minutes

2 large or 4 small loaves

Hint: Cracked wheat is available in health food stores.

Family Swedish Rye

INGREDIENTS

1 cup buttermilk

3 tablespoons butter

¾ cup sugar

6 tablespoons dark molasses

¾ cup cold water

¼ cup lukewarm water

1 package dry yeast

2 cups rye flour

¼ teaspoon baking soda

¼ to ½ cup mashed potatoes

4 to 4½ cups white flour

2 tablespoons melted butter

- In a saucepan over medium heat, combine buttermilk, butter, sugar and molasses until butter melts. Stir frequently. Add cold water and blend.

- In small bowl, combine yeast and warm water. Let set 5 minutes then add to buttermilk mixture.

- Stir in rye flour, soda, potatoes and 2 cups white flour. Beat well.

- Gradually add remaining flour. Turn onto floured surface and knead 10 minutes.

- Let rise until doubled in volume, approximately 1 hour.

- Punch down and divide into 2 well-oiled 5 x 9-inch loaf pans. Let rise again, until doubled in volume, approximately 1 hour.

- Bake 35 to 40 minutes.

- Remove from oven and brush tops of loaves with melted butter. Cool slightly and remove bread from pans to a rack.

Temperature: 350°

Time: 35 to 40 minutes

2 loaves

Hint: Try this bread toasted with cream cheese!

BREAKFAST PIZZA

1 package (8 ounces) refrigerated crescent rolls

1 pound pork sausage, cooked and drained

1 cup frozen hash brown potatoes, thawed

1 cup shredded cheddar cheese

3 to 4 eggs

¼ cup milk

½ teaspoon salt

⅛ teaspoon pepper

2 tablespoons grated Parmesan cheese

- Pat rolls to form a pastry base in pizza pan.

- Top with sausage, potatoes and cheese.

- Beat eggs, milk, salt and pepper. Gently pour over crust.

- Sprinkle with Parmesan cheese. Bake 20 to 25 minutes. Cut into wedges to serve.

Temperature: 375°

Time: 20 to 25 minutes

4 servings

BLINTZ SOUFFLÉ

12 frozen blintzes

¼ cup margarine, melted

2 cups sour cream

6 eggs

4 tablespoons orange juice

2 teaspoons vanilla

4 tablespoons sugar

Cinnamon sugar

Sour cream, fresh strawberries or canned fruit pie fillings

- Brush blintzes with margarine and arrange in 9 x 13 inch pan.

- Beat remaining ingredients with hand mixer or blender. Pour over blintzes.

- Refrigerate 8 hours or overnight.

- Sprinkle with cinnamon sugar.

- Bake 45 minutes.

- Serve with dollop of sour cream, fresh berries or canned fruit.

Temperature: 350°

Time: 45 minutes

8 to 12 servings

BREAKFAST EXTRAORDINAIRE

INGREDIENTS

12 slices Canadian bacon

12 1-ounce slices Swiss cheese

12 eggs

1 cup heavy cream

⅓ cup grated Parmesan cheese

Pepper to taste

Paprika to taste

Minced fresh parsley

- Overlap bacon slices in well-oiled 9 x 13-inch pan. Cover bacon with overlapping slices of cheese.

- Break eggs one at a time and space evenly on cheese. Pour cream gently around eggs.

- Bake 10 minutes. Sprinkle with Parmesan cheese, pepper and paprika.

- Bake 8 to 10 minutes longer until eggs are set.

- Remove from oven. Sprinkle with parsley. Let stand approximately 10 minutes before serving.

Temperature: 450°

Time: 20 minutes

6 to 8 servings

Eggs in Bacon Baskets

INGREDIENTS

8 bacon strips

8 eggs

2 cups half-and-half

Paprika

- Fry bacon until limp but not crisp. Immediately wrap each warm bacon strip around sides of muffin tin to form a circle.

- Break egg into each muffin tin.

- Top each egg with 2 to 3 tablespoons half and half. Sprinkle with paprika.

- Bake 12 minutes for a medium-firm egg.

- Gently remove eggs to serve.

Temperature: 350°

Time: 12 minutes

4 servings

Hint: For zesty accents, top each egg with minced green onions, jalapeño peppers or grated cheese before baking.

Ham and Sauerkraut Puff

INGREDIENTS

2 eggs

¾ cup milk

¾ cup flour

1 cup chopped fresh broccoli

½ pound ham, diced

- In blender or food processor with steel blade, mix eggs, milk and flour. Pour into well-oiled pie plate.

- Bake at 450° for 15 minutes; reduce heat to 350° and bake 10 minutes longer.

- Cook broccoli in boiling water for 5 minutes; drain.

- In large mixing bowl, combine broccoli, ham and sauerkraut. Stir in 1 cup cheddar.
- Spoon filling into hot puff. Top with remaining ½ cup cheese. Bake at 350° for 5 minutes or until cheese melts.
- Cut into wedges and serve immediately.

Temperature: 450° – 15 minutes
350° – 15 minutes

6 servings

1 can (8 ounces) sauerkraut, drained

1½ cups shredded cheddar cheese

FEATHER-LIGHT CHEESE SOUFFLÉ

- In medium saucepan, cook flour and milk until thickened, whisking constantly. Add cayenne, mustard and salt; mix well. Stir in cheese. Remove from heat.
- Beat egg yolks and add to sauce; blend well.
- In a large bowl, combine egg whites and cream of tartar. Beat until stiff and peaks form. Carefully fold cheese mixture into beaten whites.
- Pour mixture into a well-oiled 2-quart soufflé dish. Bake 30 minutes. Serve immediately.

Temperature: 375°

Time: 30 minutes

6 servings

INGREDIENTS

1 cup milk

¼ cup flour

¼ teaspoon cayenne pepper

½ teaspoon dry mustard

¼ teaspoon salt

1 cup shredded sharp cheddar cheese

6 eggs, separated

⅛ teaspoon cream of tartar

Matzo Kugel

4 matzo crackers

3 eggs, beaten

½ teaspoon salt

¼ cup sugar

½ cup melted margarine

¼ teaspoon cinnamon

½ cup coarsely chopped nuts

½ cup golden raisins

- Break crackers into large pieces; soak in water until soft. Drain until dry; do not squeeze.

- Combine eggs with salt, sugar, margarine, cinnamon, nuts and raisins.

- Place approximately ¼ of cracker pieces in bottom of a 1½-quart casserole. Pour approximately ¼ of egg mixture on top. Repeat with alternating layers, ending with egg mixture. Dot with margarine.

- Bake 45 minutes or until lightly browned.

Temperature: 350°

Time: 45 minutes

4 to 6 servings

Ham Strudel

1 cup butter

1 large onion, finely chopped

¾ cup long-grain rice

1½ cups chicken stock

1 to 2 tablespoons minced fresh parsley

1 cup shredded Swiss cheese

1 cup shredded cheddar cheese

- In a large saucepan, melt 1 tablespoon butter. Add onion and sauté over medium heat until onion is softened, but not browned.

- Add rice and chicken stock. Bring to a boil, reduce heat and simmer approximately 15 minutes or until stock is absorbed. Set aside to cool, then stir in parsley.

- Melt remaining butter. Place one phyllo sheet on work surface; brush with melted butter. Top with another sheet; brush again with butter. Continue with all phyllo.

- Spoon rice over phyllo sheets leaving a border around outer edges. Top rice with ham. Sprinkle with cheeses.

- Beginning at narrow end, fold phyllo over once. Fold long sides in 1 inch on each side; continue rolling.
- Place strudel on lightly oiled, foil-lined baking sheet. Brush with melted butter. With a sharp knife, make a few slashes on the top of each strudel. Sprinkle with paprika.
- Bake 30 to 35 minutes until golden brown.
- Remove from oven; let stand 5 minutes. Slice and serve.

Temperature: 375°

Time: 30 to 35 minutes

6 servings

¼ pound thinly sliced ham, cut into julienne strips

10 sheets frozen phyllo dough, thawed

Paprika

Onion Cheese Strata

- Separate onion slices into rings. Set aside.
- Trim crusts from bread. Place 4 slices of bread in the bottom of buttered 9-inch square pan. Top with ½ cheese slices and onion rings. Repeat layers: bread, cheese, onions.
- In medium bowl, beat eggs, milk, salt, mustard, Worcestershire and hot pepper sauce. Pour into pan.
- Cover and refrigerate 6 to 24 hours.
- Drizzle melted butter over the top of strata. Bake for 50 to 60 minutes or until firm. Cut into squares and serve.

Temperature: 350°

Time: 50 to 60 minutes

6 servings

INGREDIENTS

1½ cups sweet Spanish onions, thinly sliced

8 slices white bread

8 ounces sharp cheddar cheese, sliced

3 eggs, beaten

2½ cups milk

1 teaspoon salt

¼ teaspoon dry mustard

¼ teaspoon Worcestershire sauce

3 drops hot pepper sauce

2 tablespoons butter, melted

2 to 3 tablespoons oil

2 potatoes, peeled and diced

10 links pork sausage, cut into bite-size chunks

1 onion, diced

1 green pepper, diced

6 eggs, separated

¼ cup milk

Salt and pepper to taste

3 tablespoons butter

SUNDAY NIGHT FRITTATA

- Heat oil in a large skillet over medium heat. Add potatoes and sauté until tender and browned. Remove potatoes to large bowl.

- Sauté sausage, onion and green pepper until sausage is browned and onion is tender. Remove from heat and combine with potatoes. Drain off excess fat.

- In a medium bowl, beat egg whites until stiff.

- In a large bowl, beat egg yolks until thick and lemon colored. Add milk, salt, and pepper. Fold in egg whites.

- In ovenproof skillet over medium heat, melt butter. Add egg mixture, sausage, potatoes, peppers and onions. Turn heat to low. Cook slowly for 10 minutes.

- Place frittata in oven. Bake 10 to 15 minutes.

Hint: Serve with salsa.

Temperature: 350°

Time: 10 to 15 minutes

4 servings

1 pound fresh broccoli, cut into spears

8 to 10 slices boiled ham

3 to 4 cups cubed French or Italian bread

SWISS BRUNCH

- Cook broccoli in boiling salted water until tender-crisp; drain.

- Wrap ham around broccoli spears; arrange in 3-quart casserole with low sides.

- Toast bread cubes on a baking sheet in oven for 10 minutes. Remove from oven. Arrange cubes around edges of casserole.

- In a saucepan over low heat, heat wine to simmering. Do not boil.

- In a large bowl, combine cheese and flour. Gradually add to wine. Stir constantly with wooden spoon until cheese melts before adding more.

- Stir in mustard and garlic powder.

- Drizzle cheese sauce over surface of casserole. Bake 40 minutes until bubbly and bread cubes are golden brown.

Temperature: 350°

Time: 40 minutes

6 servings

1½ cups dry white wine

¾ pound Swiss cheese, shredded

2 tablespoons flour

2 tablespoons prepared mustard

⅛ teaspoon garlic powder

STRASBOURG QUICHE

BON APPETIT! THIS IS AN AUTHENTIC FRENCH TREAT.

- Shape pastry in a 10½-inch diameter pie plate; set aside.

- Sprinkle cheese on pastry.

- In a small bowl, beat eggs; add salt and pepper.

- In a large mixing bowl, beat cream until stiff peaks form.

- Gently fold egg mixture into whipped cream.

- Carefully pour mixture into pan, completely covering cheese.

- Bake 30 to 35 minutes or until custard has set and is golden brown.

Temperature: 350°

Time: 30 to 35 minutes

4 to 6 servings

INGREDIENTS

1 unbaked pastry shell

½ pound Swiss or Gruyère cheese, shredded

4 eggs

½ pint heavy cream or créme fraîche

Salt and pepper to taste

INGREDIENTS

¾ cup pancake mix

½ cup water

3 eggs

¼ cup plus 1 tablespoon sugar

½ cup butter or margarine

3 cups thinly sliced, peeled apples

¼ cup chopped pecans

½ cup raisins

1 teaspoon cinnamon

BAKED APPLE PECAN PANCAKE

ENJOY THE NUTTY SWEETNESS...
A NEW TWIST FOR THAT SPECIAL BRUNCH!

- In a large bowl, combine pancake mix, water, eggs and 1 tablespoon sugar. Mix well and set aside.

- Melt butter in a skillet over medium heat. Add apples and sauté until tender, stirring frequently. Remove skillet from heat. Spoon apples into ungreased pie plate.

- Sprinkle pecans and raisins over apples. Pour batter evenly over fruit.

- In a small bowl, combine ¼ cup sugar and cinnamon; sprinkle over batter.

- Loosely cover pie plate with foil and bake 12 to 14 minutes or until pancake is puffed and sugar melted.

- Loosen sides of pancake from pie plate; cool slightly. Cut pancake into wedges and serve.

Temperature: 450°

Time: 12 to 14 minutes

4 to 6 servings

Batter-Up French Toast

INGREDIENTS

1 egg

½ cup milk

½ cup flour

1 teaspoon baking powder

¼ teaspoon salt

4 to 5 slices white or French bread

2 tablespoons melted butter or margarine

A DELICIOUS, CRISPY FRENCH TOAST TREAT!

- Beat egg, then add milk; beat well.

- Stir in sifted dry ingredients.

- Dip bread in mixture and pan fry until golden brown on both sides.

- Serve hot with maple syrup, powdered sugar or other topping.

4 to 5 slices

Marmalade Monte Cristo

INGREDIENTS

1 cup orange marmalade

8 slices raisin bread

2 eggs

2 cups milk

½ teaspoon sugar

2 to 4 tablespoons margarine or butter

Confectioners' sugar

- Spread marmalade evenly on one side of each slice of bread. Put slices together to form four sandwiches.

- In a medium mixing bowl, beat eggs, milk and sugar together.

- Dip sandwiches thoroughly in milk mixture to coat well on both sides.

- In a large skillet over medium heat, melt 2 tablespoons butter or margarine. Brown sandwiches on both sides, cooking two at a time. Melt additional margarine or butter, if needed.

- Remove sandwiches to a warm platter. Sprinkle with confectioners' sugar before serving.

4 servings

4 eggs, separated

1 cup sour cream

1 cup small-curd cottage cheese

1 cup sifted flour

1 teaspoon baking soda

2 tablespoons sugar

Blueberries or other fruit, optional

SOUR CREAM PANCAKES

- In medium bowl beat egg whites until stiff.

- In large bowl beat egg yolks slightly, then stir in sour cream, cottage cheese, flour, baking soda and sugar.

- Fold in egg whites.

- Heat griddle until drop of water sizzles. Oil slightly if surface is not non-stick.

- Use ¼ cup measure for each pancake. Scatter a few berries or other fruit over batter, if desired.

- Cook approximately 3 minutes on each side. Serve immediately.

4 servings

INGREDIENTS

1 package (8 ounces) cream cheese, softened

1 teaspoon vanilla

1 teaspoon cinnamon, divided

½ cup chopped walnuts

1 loaf French bread, sliced 1½-inch thick

4 eggs

1 cup heavy cream

½ teaspoon vanilla

FANCY FRENCH TOAST POCKETS

- In a mixing bowl beat together cream cheese, vanilla and ½ teaspoon cinnamon until fluffy. Stir in nuts.

- Cut a slit through top crust of each bread slice to form a pocket. Do not cut through bottom crust.

- Fill each pocket with a tablespoon of cream cheese filling.

- In a medium bowl, beat eggs, cream, vanilla, ½ teaspoon cinnamon and nutmeg.

- Dip each bread slice into egg mixture, coating both sides.

- In large skillet, heat oil. Pan fry pockets until golden brown on both sides.
- Transfer cooked pockets to a baking sheet and keep warm in oven until all pockets are cooked.
- In a small saucepan, heat apricot preserves and orange juice.
- Pass hot syrup to drizzle over each serving.

Temperature: 300°

Time: 5 to 10 minutes

10 to 12 slices

½ teaspoon nutmeg

1 tablespoon vegetable oil

1½ cups apricot preserves

½ cup orange juice

ORANGE WAFFLES

- In blender or food processor, grind pecans with flour, sugar, baking powder and salt until fine. Transfer to a large bowl; stir in orange peel.
- In small bowl, whisk together eggs and butter. Add to flour mixture. Stir in club soda.
- Bake waffles in preheated waffle iron.
- Heat maple syrup and orange juice in microwave or small saucepan. Pass hot syrup to drizzle over hot waffles.

4 servings

INGREDIENTS

½ cup pecans, lightly toasted

1⅓ cups flour

2 tablespoons sugar

4 teaspoons baking powder

½ teaspoon salt

2 teaspoons freshly grated orange peel

2 large eggs

¼ cup unsalted butter, melted and cooled

1½ cups club soda

SYRUP

1 cup maple syrup

¼ cup orange juice

A+ Apricots

INGREDIENTS

1 stack (4 ounces) Ritz crackers

5 cans (17 ounces each) apricots, halved and drained

⅔ cup brown sugar

½ cup butter, melted

DELICIOUS SERVED AS SIDE DISH FOR BRUNCH OR WITH PORK

- Roll crackers into crumbs.
- In 3-quart casserole, alternate layers of apricots, crumbs and sugar. Drizzle butter on top.
- Bake 30 to 45 minutes.

Temperature: 300°

Time: 30 to 45 minutes

10 servings

Spiced Peaches

INGREDIENTS

1 can (28 ounces) peach halves

⅓ cup orange marmalade, melted

¼ cup chopped walnuts

2 teaspoons ground cinnamon

½ teaspoon ground nutmeg

- Drain peach halves, reserving juice.
- In a small bowl, combine marmalade, nuts, cinnamon and nutmeg; mix thoroughly.
- Arrange peaches, cut side up, in an 8 x 10-inch casserole. Spoon mixture evenly into peach halves.
- Sprinkle ½ cup reserved juice over peaches. Pour any remaining juice around the peaches in the casserole.
- Bake 10 to 15 minutes or until hot, basting with pan juices.
- Delicious hot or chilled.

Temperature: 375°

Time: 10 to 15 minutes

6 servings

Pears Burgundy

A BEAUTIFUL ACCOMPANIMENT
WHEN YOU'RE SERVING GAME OR DUCKLING

- Drain pears, reserving ½ cup juice.

- Approximately 1 hour before serving time, combine sugar, jelly, ½ cup pear juice and food coloring in a saucepan over medium heat. Stir occasionally until jelly melts.

- Add pears. Simmer, covered. Just before serving add wine.

- Serve hot or cold. Top each serving with sour cream and sprinkle with cinnamon.

4 servings

INGREDIENTS

1 can (29 ounces) pear halves

⅓ cup sugar

⅓ cup currant jelly

¼ teaspoon red food coloring

⅓ cup Burgundy wine

Sour cream

Cinnamon

Baked Aloha

A PERFECT ACCOMPANIMENT TO BAKED HAM

- In large bowl, combine pineapple, water, eggs, cornstarch, sugar and vanilla; mix well.

- Pour the mixture into an ungreased 1½-quart casserole. Sprinkle cinnamon over the top; dot with butter or margarine.

- Bake uncovered, for 1 hour or until well thickened. Remove and serve immediately.

Temperature: 325°

Time: 1 hour

6 servings

INGREDIENTS

1 can (20 ounces) crushed pineapple, drained

¼ cup cold water

2 eggs, beaten

2 tablespoons cornstarch

1 cup sugar

1 teaspoon vanilla

¼ teaspoon cinnamon

1 tablespoon butter or margarine

INGREDIENTS

1 pound egg noodles, medium or wide

¾ cup sugar

½ cup butter, melted

1 cup orange juice

1 cup small-curd cottage cheese

1 pint sour cream

2 teaspoons vanilla

1 tablespoon orange rind

6 eggs, separated

1 jar (about 10 ounces) orange marmalade, at room temperature

ORANGE NOODLE PUDDING

- Cook noodles according to package directions; drain and rinse with cold water. Place in a large mixing bowl.

- In another large bowl, combine sugar, butter, orange juice, cottage cheese, sour cream, vanilla and orange rind. In a small bowl, beat egg yolks. Add to cottage cheese mixture, then fold this mixture into noodles.

- In a medium bowl, beat egg whites until stiff. Gently fold whites into noodles.

- Transfer pudding into a well-oiled 3-quart casserole. Bake 45 minutes.

- Remove from oven and gently spread top with orange marmalade. Return to oven and continue baking for 15 minutes.

Temperature: 350°

Time: 45 minutes
      15 minutes

10 to 12 servings

INGREDIENTS

1 jar (12 ounces) strawberry preserves

1 container (8 ounces) whipped cream cheese

2 ounces frozen non-dairy whipped topping, thawed

2 tablespoons almond liqueur

STRAWBERRY CRÉME

THIS DOUBLES AS DESSERT OR A DIP WITH STRAWBERRIES, FRESH PINEAPPLE OR MELON.

- In a large bowl, combine preserves, cream cheese and whipped topping; blend in liqueur.

- Refrigerate for 2 to 3 hours to blend flavors.

- Remove from refrigerator 30 minutes before serving.

6 to 8 servings

PASTA PLUS

Pasta Plus / Index

Pasta

Casino Linguine / 133

Confetti Pasta / 131

Garden Carbonara* / 138

Lasagne Rollatine / 137

Linguine with Brie and Fresh
  Tomato Sauce / 133

Low Cholesterol Turkey Lasagne / 136

Noodles Ontario / 135

Pasta Carbonara* / 139

Pasta Verde / 131

Sesame Linguine / 132

Summer Sunset Pasta / 132

Three Cheese Fettuccine / 134

Pizza

Gift of Garlic Pizza / 140

Pizza with Pizzazz / 142

Yes-You-Can-Grill Pizza / 141

Enchiladas

Incredulada Enchilada / 144

South-of-the-Border Enchiladas / 142

Tomato Chicken Enchiladas / 143

Confetti Pasta

A RAINBOW OF GOOD TASTES - READY IN A JIFFY

- Boil fettuccine until al dente.
- While pasta is cooking, heat oil in large skillet over medium heat. Sauté peppers until tender-crisp.
- Toss hot, drained pasta with cheese. Add peppers and toss again. Serve immediately.

4 to 6 servings

INGREDIENTS

1 pound fettuccine

1 large green pepper, cut into strips

1 large red pepper, cut into strips

1 large yellow pepper, cut into strips

2 tablespoons olive oil

8 ounces Gorgonzola cheese, crumbled

Pasta Verde

- In large skillet, sauté garlic in oil. Add red peppers and cook until almost soft. Add pine nuts and cook 1 minute longer.
- Boil and drain pasta; transfer to large bowl.
- Add vegetables; toss. Stir in cheese and pepper.

3 to 4 servings

INGREDIENTS

9 ounces fresh spinach linguine

3 cloves garlic, minced

2 tablespoons vegetable oil

2 red peppers, sliced

½ cup toasted pine nuts

2 tablespoons olive oil

1 cup grated Parmesan cheese

¼ teaspoon pepper

INGREDIENTS

3 large ripe tomatoes, peeled, seeded and coarsely chopped

2 tablespoons chopped fresh basil

1 tablespoon snipped fresh chives

2 tablespoons chopped fresh parsley

3 cloves garlic, minced

⅓ cup olive oil

½ cup grated Mozzarella cheese

¼ teaspoon salt

¼ teaspoon freshly ground pepper

12 ounces fresh rotini or linguine (8 ounces dried)

Freshly grated Parmesan cheese

SUMMER SUNSET PASTA

- In a medium bowl, combine all ingredients except pasta and Parmesan cheese. Let stand at room temperature 1 hour before serving.

- Cook pasta according to package directions. In a warm bowl, toss hot, drained pasta and sauce.

- Serve immediately with fresh Parmesan cheese.

3 to 4 servings

INGREDIENTS

12 ounces linguine

¼ cup oriental sesame oil

¼ cup soy sauce

½ teaspoon minced garlic

½ cup minced watercress

1 teaspoon hot chili oil

Salt and pepper to taste

2 to 3 green onions, chopped

SESAME LINGUINE

THIS COOL PASTA SIDE DISH HAS SPICY-HOT OVERTONES

- Cook linguine according to package directions; rinse with cold water, drain and transfer to salad bowl.

- Combine remaining ingredients except onions; toss and refrigerate overnight.

- Garnish with onions before serving.

8 servings

Linguine with Brie and Fresh Tomato Sauce

INGREDIENTS

4 to 6 large, ripe tomatoes

1 pound Brie

1 cup chopped fresh basil

2 cloves garlic, finely minced

1 cup extra virgin olive oil

½ teaspoon salt

½ teaspoon freshly ground pepper

1½ pounds linguine

Freshly grated Parmesan cheese

- Peel and seed tomatoes. Cut into cubes.

- Remove and discard rind from Brie; dice cheese.

- In a large bowl, combine tomatoes, Brie, basil, garlic, olive oil, salt and pepper. Let stand at room temperature for 2 hours.

- Prepare linguine according to package directions. Drain and toss immediately with sauce. Sprinkle with fresh Parmesan cheese.

Hint: 2 cups cooked shrimp can be added just before serving.

4 to 6 servings

Casino Linguine

INGREDIENTS

3 cans (6½ ounces each) chopped or minced clams

1 pound bacon, cut into 1-inch strips

1 medium onion, chopped

2 cloves garlic, minced

½ cup margarine

½ cup minced fresh parsley

Freshly ground black pepper

1 pound linguine, cooked and drained

- Drain clams, reserving half of the juice.

- In large skillet, fry bacon until crisp. Remove bacon, leaving drippings in pan.

- Sauté onion in bacon fat. When onion is soft, but not browned, add margarine.

- When margarine has melted, stir in remaining ingredients, except pasta.

- Toss linguine with sauce. Serve warm.

6 servings

8 ounces fettuccine

8 ounces spinach fettuccine

½ cup chopped walnuts

2 cups heavy cream

8 ounces Mozzarella cheese, shredded

6 ounces Gorgonzola cheese, crumbled

3 tablespoons grated Parmesan cheese

3 tablespoons finely minced fresh parsley

2 tablespoons finely chopped fresh basil

1 tablespoon finely chopped fresh oregano (or ½ teaspoon dried)

1 tablespoon finely chopped fresh chives

THREE CHEESE FETTUCCINE

- Cook pasta according to package directions.

- While pasta is cooking, toast walnuts in large skillet, stirring constantly.

- Drain pasta. In pot used for pasta, heat cream; boil one minute.

- Stir in all remaining ingredients. Heat until sauce is blended and thickened slightly.

- Transfer pasta to warm platter. Before serving, sprinkle with walnuts and additional Parmesan cheese.

4 servings

NOODLES ONTARIO

- Remove casing from sausage, if necessary. In saucepan over medium-high heat, brown sausage, breaking up pieces. Drain off excess fat.

- Stir in remaining sauce ingredients. Bring to boil, reduce heat and simmer uncovered 1 hour until sauce thickens, stirring occasionally.

- Discard bay leaf.

- Cook noodles in large amount of water; drain, rinse and drain again.

- In large bowl, beat eggs then stir in noodles, spinach, onions and seasonings.

- Divide one-half of noodles between two well-oiled 9-inch square pans.

- Top with ¼ of the sauce, then ¼ of the Mozzarella. Repeat layers. Sprinkle each casserole with Parmesan.

- Bake for 30 minutes. Cool 15 minutes before serving.

Temperature: 350°

Time: 30 minutes

8 servings

SAUCE

1 pound sweet Italian sausage, bulk or in casing

2 teaspoons minced garlic

2 cans (28 ounces each) crushed tomatoes

2 teaspoons sugar

1 teaspoon dried basil

½ teaspoon dried oregano

1 large bay leaf

⅛ teaspoon salt

¼ teaspoon pepper

INGREDIENTS

1 package (12 ounces) extra-wide curly egg noodles

4 large eggs

2 packages (10 ounces each) frozen chopped spinach, thawed and well-drained

4 green onions, sliced

Parmesan cheese

⅛ teaspoon ground nutmeg

⅛ teaspoon black pepper

1 pound Mozzarella cheese, coarsely shredded

¼ cup grated Parmesan cheese

INGREDIENTS

1 pound mild Italian turkey sausage

1 tablespoon olive oil

1 clove garlic, minced

1 teaspoon dried basil

1 teaspoon dried oregano

½ teaspoon salt

Ground pepper to taste

2 cups canned tomatoes

2 cans (6 ounces each) tomato paste

8 lasagne noodles, cooked and drained

Salt to taste

1 pound low-fat cottage cheese

Egg substitute (2 egg portion)

½ cup grated Parmesan cheese

1 tablespoon dried parsley flakes

1 pound part skim Mozzarella cheese

LOW CHOLESTEROL TURKEY LASAGNE

A WONDERFUL LIGHT VARIATION OF A FAMILY FAVORITE

- Remove turkey sausage from its casing and brown in olive oil in a large skillet. Add garlic and sauté for 2 minutes.

- Stir in basil, oregano, salt, pepper, tomatoes and tomato paste. Simmer for 15 minutes.

- In mixing bowl, combine cottage cheese, eggs, Parmesan cheese and parsley.

- Slice mozzarella cheese in ⅛-inch slices or grate. Reserve one slice for garnish.

- Spread ½ cup of sauce in 9 x 13-inch shallow baking dish. Top with 3 or 4 noodles.

- Spread half of cottage cheese mixture over noodles, then half of the Mozzarella, followed by half of the sauce. Repeat layers.

- Garnish with reserved cheese strips.

- Bake for 30 minutes. Let stand 10 minutes before serving.

Temperature: 375°

Time: 30 minutes

6 to 8 servings

Lasagne Rollatine

- In medium saucepan, melt butter, stir in flour and gradually add milk. Cook and stir over medium heat until thickened.

- In a small bowl, beat yolks. First stir 2 tablespoons of hot sauce into eggs, then add eggs to the sauce and simmer one to two minutes.

- Stir in cheese, remove from heat.

- Boil noodles according to package directions. Drain and arrange noodles on oiled flat baking sheet.

- In large bowl, thoroughly combine spinach, cheeses and butter. Spread filling evenly over each noodle, then roll up.

- Using two 9 x 13-inch pans, spread ¼ cup tomato sauce in each pan. Place lasagne roll-ups, seam side down, in pans.

- Cover roll-ups with mornay sauce, then with remaining tomato sauce. Sprinkle with nutmeg.

- Bake 40 minutes or until heated through. Serve immediately.

Temperature: 350°

Time: 40 minutes

10 to 12 servings

MORNAY SAUCE

8 tablespoons butter

½ cup flour

3 cups milk

2 egg yolks

½ cup grated Parmesan cheese

INGREDIENTS

1 pound lasagne noodles

3 packages (10 ounces each) frozen, chopped spinach, thawed and drained

15-ounces ricotta cheese

1 cup grated Parmesan cheese

1 cup melted butter

2 cups hearty tomato sauce

Nutmeg

INGREDIENTS

3 large eggs

½ cup cream or milk

8 slices bacon

2 tablespoons vegetable oil

1 clove garlic, minced

¼ cup sliced green onion

1 cup sliced fresh mushrooms

1 cup cauliflower florets

1 cup sliced carrots

1 cup frozen peas

1 cup sliced zucchini

16 ounces fettuccine

¼ cup melted butter

1 cup grated Parmesan cheese

GARDEN CARBONARA*

- Beat eggs and cream; set aside.
- Cook bacon until crisp; drain on paper towel.
- In large frying pan, sauté vegetables in oil 5 to 7 minutes. Cover and set aside.
- Cook fettuccine according to package directions; toss with butter.
- Add eggs and cream, toss.
- Add vegetables and bacon, toss.
- Add cheese, toss. Heat through and serve warm.

6 servings

* This recipe contains uncooked egg yolks/whites. See SPECIAL NOTE page 7.

Pasta Carbonara*

INGREDIENTS

OUR TASTERS WERE UNANIMOUS IN RECOMMENDING
THAT THIS IS THE ULTIMATE WAY TO INDULGE!

1½ pounds sugar-cured bacon

2 white onions, chopped

4 tablespoons butter

1½ pounds mushrooms, quartered

1 bunch parsley, minced

1 pound Italian semolina pasta

1 to 2 tablespoons olive oil

5 eggs

1 cup light cream

Crushed red pepper flakes, to taste

*1 cup freshly grated blended
Parmesan and Romano cheese*

1 teaspoon vinegar

- In a large skillet, cook bacon over medium heat until cooked but not crisp. Remove bacon from skillet and drain on paper towels. Pour off bacon fat and discard.

- In the same skillet melt 2 tablespoons butter. Sauté onions over medium heat until lightly golden and still moist, stirring constantly. Remove onion and drain on paper towels.

- Again in the same skillet, melt remaining 2 tablespoons butter and sauté mushrooms over medium heat for 3 to 5 minutes or until just tender. Stir constantly. Add chopped bacon, onions and half the parsley. Stir and remove from heat.

- Meanwhile, cook pasta al dente. Drain and keep warm. Sprinkle and toss with olive oil to prevent sticking.

- In a large mixing bowl beat eggs with the light cream. Add red pepper flakes and cheese.

- Heat large serving bowl or platter. Pour ½ cup of egg mixture into serving bowl.

- Add hot drained pasta and bacon mixture. Pour on remaining sauce and vinegar. Toss well.

- Sprinkle with remaining parsley. Serve immediately.

4 to 6 servings

* This recipe contains uncooked egg yolks/whites. See SPECIAL NOTE page 7.

GARLIC BUTTER

1 cup butter, softened

5 to 7 garlic cloves, minced

¼ cup olive oil

2 teaspoons dried basil

1 teaspoon minced fresh parsley

½ teaspoon dried oregano

¼ cup grated Parmesan cheese

Salt and pepper to taste

INGREDIENTS

1 pound pizza dough (or frozen bread dough)

2 to 3 tablespoons Garlic Butter

Shredded Mozzarella cheese

GIFT OF GARLIC PIZZA

FINALLY, A GARLIC PIZZA RECIPE TO CHALLENGE THE RESTAURANTS!

- Use mixer to combine butter, garlic, oil, basil, parsley, oregano, Parmesan cheese, salt and pepper; mix well.

- Refrigerate, covered, until ready to use.

- Spread dough on lightly-oiled baking sheet or pizza pan.

- Spread butter evenly on dough leaving a 1-inch border. Generously sprinkle Mozzarella on dough.

- Bake 20 to 25 minutes or until cheese is lightly browned.

- Cut into wedges and serve immediately.

Temperature: 375°

Time: 20 to 25 minutes

3 to 4 servings

Hint: For mouth-watering garlic bread, spread topping mixture on thick slice of Italian bread. Broil until golden (approximately 3 to 5 minutes).

Yes-You-Can-Grill Pizza

MAKES A WONDERFUL LIGHT SUPPER OR HORS D'OEUVRE!

- Drain tomatoes, reserving juice. Discard seeds and coarsely chop.

- Melt butter in skillet. Add tomatoes and ¼ cup of reserved tomato juice. Simmer 5 minutes.

- Stir in sour cream until hot. Remove from heat. Adjust seasonings.

- Divide dough into two portions. Flatten each piece into a 12-inch round.

- Oil grill rack. Place dough on heated grill. Close grill cover; cook until dough begins to puff slightly and grill marks appear on bottom.

- Turn dough over. Brush with olive oil. Top with half the sauce, one half the cheese, and half the oregano.

- Close lid. Cook until cheese melts and grill marks appear on bottom.

6 to 8 servings

Hint: The new non-stick grill toppers with perforations are ideal for grilling pizza.

SAUCE

1 can (16 ounces) whole tomatoes

1 tablespoon butter

½ cup sour cream

Salt to taste

INGREDIENTS

1½ pounds fresh pizza dough

Olive oil

½ cup crumbled blue or Gorgonzola cheese

3 tablespoons snipped fresh oregano

INGREDIENTS

1 can refrigerated pizza dough

4 ounces Mozzarella cheese, shredded

2 tablespoons olive oil

2 red onions, sliced

1 small red pepper, seeded and diced

½ teaspoon dried tarragon

1 pound boneless chicken breast, cubed

2 cloves garlic, minced

Salt and pepper to taste

PIZZA WITH PIZZAZZ

- Press pizza dough onto lightly greased baking sheet or pizza pan. Sprinkle cheese evenly over dough.

- In a large skillet, heat oil over medium-high heat. Add onions, red pepper, and tarragon. Sauté until tender. Spoon evenly over pizza dough.

- In same skillet, sauté chicken and garlic until chicken is done. Add salt and pepper. Spoon evenly over pizza dough.

- Bake for 15 to 20 minutes until crust is golden and crisp.

Temperature: 425°

Time: 15 to 20 minutes

4 to 6 servings

INGREDIENTS

6 tablespoons butter

3 medium onions, thinly sliced

2½ cups shredded cooked chicken

¾ cup canned diced green chiles

6 ounces cream cheese, diced

¾ cup corn oil

12 6-inch corn tortillas

1 cup heavy cream

SOUTH-OF-THE-BORDER ENCHILADAS

- In a large skillet, melt butter and sauté onions approximately 10 minutes. Remove from heat.

- Stir in chicken, chiles and cream cheese; set aside.

- In a separate skillet, quickly fry tortillas, one at a time. Turn once, when they start to blister. Drain on paper towels.

- Spoon chicken mixture on the center of each tortilla; roll up and place seam-side down in a glass baking dish.

- Top with cream and cheese. Bake until cream thickens and cheese bubbles, approximately 20 minutes.
- Serve with salsa.

Temperature: 375°

Time: 20 minutes

6 servings

TOMATO CHICKEN ENCHILADAS

- Cook chicken breasts. When cool, cut meat into bite-sized pieces.
- In a large skillet or saucepan, sauté onion and garlic in oil.
- Purée canned tomatoes in blender, then add to onion along with tomato sauce, green chiles, sugar, cumin, oregano, basil, cilantro and salt. Bring to boil, reduce heat and simmer, covered, until thickened, approximately 1 hour.
- Remove from heat and stir in ½ cup sour cream.
- In a large saucepan over low heat, melt 2 cups cheese and ½ cup sour cream, stirring constantly. Stir in chicken, olives and green onions.
- Fill tortillas with chicken mixture. Roll and place seam-side down in oiled 9 x 13-inch pan. Cover with tomato mixture.
- Bake 30 minutes. Top with remaining 1 cup cheese and bake 10 minutes more.

Temperature: 350°

Time: 40 minutes

4 to 6 servings

3 cups shredded Monterey Jack cheese

Prepared salsa

INGREDIENTS

2 large whole chicken breasts

1 cup chopped onion

2 cloves garlic, minced

2 tablespoons olive oil

2 cans (16 ounces each) tomatoes

1 can (15 ounces) tomato sauce

2 cans (4 ounces each) chopped green chiles

1 teaspoon sugar

2 teaspoons ground cumin

½ teaspoon dried oregano

½ teaspoon dried basil

1 teaspoon minced fresh cilantro

Salt to taste

1 cup sour cream

3 cups (12 ounces) shredded sharp cheddar cheese, divided

1 can (4 ounces) sliced black olives, drained

4 green onions, sliced

8 to 10 7-inch flour tortillas

INGREDIENTS

2 tablespoons cooking oil

2 tablespoons chopped onion

1 tablespoon diced green pepper

1 pound ground beef

1 package (1¼ ounces) taco seasoning mix

1 cup water

2 cups taco sauce or salsa, divided

½ cup butter

¼ cup flour

1 teaspoon salt

1 cup milk

12 6-inch corn tortillas

1½ cups shredded cheddar cheese

1 can (2.2 ounces) black olives (optional)

1 cup sour cream (optional)

INCREDULADA ENCHILADA

- In skillet, heat oil and sauté onion and green pepper 3 to 5 minutes.

- Add beef and brown lightly. Pour off excess fat; discard.

- Stir in taco seasoning mix, water and ½ cup taco sauce. Heat to boiling, reduce heat and simmer, uncovered, 10 minutes, stirring occasionally.

- In separate saucepan, melt butter. Stir in flour and salt. Add milk and 1 cup taco sauce, heat to boiling and cook 1 minute, stirring constantly.

- Warm tortillas until they are flexible. (Microwave on High one minute in tightly covered casserole. Or, place on heatproof plate that will fit into a skillet. Add ½ inch water to skillet and steam tortillas until flexible.)

- Spread remaining ½ cup taco sauce on the bottom of 9 x 13 inch pan. Fill tortillas with beef mixture. Roll and place seam-side down in pan.

- Spread cream sauce over enchiladas. Sprinkle with cheddar cheese and bake, uncovered, for 20 minutes.

- If desired, dot with olives and sour cream before serving.

Temperature: 375°

Time: 20 minutes

6 servings

VEGETABLES &
ACCOMPANIMENTS

Vegetables and Accompaniments / Index

Vegetables

Asparagus Napoli / 150

Baked Asparagus / 149

Broccoli and Artichoke Stir-Fry / 157

Broccoli Forest / 156

Broccoli with Lemon Cream Sauce / 157

Caramelized Carrots with Grand Marnier / 152

Carrot Cheddar Bake / 149

Carrot Ginger Melody / 152

Carrot Soufflé / 153

Cauliflower Bon Vivant / 154

Cauliflower Gratiné / 153

Crunchy Calico Peas / 159

Dijon Baked Tomatoes / 163

Fiesta Corn Flan / 158

German Green Beans / 155

Golden Autumn Timbales / 166

Grilled Zucchini with Basil Butter / 147

Hunan Eggplant / 154

Most-Asked-For Onion Casserole / 165

"Muddy" Mushrooms / 159

Mushroom Supreme / 160

Oktoberfest Rolt Kraut / 168

Potluck Beans / 170

Say Cheese...Zucchini / 148

Snow Pea Stir-Fry / 150

Spinach Rice Crunch / 162

Spinach-Artichoke Bake / 161

Sweet and Sour Beans / 169

Thyme for Butternut Squash / 167

Tomatoes Stuffed with Dilled Vegetables / 163

Vegetables Marinara / 169

Vidalia Tomato Bake / 164

Zesty Zucchini / 151

Potatoes

Company's Coming Potatoes / 171

Potatoes Monterey / 172

Roasted New Potatoes with Garlic and Rosemary / 172

Saucy Scalloped Potatoes / 173

"Seconds, Please" Hash Browns / 174

Sweet Potato Medley / 174

Tzimmes / 168

Rice

Bulgur Pilaf / 176

Consommé Rice / 175

Elegant Wild Rice / 175

Wild Rice with Pecans / 176

Grilled Zucchini with Basil Butter

INGREDIENTS

½ cup butter, softened

1 clove garlic, minced

1 tablespoon lemon juice

6 large fresh basil leaves, minced

6 small to medium zucchini, halved lengthwise

- Cream butter, garlic, lemon juice and basil.

- Spread cut surfaces of zucchini with basil butter.

- Grill cut-side up over medium-hot coals until tender (approximately 10 minutes). Turn once. For extra flavor, melt some basil butter and baste while grilling.

- Before serving, spread additional basil butter on cut surfaces.

6 servings

Hint: If basil butter is made ahead, refrigerate, then bring to spreadable consistency at room temperature.

INGREDIENTS

2 medium zucchini

¼ cup finely chopped onion

1 tablespoon butter or margarine

¾ cup cream-style cottage cheese

⅔ cup cooked white rice

1 egg, slightly beaten

1 tablespoon minced fresh parsley

⅛ teaspoon crushed dried basil

*2 ounces sharp American cheese,
cut into 16 strips*

SAY CHEESE…ZUCCHINI

A DELIGHTFULLY DIFFERENT VEGETABLE
SERVED AS A SIDE DISH OR AS A LIGHT SUPPER

- Trim ends of zucchini. Cook zucchini in small amount of boiling salted water for 8 minutes or until just tender.

- Halve zucchini lengthwise. Scoop out pulp to form "boats". Coarsely chop remaining pulp.

- Cook onion in butter until tender.

- In a large bowl, combine chopped zucchini with onion, cottage cheese, rice, egg, parsley and basil. Divide mixture among zucchini boats.

- Place zucchini in lightly greased 9 x 13-inch baking dish. Loosely cover and bake 25 minutes.

- Top each "boat" with 4 cheese strips. Bake, uncovered, 5 minutes more to melt cheese.

Temperature: 350°

Time: 30 minutes

4 servings

BAKED ASPARAGUS

- Cook asparagus according to package directions; drain.
- Combine asparagus, onions, eggs, white sauce, cayenne pepper and water chestnuts. Pour into 9 x 13-inch baking dish.
- Combine breadcrumbs and butter. Spread over casserole.
- Bake 30 minutes.

Temperature: 350°

Time: 30 minutes

8 to 10 servings

* Make with 2 cups milk, 4 tablespoons butter or margarine, 4 tablespoons flour.

4 cups fresh asparagus cut in 1-inch pieces and steamed until crisp-tender (or 2 packages [10 ounces each] frozen asparagus)

1 jar (14 ounces) tiny white onions, drained

4 hard-cooked eggs, chopped

2 cups medium white sauce*

¼ teaspoon cayenne pepper

1 can (8-ounces) sliced water chestnuts, drained

1 cup fresh breadcrumbs

1 tablespoon melted butter or margarine

CARROT CHEDDAR BAKE

INGREDIENTS

- Cook carrots until tender; drain. Place carrots in 8 x 11-inch buttered baking dish.
- Combine remaining ingredients; pour over carrots.
- Bake 45 minutes or until hot and puffy. Cut into squares to serve.

Temperature: 350°

Time: 45 minutes

4 to 6 servings

1 pound carrots, pared and cut into ¼-inch coins

½ cup butter, melted

2 cups shredded cheddar cheese

½ cup half-and-half

3 eggs, beaten

1 teaspoon salt

¼ teaspoon pepper

INGREDIENTS

1 tablespoon cornstarch

1 teaspoon sugar

1 tablespoon soy sauce

½ cup water

2 tablespoons salad oil

*1 pound fresh snow peas, rinsed
and strings removed*

*4 stalks celery, sliced, diagonally
into ¾ inch pieces*

*½ cup sliced green onions,
including green tops*

½ cup sliced fresh mushrooms

SNOW PEA STIR-FRY

- In small bowl, combine cornstarch, sugar, soy sauce and water; set aside.

- Heat wok to medium-high. Add oil; when hot, add vegetables and stir-fry for 2 minutes.

- Add cornstarch mixture and stir until sauce is thickened. Serve immediately.

6 to 8 servings

INGREDIENTS

1½ pounds fresh asparagus

1 to 2 tablespoons butter, melted

¼ cup grated Parmesan cheese

1 tablespoon tarragon vinegar

*⅓ cup black olives, pitted and
sliced*

*4 slices bacon, cooked and
crumbled*

ASPARAGUS NAPOLI

- Break or trim tough ends from asparagus stalks. Steam until tender-crisp, approximately 8 minutes; drain.

- While asparagus is cooking, combine butter, cheese and vinegar in large bowl. Add drained asparagus; toss.

- Before serving, top with olives and bacon. Serve immediately.

Hint: Steam asparagus upright in tall pot. Place vegetable steamer rack in bottom of pot. Add sufficient water to reach base of steamer. When water boils, add asparagus; cover and steam.

6 servings

ZESTY ZUCCHINI

INGREDIENTS

A VEGETARIAN MEAL IN ITSELF!

- In a large skillet over medium heat, sauté green onions and peppers in 1 tablespoon margarine. Remove from skillet; set aside.

- In same skillet, melt 2 tablespoons margarine over medium heat and sauté zucchini and mushrooms. Add zucchini and mushrooms to the reserved scallions and peppers; mix well.

- Use 1 tablespoon margarine to grease 4 to 5-quart Dutch oven or casserole. Layer casserole in this order: rice, Monterey Jack, vegetables, chiles, sour cream, cheddar.

- Cover and bake 1 hour.

Temperature: 350°

Time: 1 hour

20 servings

Hint: This recipe can be halved to fill a 2½-quart casserole.

4 tablespoons margarine, divided

2 bunches green onions, thinly sliced

1 red pepper, seeded and diced

4 medium zucchini, sliced

1 pound mushrooms, sliced

4 cups cooked rice

1 pound Monterey Jack cheese, shredded

1 can (7½ ounces) green chiles, drained and chopped

1 pint (16 ounces) sour cream

1 pound cheddar cheese, shredded

INGREDIENTS

1 package (24 ounces) fresh baby carrots, or frozen baby carrots

⅓ cup butter

5 tablespoons apricot preserves

3 tablespoons Grand Marnier

Minced fresh parsley

CARAMELIZED CARROTS WITH GRAND MARNIER

A SIMPLE, EXQUISITE WAY TO SERVE CARROTS

- Clean fresh carrots and cook in small amount of boiling water for 10 minutes or cook frozen carrots according to package directions. Immediately drain carrots. Run cold water over carrots to stop cooking and preserve the orange color. Set aside.

- Approximately 30 minutes before serving, melt butter in large skillet. Add preserves and Grand Marnier; stir to dissolve. Remove from heat.

- Add carrots and cook over low heat, stirring occasionally, until the carrots are hot and caramelized. Garnish with parsley.

6 to 8 servings

INGREDIENTS

3 large fresh carrots

3 tablespoons margarine

2 tablespoons lemon juice

2 tablespoons brown sugar

½ teaspoon ground ginger

¼ cup raisins

3 firm bananas, sliced

CARROT GINGER MELODY

- Slice carrots into ½-inch "coins" and cook in boiling salted water until tender-crisp. Drain and set aside.

- In a large saucepan, combine margarine, lemon juice, brown sugar and ginger; heat thoroughly.

- Stir in raisins and carrots. Remove from heat, If time permits, leave at room temperature for approximately 1 hour to allow raisins to puff.

- To serve, stir in sliced bananas and reheat.

4 servings

Carrot Soufflé

Cinnamon accents this slightly sweet golden soufflé

- Cook carrots in small amount of water until tender. In food processor or blender, purée until smooth.

- Combine carrots with remaining ingredients; blend well.

- Pour into a 2-quart lightly buttered soufflé dish or casserole.

- Bake 45 minutes or until center is firm to touch.

Temperature: 350°

Time: 45 minutes

8 servings

INGREDIENTS

2 cups sliced carrots

2 teaspoons lemon juice

1½ tablespoons grated or minced onion

½ cup butter, softened

¼ cup sugar

1 tablespoon flour

½ teaspoon salt

¼ teaspoon cinnamon

1 cup milk

3 eggs

Cauliflower Gratiné

- In a large saucepan, boil carrots in water for 5 minutes. Add cauliflower and boil 5 minutes longer; drain.

- In well-oiled 4-quart casserole, repeat layers using half the vegetables and half the cheese. Repeat.

- In a bowl, stir undiluted soup until smooth; carefully spread on top of casserole.

- Combine cornflakes and butter; sprinkle over casserole.

- Bake uncovered for 45 minutes.

Temperature: 350°

Time: 45 minutes

10 to 12 servings

INGREDIENTS

10 carrots, peeled and cut into 1-inch pieces

1 large head cauliflower, rinsed and broken into florets

2 cups shredded cheddar cheese

2 cans (10¾ ounces each) cream of celery soup

1 cup crushed corn flakes

3 tablespoons melted butter

INGREDIENTS

1 head cauliflower

½ cup butter or margarine

¼ pound mushrooms, thinly sliced

⅓ cup thinly sliced green onions

1 tablespoon instant chicken bouillon (dry)

1 tablespoon cornstarch

1 cup water

⅓ cup toasted, slivered almonds

CAULIFLOWER BON VIVANT

- Break cauliflower into florets. Cook in salted water, or steam approximately 10 minutes. Drain and set aside.

- Melt butter in small saucepan. Add mushrooms and onion. Cook over medium heat for two minutes. Stir in dry bouillon.

- Dissolve cornstarch in water and add to onion mixture. Stir to mix. Cook until thickened, approximately 5 minutes. Pour over cooked cauliflower.

- Top with almonds.

8 to 10 servings

INGREDIENTS

6 tablespoons peanut oil

1½ pounds eggplant, cut into 1-inch chunks

3 cloves garlic, minced

1 tablespoon bottled chili paste

1½ teaspoons minced fresh ginger

½ cup chicken stock

1 tablespoon soy sauce

2 teaspoons sugar

1 tablespoon rice vinegar

2 tablespoons finely chopped green onion

1 teaspoon oriental sesame oil

HUNAN EGGPLANT

- In a wok or large skillet, heat ¼ cup peanut oil over medium heat. Add eggplant and stir-fry until soft. Remove eggplant from pan; set aside.

- Heat remaining peanut oil in wok or skillet. Add garlic, chili paste and ginger. Cook 15 seconds, stirring constantly.

- Add stock, soy sauce and sugar. Mix well and bring to a boil. Add vinegar and reserved eggplant. Toss eggplant until it has absorbed most of the sauce, about 1 minute.

- Stir in green onion and sesame oil. Serve hot.

6 servings

German Green Beans

- In a large skillet, fry bacon until crisp. Drain and reserve ¼ cup drippings; crumble bacon.

- In a medium bowl, beat eggs; add vinegar, water, sugar and salt.

- Return reserved drippings to skillet; add egg mixture. Cook over low heat, stirring constantly, until thickened.

- Prepare beans: drain canned beans or cook frozen or fresh beans until tender-crisp and drain.

- Add beans to skillet; toss well.

- Sprinkle with crumbled bacon and diced pimiento before serving.

6 servings

Hint: Can also be chilled and served as a salad with crisp greens.

INGREDIENTS

½ pound sliced bacon

2 eggs

⅓ cup vinegar

¼ cup water

3 tablespoons sugar

¼ teaspoon salt

2 pounds frozen or canned green beans (or 1½ pounds fresh green beans, rinsed and snipped)

1 tablespoon diced pimiento

INGREDIENTS

4 pounds fresh broccoli

½ cup fresh parsley

¾ cup frozen peas, thawed

4 tablespoons unsalted butter, divided

¼ cup ricotta cheese

2 tablespoons plain yogurt

2 teaspoons salt

½ teaspoon freshly ground nutmeg

¼ teaspoon ground pepper

BROCCOLI FOREST

- Rinse broccoli. Break into small florets and cut stalks into 2-inch pieces.

- In a large saucepan, cook florets in boiling water for 2 minutes. Remove and submerge in ice water to stop cooking. Drain and set aside.

- Cook stems in same water until tender, approximately 20 minutes; drain and set aside until cool enough to handle.

- In a food processor, use steel blade to mince parsley.

- Add broccoli stems, peas, 2 tablespoons butter, ricotta, yogurt, salt, nutmeg and pepper. Purée.

- Turn purée into buttered 10-inch round baking dish.

- Arrange broccoli florets, stem side down, over purée. Dot with remaining 2 tablespoons butter.

- Cover loosely with a foil "tent" and bake 30 minutes.

Temperature: 325°

Time: 30 minutes

8 servings

Broccoli and Artichoke Stir-Fry

INGREDIENTS

3 tablespoons olive oil

3 tablespoons butter

1 clove garlic, minced

4 cups broccoli florets

1 can (14 ounces) artichoke hearts, drained and quartered

½ teaspoon crushed red pepper

Salt to taste

- In a large skillet or wok, heat oil and butter over medium heat.

- Add garlic and broccoli. Sauté, stirring constantly, until broccoli turns bright green, about 3 to 4 minutes.

- Add artichokes and red pepper.

- Continue cooking, stirring constantly, until broccoli is tender-crisp, approximately 3 to 4 minutes longer.

- Add salt to taste. Serve immediately.

6 to 8 servings

Broccoli with Lemon Cream Sauce

INGREDIENTS

1 bunch broccoli

2 tablespoons butter

1 tablespoon minced, fresh mint, optional

1 cup half-and-half

1 egg yolk, lightly beaten

¼ teaspoon salt

1 tablespoon fresh lemon juice

- Break broccoli into florets. Cook broccoli in boiling water approximately 10 minutes. Drain and remove to serving dish.

- In a small saucepan over medium heat, melt butter; add mint, if desired. Stir in half-and-half and heat to boiling. Boil 5 minutes until mixture is slightly reduced, stirring often; remove from heat.

- Stir a small amount into egg yolk, then slowly combine mixture with that in saucepan.

- Stir in salt and lemon juice. Return to heat and cook on low, stirring constantly, for 2 minutes.

- Pour sauce over broccoli and serve immediately.

4 servings

Fiesta Corn Flan

INGREDIENTS

1 tablespoon unsalted butter

2 tablespoons finely chopped onion

3 tablespoons finely chopped green
pepper

1½ cups corn, divided

1½ tablespoons flour

½ cup milk

1 cup heavy cream

3 eggs

1 teaspoon salt

Freshly ground pepper to taste

¼ teaspoon freshly ground nutmeg

Pinch allspice

2 cups shredded Monterey Jack
cheese with jalapeños

- Sauté onion and pepper in butter for 5 minutes.

- Add 1 cup corn and sauté 6 to 8 minutes or until tender.

- Combine remaining corn, flour, milk, cream and eggs in blender or food processor; process until smooth.

- Add seasonings; combine with sautéed vegetables and cheese.

- Pour into 1½-quart baking dish.

- Place baking dish in pan of hot water and bake 60 minutes or until firm.

- Let stand 15 minutes before serving.

Temperature: 350°

Time: 60 minutes

6 servings

CRUNCHY CALICO PEAS

INGREDIENTS

4 tablespoons butter

1 cup sliced celery

1 cup sliced mushrooms

¼ cup chopped pimiento

¼ cup finely chopped onion

¼ cup sliced water chestnuts

Salt to taste

Freshly ground pepper

1 bag (20 ounces) frozen peas,
thawed and drained

- In a large skillet, melt butter. Add celery, mushrooms, pimiento, onion and water chestnuts. Sauté, stirring frequently, until celery is tender-crisp, approximately 6 minutes. Season to taste.

- Add peas; heat and serve.

8 servings

"MUDDY" MUSHROOMS

INGREDIENTS

3 bouillon cubes each beef,
chicken, vegetable

4 to 5 pounds fresh whole
mushrooms, cleaned

1 pound butter

1 quart Burgundy wine

1½ tablespoons Worcestershire sauce

1 teaspoon dried dill weed

1 teaspoon ground pepper

1 teaspoon garlic powder or
1 clove garlic, minced

- In a large saucepan, bring 2 cups water to boiling. Stir in bouillon cubes until dissolved. Add remaining ingredients. Slowly bring to a boil over medium heat; reduce to simmer. Cover and simmer 5 to 6 hours.

- Uncover; simmer 3 to 5 hours more until liquid is reduced so it just covers the mushrooms.

- Before serving, adjust seasonings.

8 to 10 servings

Hint: Leftovers can be frozen. Defrost in refrigerator then simmer 1 hour before serving.

INGREDIENTS

1½ pounds mushrooms, sliced

2 tablespoons butter

3 tablespoons flour

1 tablespoon minced fresh parsley

1 cup half-and-half, divided

Juice of ½ lemon

Paprika

1 egg yolk

6 ounces Ritz crackers, coarsely crushed

½ cup butter, melted

MUSHROOM SUPREME

- In large skillet, sauté mushrooms in butter for 3 to 5 minutes; add flour and parsley. Cook 10 minutes, covered, over low heat, stirring often.

- Add half-and-half (reserving 1 tablespoon), lemon juice, and paprika. Remove from heat and set aside.

- In separate bowl, whisk egg yolk with remaining half-and-half. Stir into mushroom mixture. Pour into 3-quart casserole.

- Combine crackers and butter. Sprinkle over casserole.

- Refrigerate several hours or overnight.

- Bake 15 to 20 minutes until hot and topping is golden.

Temperature: 300°

Time: 15 to 20 minutes

8 servings

SPINACH-ARTICHOKE BAKE

- Cut each artichoke heart in half. Arrange on bottom of a 1½-quart casserole.

- Cover with cooked spinach and sprinkle with pepper.

- In a medium bowl, combine cream cheese, margarine and milk; beat thoroughly. Spread over spinach.*

- Sprinkle Parmesan cheese evenly over top.

- Bake, uncovered, 30 to 40 minutes, or until bubbly and cheese is golden brown.

Temperature: 375°

Time: 30 to 40 minutes

6 servings

*Hint: May be prepared ahead to this point. Cover and refrigerate.

INGREDIENTS

2 cans (14 ounces each) plain artichoke hearts, drained

3 packages (10 ounces each) frozen leaf spinach, defrosted and drained well

Pepper to taste

1 package (8 ounces) cream cheese, softened

¼ cup margarine

⅓ cup milk

⅓ cup grated Parmesan cheese

Spinach Rice Crunch

6 cups cooked rice

½ cup butter

½ pound mushrooms, sliced

1 clove garlic, minced

1 small onion, chopped

3 packages (10 ounces each) frozen, chopped spinach, defrosted and drained well

2 jars (4 ounces each) chopped pimiento, drained

1 can (8 ounces) water chestnuts, drained and sliced

Salt and pepper

- In large skillet over medium heat, melt butter. Add mushrooms, garlic and onion. Sauté, stirring often, until mushrooms are just tender.

- Remove skillet from heat; add rice, spinach, pimiento, and water chestnuts. Season to taste.

- Pack mixture in a well-oiled ring mold or other decorative mold.* Place mold in a large pan. Pour water into the larger pan until it reaches halfway up the sides of mold.

- Bake 1 hour. Remove from oven and invert onto a serving platter.

- If ring mold is used, fill center with peas, carrots or similar vegetable. If decorative mold is used, garnish with a border of fresh herbs or vegetables.

Temperature: 350°

Time: 1 hour

12 servings

*Hint: May be prepared ahead to this point. Cover and refrigerate; bring to room temperature before baking.

Dijon Baked Tomatoes

INGREDIENTS

3 large tomatoes, cored and halved crosswise

Salt and freshly ground pepper

2 tablespoons Dijon mustard

½ cup sour cream

3 green onions, thinly sliced

1 garlic clove, minced

2 tablespoons minced fresh parsley

COLORFUL AND FLAVORFUL,
EVEN WHEN TOMATOES AREN'T HOMEGROWN

- Sprinkle tomato halves with salt and pepper. Place on a baking sheet.

- In a small bowl, combine mustard, sour cream, onions and garlic. Spread on tomatoes.

- Bake 5 to 8 minutes. Sprinkle with parsley before serving.

Hint: An easy way to keep tomatoes upright is to place each half in a muffin tin.

Temperature: 500°

Time: 5 to 8 minutes

6 servings

Tomatoes Stuffed with Dilled Vegetables

INGREDIENTS

8 to 10 large ripe tomatoes

2 bags (20 ounces each) frozen mixed vegetables

2 stalks celery, finely chopped

6 to 8 green onions, finely chopped

½ teaspoon salt

6 tablespoons mayonnaise

6 tablespoons sour cream

1 can (8 ounces) water chestnuts, drained and chopped

2½ teaspoons dill weed

Fresh dill sprigs

- Rinse tomatoes, core and halve crosswise. Remove seeds and pulp. Discard. Set hollow tomato halves aside.

- Steam mixed vegetables just until tender-crisp. Drain and cool.

- In a large bowl, combine all ingredients.

- Generously stuff tomato shells. Refrigerate 4 to 6 hours before serving. Garnish with dill.

8 servings

2 cups seasoned breadcrumbs

5 fresh tomatoes, sliced

2 medium Vidalia onions, thinly sliced and separated into rings

½ cup butter, divided

1½ cups sour cream

1 tablespoon chopped fresh basil

2 tablespoons minced fresh parsley

2 to 3 tablespoons minced fresh chives

1 tablespoon brown sugar

Salt and pepper to taste

VIDALIA TOMATO BAKE

- Line a well-oiled 9 x 13-inch casserole with 1 cup breadcrumbs. Alternately layer tomatoes and onions. Dot with ¼ cup butter.

- In a small bowl, combine sour cream, basil, parsley, chives and brown sugar. Spread over vegetables.

- Sprinkle with remaining breadcrumbs. Dot with remaining ¼ cup butter.

- Bake uncovered for 50 minutes or until hot and lightly browned. Serve immediately.

Temperature: 350°

Time: 50 minutes

8 servings

Hint: If Vidalia onions are out of season, substitute any sweet, mild onion.

Most-Asked-For Onion Casserole

INGREDIENTS

4 large white Bermuda or Vidalia onions

Salt and pepper

Paprika

4 tablespoons butter

¼ cup flour

4 to 6 cups heavy cream

1 cup prepackaged stuffing crumbs

THE TITLE SAYS IT ALL!

- Peel and thinly slice onions.

- In a 2½-quart deep casserole, layer onions, seasoning each layer with salt, pepper and paprika; dot each layer with butter and sprinkle with flour.

- Pour heavy cream over casserole until it comes to ½-inch from top and covers the top layer completely.

- Cover and bake 4 to 5 hours.

- Half an hour before serving, remove cover, pour stuffing evenly over top layer, and bake 30 minutes more. Serve immediately.

Temperature: 325°

Time: 4 to 5 hours

6 to 8 servings

INGREDIENTS

1 cup canned pumpkin

*¾ cup cooked, mashed
butternut squash*

5 eggs

1 cup heavy cream

½ cup chicken broth

½ teaspoon salt

½ teaspoon paprika

⅛ teaspoon freshly grated nutmeg

Minced fresh parsley

GOLDEN AUTUMN TIMBALES

THIS IS AN ELEGANT ACCOMPANIMENT
FOR A SPECIAL HARVEST DINNER.

- In a large mixing bowl, combine pumpkin, squash, eggs, cream, broth, salt, paprika and nutmeg. Stir to blend.

- Generously grease 6 to 8 individual ramekins or ovenproof molds.

- Divide mixture evenly among the molds. Place molds into a 9 x 13-inch pan. Set the pan on oven rack; carefully pour enough hot water into pan to reach halfway up sides of molds.

- Bake 30 minutes or until a knife inserted into the center comes out clean.

- To serve, carefully invert molds onto warm plates. Garnish with additional nutmeg and parsley.

Temperature: 325°

Time: 30 minutes

6 to 8 servings

Thyme for Butternut Squash

INGREDIENTS

1 medium butternut or buttercup squash, halved

4 tablespoons unsalted butter, cut in pieces

3 tablespoons honey

1½ teaspoons dried thyme

Salt and pepper to taste

- Place squash cut-side down on a greased baking sheet.

- Bake 45 minutes or until it pierces easily with a kitchen fork; remove from oven.

- Turn squash cut-side up to cool, then remove seeds and discard.

- Scoop out pulp and place in a food processor fitted with steel blade. Add butter, honey, thyme, salt and pepper. Process until smooth (approximately 30 seconds).

- Place mixture in well-oiled casserole dish and bake 20 minutes or until hot. Serve immediately.

Temperature: 400°

Time: 45 minutes
      20 minutes

4 servings

INGREDIENTS

1 head red cabbage (approximately 3 pounds)

2 large cooking apples, peeled and chopped

1 large onion, chopped

¼ cup sugar

¼ cup vinegar

6 slices bacon, cooked and crumbled

2 tablespoons bacon drippings

1 teaspoon salt

Ground pepper to taste

½ cup boiling water

OKTOBERFEST ROLT KRAUT

A "MUST" WITH GERMAN FARE, OR AS A SPICY ACCENT ANYTIME TO POULTRY OR PORK

- Coarsely shred cabbage.

- In large saucepan, combine all ingredients.

- Bring to boil, reduce heat and simmer, covered, for 1 hour.

8 servings

INGREDIENTS

3 cans (16 ounces each) yams

1 can (21 ounces) apple pie filling

¼ cup brown sugar, firmly packed

1 cup dark raisins

TZIMMES

THIS IS A QUICK AND EASY VARIATION OF THE TRADITIONAL JEWISH DISH FOR ROSH HASHANAH.

- Drain yams, reserving liquid. Cut yams into 1-inch cubes.

- Combine all ingredients (including reserved liquid) in a well-oiled 9 x 13-inch casserole. Cover and bake 35 minutes.

Temperature: 350°

Time: 35 minutes

8 to 10 servings

Sweet and Sour Beans

- Place beans in a 3-quart casserole.
- Cut bacon into 1-inch pieces. Fry until nearly crisp. Remove bacon; drain on paper towel.
- Discard half of drippings. To remaining drippings in skillet, add vinegar, onions, brown sugar, mustard, salt and garlic powder. Cook 20 minutes or until onions are tender, stirring often.
- Add mixture and bacon to casserole. Stir to mix.
- Bake uncovered, 1 to 1½ hours, stirring every 30 minutes. Serve hot.

Temperature: 350°

Time: 1 to 1½ hours

10 to 12 servings

INGREDIENTS

2 cans (15 ounces each) butter beans, drained

1 can (16 ounces) pork and beans

1 can (16 ounces) lima beans, drained

1 can (15 ounces) kidney beans, drained

½ pound sliced bacon

½ cup vinegar

4 medium onions, sliced

1 cup brown sugar

1 teaspoon prepared mustard

½ teaspoon salt

Dash garlic powder

Vegetables Marinara

- Place rice in 2-quart baking dish.
- Cook vegetables until tender-crisp; drain. Spoon over rice.
- Top with marinara sauce. Cover and bake 30 minutes.
- Combine cheeses; sprinkle over casserole. Bake 5 to 10 minutes more to melt cheese.

Temperature: 375°

Time: 35 to 40 minutes

6 to 8 servings

INGREDIENTS

2 cups cooked brown rice

2 cups broccoli florets

2 medium carrots, cut into strips

1 medium zucchini, shredded

1 cup green beans, French cut

1 jar (16 ounces) marinara sauce

4 ounces shredded longhorn cheese

4 ounces shredded Monterey Jack cheese

INGREDIENTS

1¼ pounds ground beef

½ cup diced bacon

1 small onion, diced

¼ cup barbecue sauce

⅓ cup brown sugar

½ cup sugar

¼ cup ketchup

1 tablespoon prepared mustard

¼ cup molasses

½ teaspoon chili powder

½ teaspoon pepper

½ teaspoon salt

1 can (27 ounces) kidney beans

1 can (16 ounces) pork and beans

1 can (16 ounces) white beans

POTLUCK BEANS

- Brown ground beef, bacon and onion in large saucepan. Drain fat.

- Add remaining ingredients, mix together and simmer for 1 hour.

- Serve warm.

8 to 10 servings

Company's Coming Potatoes

INGREDIENTS

8 to 10 medium potatoes

1 package (8 ounces) cream cheese, softened

2 cups sour cream

⅓ cup chopped chives

Salt and freshly ground pepper to taste

4 tablespoons margarine

Paprika

This special potato dish can be refrigerated for 4 to 5 days and baked as needed, or cook all at once and reheat for delicious leftovers.

- Peel potatoes; boil until tender.

- Beat cream cheese and sour cream together. Add potatoes and beat until smooth. Stir in chives, salt and pepper.

- Pour into well-oiled 2-quart casserole. Dot with margarine and sprinkle with paprika. Bake 30 minutes.

Temperature: 350°

Time: 30 minutes

8 to 10 servings

INGREDIENTS

3 tablespoons butter

3 medium potatoes, baked in skins, cooled and sliced crosswise

1¼ cups shredded Monterey Jack cheese

1¼ cups shredded cheddar cheese

⅔ cup diced fresh tomatoes

¼ cup finely chopped green onion

Salt to taste

½ avocado, diced

½ cup sour cream

POTATOES MONTEREY

BAKE EXTRA POTATOES FOR THIS SCRUMPTIOUS TREAT!

- In a heavy skillet over medium heat, melt butter. Add potatoes and fry until crispy, stirring frequently.

- Add cheeses, tomatoes, and onion. Cook, stirring until cheeses melt. Season to taste.

- Gently mix in avocado.

- Spoon onto serving plates. Top each serving with sour cream.

3 to 4 servings

INGREDIENTS

3 pounds small red potatoes, quartered

¼ cup olive oil

½ teaspoon salt

½ teaspoon freshly ground pepper

3 large garlic cloves, thinly sliced

2 teaspoons dried rosemary

2 tablespoons minced fresh parsley

2 tablespoons minced fresh chives

—

ROASTED NEW POTATOES WITH GARLIC AND ROSEMARY

- In a large roasting pan, combine oil, salt, pepper, garlic and rosemary. Stir in potatoes until well coated.

- Roast uncovered 1 hour or until potatoes are tender, turning them 2 to 3 times.

- Remove from the oven. Before serving, toss with parsley and chives.

Temperature: 375°

Time: 1 hour

8 to 10 servings

Saucy Scalloped Potatoes

INGREDIENTS

8 to 9 red-skinned potatoes

1 cup milk

1 cup heavy cream

½ pound cheddar cheese, shredded

1 teaspoon dry mustard

1½ teaspoons salt

½ teaspoon ground nutmeg

Dash of pepper

¼ pound butter

Paprika

RED-SKINNED POTATOES MAKE THIS UNIQUELY WONDERFUL!

- Boil red potatoes with skins on until tender.

- In saucepan, combine milk, cream, cheddar, mustard, salt, nutmeg and pepper. Cook over medium heat until cheese melts; do not boil.

- In a well-oiled 9 x 13-inch casserole dish, slice potatoes; cover with sauce. Dot with butter and paprika.*

- Bake, uncovered, for 1 hour.

Temperature: 350°

Time: 1 hour

8 servings

Hint: May be refrigerated up to 24 hours at this point.

INGREDIENTS

1 bag (32 ounces) frozen hash browns, partially thawed

½ cup melted butter

½ teaspoon pepper

½ teaspoon salt

1 can (10¾ ounces) cream of chicken soup

1 pint sour cream

2 cups shredded sharp cheddar

½ cup chopped onion

TOPPING

3 cups crushed cornflakes

3 tablespoons melted butter

"SECONDS, PLEASE" HASH BROWNS

- In a large mixing bowl combine all ingredients. Place in a well-oiled 9 x 13-inch casserole.
- In small bowl, mix cornflakes and butter; spread over casserole. Bake 1 hour.

Temperature: 350°

Time: 1 hour

8 servings

INGREDIENTS

2 cans (1 pound each) whole sweet potatoes, drained

½ teaspoon salt

½ cup brown sugar

1 tablespoon cornstarch

¼ teaspoon salt

1 cup orange juice

¼ cup light raisins

2 tablespoons dry sherry

1½ teaspoons shredded orange peel

2 tablespoons chopped walnuts or pecans

SWEET POTATO MEDLEY

- Arrange potatoes in a 9 x 13-inch casserole; sprinkle with salt.
- Place remaining ingredients, except nuts, in saucepan. Cook 2 to 4 minutes until sauce thickens. Remove from heat; pour over potatoes.
- Sprinkle with nuts. Bake 25 to 30 minutes.

Temperature: 350°

Time: 25 to 30 minutes

8 servings

Consommé Rice

- In skillet, melt butter and sauté onion until transparent.
- Add rice and cook until toasted.
- Add consommé, water, salt, pepper and parsley.
- Place in 1½-quart casserole; bake, covered, for 1 hour, stirring occasionally.

Temperature: 350°

Time: 1 hour

6 servings

INGREDIENTS

½ cup butter

1 onion, finely chopped

1 cup long grain white rice

1 can (14½ ounces) beef consommé

1 cup water

Salt and pepper to taste

1 tablespoon minced fresh parsley

Elegant Wild Rice

- Add wild rice to 3 cups boiling water. Cover, reduce heat, and cook 15 minutes; drain.
- Melt 3 tablespoons butter in saucepan over medium heat. Add carrots, onions and celery, and cook until onion is transparent, stirring frequently.
- Add wild rice, white rice and tarragon; mix well.
- Add broth; bring to boil. Reduce heat, cover and simmer 40 minutes or until liquid is absorbed.
- Melt remaining 2 tablespoons butter; add mushrooms, and cook about 3 minutes. Add snow peas and stir-fry for 2 more minutes. Add to rice; season with salt and pepper to taste.

6 to 8 servings

INGREDIENTS

1 cup wild rice

5 tablespoons butter

¼ cup chopped carrot

¼ cup chopped onion

¼ cup chopped celery

½ cup long grain white rice

1 teaspoon dried tarragon, crumbled

2⅔ cups beef broth

12 mushrooms, cleaned, stemmed, and sliced thin

⅓ pound snow peas, stemmed and sliced into thirds

Salt and fresh ground pepper

BULGUR PILAF

INGREDIENTS

6 green onions

1 teaspoon cumin

2 tablespoons vegetable oil

1 cup bulgur

1½ cups water

1 teaspoon salt

½ cup yellow raisins

- Thinly slice white bulbs of green onions and enough of the green stems to measure ⅓ cup, keeping white and green parts separate.

- In a heavy medium saucepan, sauté the white onions with cumin and oil.

- Add bulgur and cook, stirring for 1 minute.

- Add water and salt; bring to boil. Cover, reduce heat, and cook for 15 minutes or until liquid is absorbed.

- Stir in raisins and onion greens; remove from heat. Let sit, covered, for 5 to 10 minutes to plump raisins. Serve hot.

4 servings

WILD RICE WITH PECANS

INGREDIENTS

1 cup wild rice

½ lemon

2 cups chicken stock

1 tablespoon fresh lemon juice

1 tablespoon unsalted butter

½ cup pecans, lightly toasted and chopped

3 to 4 tablespoons minced green onions

¼ cup minced fresh parsley

Salt and pepper

- Place wild rice in a medium bowl; add water to cover. Set aside 4 to 6 hours or overnight; drain before cooking.

- Using a vegetable peeler, remove rind from lemon in julienne strips.

- In a heavy saucepan, combine chicken stock, half of the lemon rind, lemon juice and butter. Bring mixture to a boil; stir in rice. Cook rice, covered, over low heat until tender and liquid is absorbed (approximately 40 to 50 minutes).

- Remove pan from heat. Add pecans, green onions, parsley and the remaining rind. Season to taste with salt and pepper.

4 servings

MEAT

Meat / Index

Beef

Baked in a Pie / 185
Baked Steak / 179
Beijing Beef / 182
Estofado / 183
Grilled Beef Kabobs / 180
Indonesian Spiced Beef / 184
Korean Beef / 185
Mustard Flank Steak / 180
Stuffed Filet of Beef with Bordelaise Sauce / 181

Lamb

Greek Lamb / 202
Infamous Patio Kabobs / 200
Lake George Lamb / 198
Lamb Chops with Fresh Rosemary / 201
Marinated Butterflied Leg of Lamb / 199
Roast Rack of Lamb / 201
Saucy Lamb Shanks / 202
Spring Lamb / 198

Pork & Ham

Apple-Kraut Pork Chops / 186
Ariste Con Carne / 188
Back-Country Cook Out / 190
Dramatic Crown Roast / 189
Grilled Pork Tenderloin with Mustard Cream
   Sauce / 186
Ham Asparagus Tetrazzini / 188

Lo Mein / 190
Pepper Sausage Ragout / 191
Pork Loin Roast with Peach Sauce / 191
Spiedis / 192
True Cajun Jambalaya / 187

Veal

Arrivederci Veal / 197
Roast Veal Dijon / 195
Veal Bolognese / 196
Veal Forestière / 195
Veal Pistachio / 194
Veal Tarragon / 193

Sauces

Blue Ribbon Pork Marinade / 206
Dilly Dijon Sauce / 203
Dynamite Cocktail Sauce / 203
Hacienda Sauce / 207
Lemon Barbecue Marinade / 205
Lime Butter / 208
Memorable Marinade / 204
Mustard Street Sauce / 206
My Bleu Heaven Sauce / 208
Prairie Sauce / 204
Szechwan Beef Marinade / 207
Upper Crust Marinade / 205

BAKED STEAK

INGREDIENTS

*3-inch thick boneless sirloin steak
(3 to 4 pounds)*

3 tablespoons butter, melted

1 cup chili sauce

3 tablespoons Worcestershire sauce

¼ cup chopped onion

A VERY SPECIAL RECIPE THAT'S ALMOST TOO GOOD TO BE TRUE!

- Sear sirloin steak on all sides under broiler.

- Combine butter, chili sauce, Worcestershire sauce and onion.

- Pour over steak; bake 45 minutes for rare.

- While steak is baking, sauté mushrooms in butter; add remaining ingredients and cook over medium heat until slightly thickened (about 15 minutes).

- After baking, let steak stand 2 minutes, then slice. Serve with mushroom sauce.

MUSHROOM SAUCE

2 tablespoons butter

1 pound mushrooms, sliced

1 tablespoon Worcestershire sauce

¼ cup chili sauce

1 cup heavy cream

Temperature: 350°

Time: 45 minutes

6 to 8 servings

Hint: Sauce is great on baked potatoes, too!

Wine Suggestions: French Bordeaux Red
California Carbernet
Australian Red
French Red Burgundy
Chilean Red

INGREDIENTS

⅓ cup Dijon mustard

2 tablespoons soy sauce

1 tablespoon heavy cream

1 teaspoon dried thyme

1 teaspoon minced fresh ginger

¼ teaspoon cracked peppercorns

2 cloves garlic, minced

Large flank steak (about 1 pound)

MUSTARD FLANK STEAK

- In small bowl, mix together first 7 ingredients. Spread on both sides of steak. Place steak in ceramic or plastic container and marinate meat for 2 to 4 hours at room temperature or 18 hours in refrigerator.

- Bring steak to room temperature. Grill over hot coals (5 minutes on each side for rare).

- To serve, slice on an angle.

3 to 4 servings

INGREDIENTS

½ envelope dry onion soup mix

2 tablespoons sugar

½ cup water

½ cup ketchup

¼ cup vinegar

¼ cup salad oil

¼ teaspoon salt

1 tablespoon mustard

1½ pounds beef chuck or sirloin tip, cut into 1-inch cubes

1 green pepper, cut into 2-inch chunks

1 red pepper, cut into 2-inch chunks

1 can (14 ounces) small onions

12 ounces fresh mushrooms

1 pint cherry tomatoes

GRILLED BEEF KABOBS

- In saucepan, combine first 8 ingredients. Simmer 20 minutes; cool, then add meat and marinate 2 hours at room temperature or refrigerated 4 to 18 hours.

- Thread meat with vegetables on skewers.

- Grill over medium coals 10 to 20 minutes, turning once. Brush occasionally with marinade.

4 to 6 servings

Stuffed Filet of Beef with Bordelaise Sauce

- Sauté onions in oil and butter until limp.

- Add garlic, ham, pepper, salt, and thyme. Stir in egg yolk and parsley.

- Cook for 3 minutes over medium heat.

- Slice the tenderloin, but not quite through, into 8 thick sections. Spoon mixture between each slice.

- Tie roast securely with string. Place meat on a roasting rack. Brush with additional oil or butter.

- Roast 45 to 50 minutes or until meat thermometer reaches 125° (for rare).

- Let meat set for 10 minutes. Remove string. Serve with Bordelaise Sauce.

Bordelaise Sauce

- In a saucepan, melt butter and sauté green onion until transparent.

- Add wine; simmer until it is reduced by one-half. Add the remaining ingredients and heat thoroughly.

Temperature: 300°

Time: 45 to 50 minutes

8 servings

INGREDIENTS

2 large onions, thinly sliced

¼ cup vegetable oil

3 tablespoons butter

1 clove garlic, minced

⅓ cup chopped, cooked ham

1 teaspoon fresh ground pepper

1 teaspoon salt

¾ teaspoon dried thyme

1 egg yolk, beaten

¼ cup minced fresh parsley

4 pounds beef tenderloin

BORDELAISE SAUCE

2 tablespoons butter

2 tablespoons finely chopped green onion

¾ cup dry red wine

1½ cups brown sauce or canned beef gravy

2 tablespoons lemon juice

2 tablespoons minced parsley

Salt to taste

Cayenne pepper to taste

¾ cup sliced, cooked mushrooms

Beijing Beef

INGREDIENTS

*2 pounds stewing beef, cut into
1-inch cubes*

⅓ cup flour

2 tablespoons peanut oil

1 can (30 ounces) plums in syrup

⅔ cup low-sodium soy sauce

¼ cup dry white wine

*2 tablespoons finely chopped
fresh ginger*

*3 large carrots, cut into
julienne strips*

*1 package (6 ounces) frozen pea
pods, thawed*

2 cups sliced fresh mushrooms

*3 green onions, sliced into
½-inch pieces*

*1 red bell pepper, cut into
julienne strips*

*1 can (8 ounces) bamboo
shoots, drained*

4 cups hot cooked rice

- Dredge beef in flour. Brown beef in oil in a Dutch oven over medium heat. Remove meat, drain oil, return beef to pan.

- Drain plums, reserving syrup. Remove and discard plum pits. In blender, purée plums and syrup.

- Add plums, soy sauce, wine and ginger to beef. Bring to a boil, cover and reduce heat. Simmer 1 to 2 hours or until meat is tender.

- Add carrots. Cover and simmer 7 minutes.

- Add next 5 ingredients. Cover and simmer 7 to 10 minutes more or until vegetables are tender-crisp.

- Serve over rice in individual bowls.

6 servings

Estofado

THE ADDITION OF FRUIT TO THIS TRADITIONAL STEW
ADDS A FLAVORFUL TWIST.

- In skillet over medium heat, melt butter. Sear beef cubes, but do not brown.

- Add red wine, beef broth, tomato paste, vinegar, sugar, cumin, garlic, allspice, bay leaf, salt and pepper.

- Simmer, covered, until almost tender (approximately 1½ hours).

- Add onions, mushrooms, prunes and apricots.

- Simmer 30 minutes more or until tender.

- If desired, broth can be thickened with 1 tablespoon flour mixed with 2 tablespoons cold water.

8 servings

Wine Suggestions: Spanish Red
                 Italian Red

INGREDIENTS

¼ cup butter

3 pounds stew meat or round
steak, cubed

2 cups red wine

2 cups beef broth

1 can (6 ounces) tomato paste

¼ cup red wine vinegar

2 tablespoons brown sugar

1½ teaspoons ground cumin

1 teaspoon minced garlic

½ teaspoon ground allspice

1 bay leaf

Salt and pepper

1 jar (14 ounces) small onions,
drained

½ pound large mushrooms,
quartered

6 ounces dried prunes, halved

4 ounces dried apricots, halved

INGREDIENTS

1 pound beef tenderloin or top round, partially frozen

2 tablespoons peanut oil

1 clove garlic, minced

1 medium onion, coarsely chopped

½ pound fresh snow peas, trimmed

MARINADE

2 teaspoons soy sauce

Dash pepper

2 teaspoons oriental sesame oil

2 teaspoons cornstarch

SAUCE

1 tablespoon satay sauce*

2 tablespoons dry sherry

½ teaspoon curry powder

Dash salt

2 tablespoons water

2 teaspoons soy sauce

½ teaspoon sugar

INDONESIAN SPICED BEEF

- Trim meat. While meat is still at least half frozen, slice across grain into ¼-inch pieces. Pound each slice on both sides to ⅛-inch thickness.

- In a medium bowl, combine marinade ingredients; mix thoroughly. Add beef and stir to cover each piece. Refrigerate, covered, 4 to 18 hours, stirring occasionally.

- In a small bowl, combine sauce ingredients; set aside.

- Drain meat and separate slices. Heat oil in a wok over medium high heat. Sear meat in hot oil, browning it quickly on both sides. Remove to platter and keep warm.

- Add garlic and onion to meat juices in wok. Stir constantly until onion is transparent; do not burn.

- Add sauce; stir until boiling. Add meat and snow peas, stirring constantly, until snow peas are tender-crisp. Serve immediately.

4 servings

*Available in gourmet food section or Southeast Asian market.

Satay sauce substitute: 2 teaspoons Worcestershire sauce, 1 teaspoon honey, 1 tablespoon chili sauce.

BAKED IN A PIE

- Brown ground beef and chopped onion. Pour off drippings, season meat with pepper; set aside.
- In a large saucepan over medium heat, mix flour, salt, garlic salt, 1¼ cups milk and cream cheese. Cook and stir until mixture is thick and smooth.
- Add beaten egg; cook and stir 1 to 2 minutes more. Stir in broccoli and beef.
- Line pie pan with one crust. Pour in filling. Top with cheese. Add top crust; seal edges. Brush crust with 1 tablespoon milk; prick with fork.
- Cover loosely with foil; bake 20 minutes. Remove foil and bake 20 minutes longer or until crust is golden brown.

Temperature: 350°
Time: 40 minutes
6 to 8 servings

INGREDIENTS

1 pound ground beef

¼ cup chopped onion

¼ teaspoon freshly ground pepper

2 tablespoons flour

½ teaspoon salt

½ teaspoon garlic salt

1¼ cups plus 1 tablespoon milk, divided

1 package (3-ounce) cream cheese

1 egg, beaten

1 package (10 ounces) frozen chopped broccoli, cooked

4 ounces Monterey Jack cheese, sliced

2 8-inch or 9-inch pie crusts

KOREAN BEEF

THIS AUTHENTIC KOREAN RECIPE IS DELICIOUS SERVED WITH RICE AND ORIENTAL VEGETABLES.

- Slice meat into 3-inch by ¾-inch pieces. Place in large bowl.
- Add sugar; let sit 30 minutes.
- Add soy sauce, sesame seeds, onions, garlic and pepper; mix well.
- Add oil, mix well and allow to sit an additional 30 minutes.
- Cook over high heat, preferably in a wok.

4 to 6 servings

INGREDIENTS

2 pounds round steak or London broil

½ cup sugar

½ cup soy sauce

3 tablespoons sesame seeds

3 tablespoons sliced green onions

3 cloves garlic, minced

1½ teaspoons black pepper

3 tablespoons oriental sesame oil

¾ cup vegetable oil

1 cup dry white wine, divided

3 garlic cloves, crushed

⅛ teaspoon ground ginger

1½ pounds pork tenderloin, trimmed

1 cup heavy cream

3 tablespoons Dijon mustard

Freshly ground white pepper

Salt

GRILLED PORK TENDERLOIN WITH MUSTARD CREAM SAUCE

- In a baking dish just large enough to hold pork, combine oil, ¼ cup wine, garlic and ginger.

- Add pork, turning to coat thoroughly. Marinate overnight in refrigerator.

- Drain pork and grill on oiled rack over medium-hot coals for approximately 25 minutes, turning frequently. Let roast stand for 5 to 10 minutes before slicing.

- In large saucepan, boil remaining ¾ cup wine until reduced to about ¼ cup. Stir in cream and simmer until thickened.

- Whisk in mustard, pepper and salt.

- Serve pork with sauce on the side.

4 to 6 servings

1 tablespoon vegetable oil

2 pork chops (½-inch thick)

1 cup sauerkraut, drained

¼ cup water

½ teaspoon caraway seeds

½ cup cinnamon applesauce

1 tablespoon chopped onion

1½ tablespoons brown sugar

½ teaspoon pepper

APPLE-KRAUT PORK CHOPS

- Heat oil in skillet. Brown pork chops on both sides. Remove pork chops and set aside. Drain pan drippings.

- Add sauerkraut, water and caraway seeds to skillet and stir well. Place pork chops on top.

- Combine remaining ingredients and spoon on top of pork chops.

- Cover, reduce heat and simmer 35 to 40 minutes.

2 servings

TRUE CAJUN JAMBALAYA

A TRADITIONAL LOUISIANA FAVORITE! SERVE WITH A SALAD AND
WARM FRENCH BREAD FOR A DELIGHTFUL MEAL.

- In a stockpot or Dutch oven, melt butter and sauté sausage
  and ham until lightly browned. Stir in flour. Add onions,
  green onions, green pepper, garlic and sauté until vegetables
  are soft.

- Stir in tomatoes, bay leaf, thyme, cayenne, black pepper,
  chicken, broth, shrimp and rice. (Liquid in pot should just
  cover the contents).

- Bring to a boil, stirring occasionally, then lower heat, cover
  pot and simmer until all liquid is absorbed and rice is
  tender. Before serving, remove bay leaf and add salt to taste.

10 to 12 servings

Wine Suggestions: Cotes du Rhone
California Zinfandel
Australian Red

INGREDIENTS

¼ cup butter

1 pound smoked sausage (hot or
mild), chopped

½ pound ham, diced

¼ cup flour

3 medium onions, chopped

6 green onions, chopped

1 green pepper, chopped

4 cloves garlic, minced

4 ripe tomatoes, peeled
and chopped

1 bay leaf

½ tablespoon dried thyme

¼ teaspoon cayenne

Black pepper

1 cup diced, cooked chicken

3 cups chicken broth

2 pounds raw shrimp, shelled
and deveined

2 cups uncooked long-grain rice

1 tablespoon salt (optional)

*4 pounds boneless pork loin roast
(2 2-pound loins, butterflied)*

4 large cloves garlic, sliced thinly

*2 tablespoons fresh, or 1 scant
tablespoon dried rosemary*

2 teaspoons black pepper

1 tablespoon olive oil

ARISTE CON CARNE

- In a small bowl, combine garlic, rosemary and pepper.

- Press ¼ of mixture into butterflied side of each pork loin. Roll and tie.

- Score top of each roast and fill with remaining mixture. Rub olive oil over meat. Place roast on rack in open roasting pan. Roast for 30 minutes per pound or until meat thermometer reaches 165°. Turn meat over halfway through cooking.

- Let meat stand 10 minutes before carving. Slice thinly.

Temperature: 375°
Time: 2 hours
8 servings

6 tablespoons butter

½ cup flour

2 cups half-and-half

1 cup milk

1½ cups chicken broth

1 cup shredded cheddar cheese

¼ cup grated Parmesan cheese

¼ cup lemon juice

¼ cup sliced green onion

2 tablespoons minced fresh parsley

HAM ASPARAGUS TETRAZZINI

- In medium saucepan, melt butter; stir in flour. Add half-and-half, milk and chicken broth. Cook over medium heat 5 minutes or until thick, stirring constantly.

- Stir in cheeses, lemon juice, onion, parsley, mustard and salt. Remove from heat and stir in mayonnaise.

- Cut asparagus into 1½-inch lengths and cook until tender-crisp; drain.

- Cook spaghetti al dente; drain and rinse.

- In well-oiled 9 x 13-inch baking dish, layer asparagus, ham, spaghetti and sauce.
- Bake for 30 to 40 minutes.

Temperature: 350°
Time: 30 to 40 minutes
8 servings

2 tablespoons prepared mustard

2 teaspoons salt

¾ cup mayonnaise

1¾ pounds asparagus

8 ounces spaghetti

4 cups cubed cooked ham

DRAMATIC CROWN ROAST

- Cook rice according to package directions.
- Brown ground pork with onion, celery and garlic until vegetables are tender and meat is browned; drain off fat.
- Combine meat and vegetable mixture with rice, pecans, apricots, allspice and ginger in large bowl. Spoon stuffing lightly into center of roast. Protect ends of bones and top of stuffing with foil.
- Roast at 400° for 10 minutes. Lower temperature to 325° and continue to bake 30 more minutes per pound or until meat thermometer inserted in thickest part of roast reaches 170°.
- Remove roast to heated serving platter; keep warm.
- Skim off fat from pan juices. Add cloves, bay leaves, wine and broth to juices. Cook over medium heat, stirring frequently, until gravy is reduced to two-thirds of its original volume.
- To serve, strain gravy into gravy boat.

Temperature: 400°, then 325°
Time: approximately 3½ hours
8 to 10 servings

INGREDIENTS

1 6-ounce package long-grain wild rice mix

¼ pound ground pork

1 medium onion, chopped

⅓ cup chopped celery

2 cloves garlic, minced

½ cup chopped pecans

1½ cups chopped dried apricots

½ teaspoon ground allspice

½ teaspoon ground ginger

1 7-pound crown roast of pork

6 cloves

2 bay leaves

¾ cup Marsala wine

1 can (13¾-ounces) beef broth

INGREDIENTS

2 cans beer

2 cans water

1 pound smoked sausage, cut into 2-inch pieces

6 to 8 ears corn, cut into 2-inch pieces

1 medium zucchini, cut into large julienne slices

1 pound large shrimp with shells

Melted butter

BACK-COUNTRY COOK OUT

THIS IS A FABULOUS FEAST FOR SUMMER ENTERTAINING!

- In a large Dutch oven, bring beer and water to boil.
- Add sausage, cover and simmer for 15 minutes.
- Add corn, cook for 5 more minutes.
- Add zucchini and shrimp. Cook 3 to 5 more minutes, covered.
- Heap all on a platter. Serve with ramekins of melted butter, lots of napkins and beer to drink!

4 servings

INGREDIENTS

½ pound fine egg noodles

2 tablespoons vegetable oil

3 cloves garlic, minced

8 green onions, cut in 1-inch pieces, greens included

½ pound lean cooked pork, cut in julienne strips

3 tablespoons oyster sauce

2 tablespoons soy sauce

2 tablespoons sugar

⅛ teaspoon (or more) crushed red pepper

Oriental sesame oil

LO MEIN

- Cook egg noodles according to package directions; drain and set aside.
- In wok or large skillet, heat oil. Add garlic, onion and pork. Stir-fry 2 to 3 minutes.
- Add oyster sauce, soy sauce, sugar and red pepper; heat.
- Stir in noodles and heat through. Sprinkle with sesame oil to taste.

4 servings

Pork Loin Roast with Peach Sauce

INGREDIENTS

¼ cup sherry

¼ cup soy sauce

3 to 6 pound pork loin

1 can (16 ounces) sliced peaches, drained

½ cup dark brown sugar

⅓ cup ketchup

⅓ cup white vinegar

2 tablespoons soy sauce

2 large cloves garlic

2 teaspoons ground ginger

- Combine sherry and soy sauce. Pour over pork loin and marinate, refrigerated, overnight.
- In blender or food processor fitted with steel blade, process remaining ingredients.
- Transfer meat to open roasting pan and roast pork for ½ hour per pound, basting the last ½ hour with the peach sauce.

Temperature: 325°

Time: ½ hour per pound

6 to 12 servings

Pepper Sausage Ragout

INGREDIENTS

3 pounds Italian sausage in casing

¼ cup olive oil

2 green peppers, cut into strips

2 red peppers, cut into strips

1 yellow pepper, cut into strips

1 large onion, coarsely chopped

3 cloves garlic, minced

3 large tomatoes, diced

1 cup tomato sauce

½ cup chopped fresh basil

½ cup red wine

A GREAT RECIPE FOR THE ELECTRIC SKILLET

- Cut sausage into ½-inch slices, and brown in skillet. Pour off excess fat.
- Add olive oil and sauté peppers, onion and garlic 5 minutes over medium heat.
- Add tomatoes, tomato sauce, basil and wine. Simmer, uncovered, for 30 minutes.

8 to 10 servings

INGREDIENTS

4 pounds pork butt (may substitute beef or lamb roast)

1 cup red wine vinegar

½ cup salad oil

Juice of 2 medium lemons

5 cloves garlic, minced

2 tablespoons dried basil

1 tablespoon salt

2 teaspoons black pepper

1 tablespoon dried oregano

Fresh Italian bread, sliced

SPIEDIS

A REGIONAL SPECIALTY FROM NEW YORK'S SOUTHERN TIER

- Cut pork butt or roast into 1-inch cubes.

- In a large bowl, combine all other ingredients except bread. Add meat and marinate, refrigerated, for a minimum of 24 hours, stirring once.

- Place meat on skewers and broil until browned, turning once to ensure even cooking.

- To serve, remove meat from skewers. Serve on thick slices of buttered Italian bread. Pour pan drippings into small pitcher to serve with Spiedis.

Variation: Skewer meat alternately with onions and green peppers; serve as shish-kabobs.

8 servings

Veal Tarragon

INGREDIENTS

- Pound veal to ¼-inch thickness; cut into julienne strips.

- In a shallow bowl, combine flour, salt and pepper. Dredge veal lightly in flour mixture.

- In a large skillet, melt 2 tablespoons butter over medium heat. Add veal and sauté until tender, about 5 to 7 minutes. Remove from skillet and keep warm. Reserve pan drippings.

- In the same skillet, melt remaining 2 tablespoons butter over medium heat. Add mushrooms and green onions. Stir and cook until tender. Add lemon juice, white wine and tarragon. Dissolve bouillon in boiling water; add to sauce.

- Place cold water in a small bowl or cup. Add cornstarch and rapidly stir to blend. Add mixture to the sauce, stirring constantly. Cook until thickened and clear. Add cognac; stir. Pour over veal, garnish with lemon and serve.

4 servings

1 pound veal cutlet, trimmed

⅓ cup flour

Salt and pepper to taste

4 tablespoons butter

½ pound mushrooms, sliced

4 green onions, chopped

2 teaspoons lemon juice

½ cup dry white wine

½ teaspoon dried tarragon

1 teaspoon beef bouillon granules

½ cup boiling water

¼ cup cold water

2 tablespoons cornstarch

2 tablespoons cognac

Lemon, thinly sliced

VEAL PISTACHIO

INGREDIENTS

¼ teaspoon ground nutmeg

2 teaspoons salt

¼ teaspoon dried rosemary

2 pounds veal scallops

½ pound bulk pork sausage

2 tablespoons chopped onion

2 cloves garlic, minced

2 tablespoons minced fresh parsley

¼ cup chopped pistachio nuts

2 slices white bread, cubed

¼ cup butter or margarine

1 cup dry white wine

½ pound sliced mushrooms

½ cup sour cream

- In a small bowl combine nutmeg, salt and rosemary. Season all sides of veal.

- In a medium bowl, combine sausage, onion, garlic, parsley, nuts and bread. Place 1 tablespoon of filling on each piece of meat. Roll and secure with toothpicks.

- In a large skillet over medium high heat, melt butter. Add veal and brown on all sides. Remove veal to a 9 x 13-inch baking pan. Save skillet drippings in small bowl.

- Add wine and mushrooms to veal. Cover tightly with foil. Bake 40 minutes.

- Remove casserole from oven and place veal on serving platter; keep warm.

- Add skillet drippings to casserole and cook over medium heat. Carefully add sour cream, stirring constantly. Do not boil.

- Pour sauce over meat and serve.

Temperature: 375°

Time: 40 minutes

6 servings

Wine Suggestions: Beaujolais
Chardonnay
White Bordeaux
Sauvignon Blanc
Italian Red
California Pinot Noir

Veal Forestière

- Rub cutlets with garlic. Cut veal into serving sizes. Dredge lightly in flour.
- Melt butter in electric skillet heated to 325°. Sauté veal until golden brown on both sides.
- Squeeze juice from lemon into a measuring cup. Add chicken broth to juice to equal 1 cup.
- Heap mushrooms on veal. Add salt, pepper and chicken broth.
- Reduce skillet heat to 215° and simmer, covered, for 20 minutes or until veal is fork tender. (If pan juices cook dry while veal is simmering, add additional lemon juice and chicken broth.)

4 servings

INGREDIENTS

1 pound thin veal cutlets

1 clove garlic, halved

½ cup flour

¼ cup butter

1 whole lemon

½ to 1 cup chicken broth

½ pound fresh mushrooms, sliced

½ teaspoon salt

Pepper

Roast Veal Dijon

- Place meat in roasting pan.
- Combine melted butter and mustard. Pour over veal, covering all surfaces. Roast 4 hours.
- Combine consommé, broth and sherry. Use to baste roast every 20 minutes during final hour of roasting.
- Remove roast from pan; keep warm. Thicken pan juices with flour to make gravy. Serve gravy separately, garnished with parsley.

Temperature: 300°

Time: 4 hours

4 to 6 servings

INGREDIENTS

1 small leg of veal, boned and rolled

½ cup butter, melted

1 jar (8 ounces) Dijon mustard

½ cup beef consommé

¾ cup beef broth

¼ cup cooking sherry

Flour

Minced fresh parsley

VEAL BOLOGNESE

INGREDIENTS

1 cup unseasoned breadcrumbs

2 tablespoons grated Parmesan cheese

½ teaspoon salt

½ teaspoon garlic powder

½ teaspoon oregano

¼ teaspoon pepper

2 tablespoons minced fresh parsley

1 ½ pounds veal, trimmed and cut into 2 x 3-inch pieces

1 egg, beaten

½ cup vegetable oil

1 to 2 tablespoons butter or margarine

½ pound mushrooms, sliced

1 package (10 ounces) frozen chopped spinach, thawed and drained

½ teaspoon salt

½ cup chopped green onions

1 cup tomato sauce

1 cup white wine

1 cup water

- In a shallow bowl, combine crumbs, Parmesan cheese, salt, garlic powder, oregano, pepper and parsley. Set aside.

- Dip each piece of meat in beaten egg, then in crumb mixture. Reserve extra crumb mixture.

- Heat oil in a large skillet on medium heat. Add veal and brown lightly on both sides; remove and set aside.

- Add reserved crumb mixture to the skillet drippings; brown slightly. Remove and set aside.

- In the same skillet over medium heat, melt butter or margarine. Sauté mushrooms. Remove and set aside.

- Spread spinach in bottom of well-oiled 2-quart baking dish. Sprinkle with salt.

- Top spinach with chopped green onions, then with layer of mushrooms. Next, add veal.

- In a medium bowl, combine tomato sauce, wine and water. Gently pour mixture into casserole. Top with reserved crumbs. (May be made ahead and refrigerated at this point. Bring to room temperature before baking.)

- Bake uncovered for 1 hour.

Hint: For a sweeter, richer flavor, substitute sherry for the white wine in the sauce.

Temperature: 325°

Time: 1 hour

5 to 6 servings

ARRIVEDERCI VEAL

- Pound veal to ¼-inch thickness; cut into 2 to 3-inch pieces.

- In a shallow bowl, combine flour, salt and pepper. Dredge veal in flour mixture.

- In a large skillet over medium heat, combine margarine and oil. Sauté veal until lightly brown. Remove veal from skillet to paper towel-lined platter.

- In the same skillet over medium heat, sauté mushrooms and garlic until mushrooms are tender and liquid has cooked off. Stir in parsley, basil, tomato, wine and broth. Bring to a boil, then remove from heat.

- Transfer veal to a 2-quart casserole. Gradually pour sauce over meat. Sprinkle with Parmesan cheese.

- Bake uncovered for 45 minutes. Serve with rice or pasta.

Temperature: 325°

Time: 45 minutes

8 servings

INGREDIENTS

2 pounds veal scallops, trimmed

½ cup flour

Salt and pepper to taste

2 tablespoons margarine

2 tablespoons oil

1 pound mushrooms, thinly sliced

1 clove garlic, minced

4 tablespoons minced fresh parsley

1 tablespoon minced fresh basil

1 cup chopped tomato

2 cups Marsala wine

1 can (10½ ounces) beef broth

2 tablespoons grated Parmesan cheese

INGREDIENTS

1 jar (8 ounces) Dijon mustard

3 tablespoons soy sauce

3 tablespoons peanut oil

2 teaspoons crushed rosemary

2 teaspoons ground ginger

1 clove garlic, minced

6 pound leg of lamb, butterflied

LAKE GEORGE LAMB

THIS DELECTABLE SUMMER FEAST
WILL MAKE A LAMB LOVER OUT OF EVERYONE!

- Combine all marinade ingredients.

- Spread marinade on all surfaces of meat. Marinate for at least 6 hours or overnight, covered and refrigerated.

- Grill over hot coals 12 to 15 minutes per side. Do not overcook.

6 to 8 servings

INGREDIENTS

1 cup chopped onion

1 teaspoon salt

1 teaspoon freshly ground pepper

½ cup fresh lemon juice

½ cup olive oil

3 large cloves garlic, minced

¼ cup minced fresh parsley

½ teaspoon dried marjoram

1 teaspoon dried thyme

1 2- to 3-pound leg of lamb, boned and butterflied

SPRING LAMB

- In a medium bowl, combine marinade ingredients.

- Pour marinade over lamb in shallow baking dish.

- Refrigerate, covered, overnight, turning meat occasionally.

- Grill lamb over hot coals 15 to 20 minutes per side, basting with marinade.

Variation: Cut lamb into steaks; grill 8 to 10 minutes on each side.

8 to 10 servings

Marinated Butterflied Leg of Lamb

INGREDIENTS

¾ cup mint jelly

2 tablespoons water

2 tablespoons olive oil

1 teaspoon dried rosemary

½ teaspoon ground ginger

2 to 3 tablespoons soy sauce

2 cloves garlic, minced

½ cup Dijon mustard

Freshly ground pepper

2 to 3 pounds leg of lamb, butterflied

- In a small saucepan over medium heat, melt mint jelly with water, stirring constantly.

- Add remaining marinade ingredients; mix well.

- Place lamb in shallow dish. Reserve ⅓ cup marinade. Pour remaining marinade over meat. Refrigerate, covered, 24 to 48 hours, turning meat occasionally.

- Grill lamb over hot coals 12 to 20 minutes per side, basting with reserved marinade.

8 servings

Wine Suggestions: French Red Bordeaux
Chilean Cabernet
California Cabernet

INFAMOUS PATIO KABOBS

BASTING SAUCE

2 cups olive or vegetable oil

½ cup water

¼ cup soy sauce

½ teaspoon salt

½ teaspoon freshly ground pepper

1 clove garlic, crushed

¼ teaspoon dried rosemary

MARINADE

1 cup basting sauce

½ cup wine vinegar

½ cup water

INGREDIENTS

2 pounds lean lamb, cut into
1½-inch cubes

18 small onions, peeled

2 green peppers, seeded and cut
into 2 inch squares

Metal or bamboo skewers

- In a medium bowl, combine all basting sauce ingredients. Transfer to a jar and refrigerate, covered, until needed.

- In a small bowl, combine all marinade ingredients. Refrigerate, covered, until needed.

- Place lamb in large bowl or casserole. Add marinade. Refrigerate, covered, overnight, stirring occasionally.

- Thread lamb cubes, peppers and onions on metal or water-soaked bamboo skewers.

- Grill 30 to 40 minutes over a slow fire, turning often and basting with sauce.

6 servings

Lamb Chops with Fresh Rosemary

- Place first eight ingredients in food processor fitted with steel blade. Process until smooth.
- Score both sides of chops.
- Rub marinade over chops, pressing into incisions.
- Marinate at room temperature for 1 to 2 hours.
- Grill about 4 to 5 inches from heat. Cook 5 minutes per side for medium rare.
- Serve with sprigs of fresh rosemary.

4 servings

INGREDIENTS

2 teaspoons chopped garlic

2 tablespoons fresh rosemary leaves

¼ cup minced fresh parsley

½ teaspoon dried thyme

½ teaspoon salt

½ teaspoon pepper

3 tablespoons olive oil

2 tablespoons red wine

8 ¾ to 1-inch thick lamb loin chops, fat trimmed

8 fresh rosemary sprigs

Roast Rack of Lamb

- In a small mixing bowl, combine garlic, breadcrumbs, parsley, salt, pepper and mustard. Add olive oil in a stream, beating until mixture forms a paste.
- Lightly score tops of lamb racks. Spread with mustard mixture; refrigerate until roasting time. Bring to room temperature before roasting.
- Place racks of lamb, meat side up, in roasting pan. Cover rib ends with foil to prevent burning.
- Bake 40 to 50 minutes for medium rare; longer for well-done chops.

Temperature: 375°

Time: 40 to 50 minutes

6 to 8 servings

INGREDIENTS

3 to 4 cloves garlic, minced

2 cups breadcrumbs

¾ cup minced fresh parsley

1 to 2 teaspoons salt

½ teaspoon pepper

¼ cup Dijon mustard

½ cup olive oil

2 meaty racks of lamb

INGREDIENTS

1 can (15 ounces) tomato sauce

2 cans (10¾ ounces each) beef broth

2 large onions, sliced

½ cup light brown sugar

2 large garlic cloves, minced

2 teaspoons dried dill weed

1 teaspoon dried oregano

2 teaspoons dried rosemary

4 meaty lamb shanks (approximately 1 pound each)

Cooked egg noodles

SAUCY LAMB SHANKS

- Mix all ingredients except lamb and noodles in casserole large enough to hold the lamb shanks in one layer.

- Add lamb, turning to coat with sauce. Cover casserole; bake for 3 hours. Turn shanks twice during cooking.

- Remove lamb and some onion from casserole; keep warm. Strain sauce into medium saucepan pressing solids with large spoon to extract lots of flavor. Rapidly boil sauce until slightly thicker, approximately 6 to 7 minutes.

- Serve lamb with hot noodles, pouring sauce over noodles.

Temperature: 300°

Time: 3 hours

4 servings

INGREDIENTS

2½ pounds stewing lamb

4 tablespoons butter

1 can (8 ounces) tomato sauce

1 clove garlic

1 bay leaf

1 cinnamon stick

½ cup water

Salt and pepper to taste

Cooked noodles

GREEK LAMB

- Cut lamb into 1-inch cubes.

- Melt butter in Dutch oven over medium heat. Sear lamb until browned.

- Add remaining ingredients. Simmer, covered, for 2 hours or until lamb is tender.

- Serve over noodles.

4 servings

Dynamite Cocktail Sauce

INGREDIENTS

¾ cup chili sauce

2 tablespoons chopped celery

2 tablespoons chopped onion

2 tablespoons chopped green pepper

¼ teaspoon paprika

⅛ teaspoon garlic powder

Hot pepper sauce

Hot horseradish to taste

GREAT FOR BOTH SHELLFISH AND SHRIMP

- Mix all ingredients, using about 4 shakes of hot pepper sauce.

- Before serving, let stand at least 1 hour for the flavors to blend.

Dilly Dijon Sauce

INGREDIENTS

1 cup Dijon mustard

⅓ cup sour cream

⅓ cup sugar

⅓ cup white wine vinegar

1 cup olive oil

2 tablespoons dried dill weed

Salt and pepper to taste

A SINFULLY RICH SAUCE, ESPECIALLY GREAT WITH NANTUCKET SWORDFISH

- In blender or food processor, combine mustard, sour cream, sugar and vinegar. Gradually add olive oil while machine is running.

- Transfer sauce to covered container; fold in dill and refrigerate.

3 cups

INGREDIENTS

½ cup vegetable oil

¼ cup soy sauce

½ cup red wine

1½ teaspoons ground ginger

2 cloves garlic, minced

1 tablespoon curry powder

2 tablespoons ketchup

½ teaspoon hot pepper sauce

½ teaspoon black pepper

MEMORABLE MARINADE

A GREAT MARINADE FOR LONDON BROIL

- In a medium bowl, mix all ingredients. Use to marinate beef.

1½ cups

INGREDIENTS

1 tablespoon olive oil

1 cup chopped onion

2 cloves garlic, minced

1 can (8 ounces) tomato sauce

¼ cup brown sugar

¼ cup lemon juice

3 tablespoons Worcestershire sauce

¼ teaspoon paprika

2 tablespoons dry mustard

¼ teaspoon crushed red pepper flakes

Salt and pepper to taste

PRAIRIE SAUCE

- In skillet over medium heat, heat oil and sauté onion and garlic until soft. Stir in remaining ingredients. Cook over medium heat for 10 to 15 minutes.
- Cool and refrigerate, covered. Use as a barbecue sauce over chicken, pork or fish.

1⅛ cups

Upper Crust Marinade

- In blender, combine mustard, soy sauce, garlic, rosemary and ginger. Process on medium-high speed for 10 to 15 seconds.
- While motor is running, partially uncover blender and gradually add oil. When all oil is added, cover tightly and process an additional 10 to 15 seconds.

1 cup

Hint: Coat a leg of lamb with the marinade before roasting or spread the marinade generously on lamb or pork chops before broiling or grilling.

INGREDIENTS

½ cup Dijon mustard

2 tablespoons soy sauce

1 clove garlic, minced

1 teaspoon dried rosemary

¼ teaspoon ground ginger

2 tablespoons olive oil

Lemon Barbecue Marinade

TERRIFIC ON PORK TENDERLOIN KABOBS!

- In a small bowl, whisk together all ingredients. Use immediately or refrigerate, covered, up to one week.

¾ cup

INGREDIENTS

½ cup fresh lemon juice

¼ cup olive oil

½ teaspoon salt

1 garlic clove, crushed

½ teaspoon black pepper

1½ teaspoons finely chopped fresh thyme (or ½ teaspoon dried)

1 teaspoon Worcestershire sauce

2 tablespoons finely chopped green onions

BLUE RIBBON PORK MARINADE

INGREDIENTS

½ cup water

¼ cup cider vinegar

1 whole lemon, sliced

1 medium onion, chopped

2 tablespoons dry mustard

⅛ teaspoon paprika

½ teaspoon salt

¼ teaspoon pepper

½ cup butter

1 cup ketchup

2 tablespoons Worcestershire sauce

ALWAYS A FIRST-PRIZE WINNER!

- In a medium saucepan, combine water, vinegar, lemon, onion, dry mustard, paprika, salt, pepper and butter. Bring to a boil, uncovered, over medium-high heat. Reduce heat to low, cover and simmer for 15 to 20 minutes.

- Stir in ketchup and Worcestershire sauce; increase heat to medium-high and heat to boiling.

- Cool to room temperature, then refrigerate, covered, at least 8 hours before using.

1½ to 1¾ cups

Hint: Use to marinate and baste pork tenderloin, chops, ribs and other meats. Marinate 2 hours before cooking.

MUSTARD STREET SAUCE

INGREDIENTS

1 cup light brown sugar

1 cup cider vinegar

⅔ cup currant jelly

4 large eggs

3 tablespoons dry mustard

1 tablespoon flour

A WONDERFUL SWEET-SOUR MUSTARD SAUCE, GREAT SERVED WITH CHICKEN NUGGETS, DIM SUM OR BEEF STICK.

- In a heavy saucepan, heat sugar, vinegar and jelly, until jelly melts and sugar dissolves. Cool slightly.

- In food processor fitted with a steel blade, combine eggs, mustard and flour. Process for 5 to 8 seconds or until blended.

- Combine two mixtures in saucepan. Cook on low heat, uncovered, for 20 to 30 minutes or until mixture is thick. Stir frequently.

- May be served warm or cold. Keeps refrigerated up to one week.

3 cups

Szechwan Beef Marinade

INGREDIENTS

2 cloves garlic, minced

1 teaspoon crushed dried red pepper flakes

1½ teaspoons oriental sesame oil

¼ cup lime juice

2 tablespoons soy sauce

2 tablespoons white wine vinegar

¼ teaspoon sugar

- In small skillet, sauté garlic and red pepper in hot oil. When slightly cool, stir in lime juice, soy sauce, vinegar and sugar. Use to marinate beef, refrigerated, for at least 6 hours or overnight.

¾ cup

Hacienda Sauce

INGREDIENTS

2½ cups ketchup

¼ cup Worcestershire sauce

¾ teaspoon black pepper

1 tablespoon chili powder

½ cup vinegar

½ cup lemon juice

½ cup sugar

½ cup vegetable oil

1 clove garlic, minced

1 tablespoon onion salt

1 tablespoon hot pepper sauce

- In a medium saucepan, combine all ingredients, bring to a boil, then simmer 10 to 15 minutes or until slightly thick.
- Brush on meat or poultry before baking or grilling, basting frequently with more sauce.
- Pass additional warm sauce at the table.

3 cups

INGREDIENTS

1 cup unsalted butter, softened

1 tablespoon dried ground coriander

1 tablespoon freshly squeezed lime juice

¾ teaspoon grated lime peel

3 tablespoons minced fresh parsley

Salt to taste

¼ teaspoon freshly ground pepper

LIME BUTTER

- In a food processor, combine all ingredients and process until blended about 5 to 8 seconds. Transfer to bowl and refrigerate for 3 to 4 hours before serving to allow the flavors to blend.

6 servings

Serving Suggestions

- Grill or bake a 1½ to 2 pound pork tenderloin until medium-well done. Thinly slice the meat on the bias and place ½ teaspoon lime butter between each slice of hot meat. Serve immediately.

- Grill salmon or swordfish steaks until done and serve with a soft dollop of lime butter.

- Freezes well for future use.

INGREDIENTS

¼ cup mayonnaise

¼ cup applesauce

4 ounces bleu cheese

4 teaspoons horseradish

1 tablespoon Dijon mustard

MY BLEU HEAVEN SAUCE

A DIVINE DIP FOR VEGGIES OR SAUCE FOR BURGERS

- Blend all ingredients in food processor or blender until chunky smooth.

6 servings

POULTRY

Poultry / Index

Bella's Special Chicken / 214

Berried Chicken / 212

Black Tie Chicken / 212

Cheesy Blue Chicken / 216

Chicken Breasts with Pecan Stuffing / 213

Chicken French / 216

Chicken Italiano / 211

Chicken Tarragon / 215

Chicken with Endive / 217

Chicken with Sage Biscuits / 218

Chinois Chicken / 220

Cornish Hens with Purple Plum Sauce / 222

Country Cinnamon Chicken / 214

Dill Chicken and Artichokes / 219

Gregoire's Favorite Chicken / 220

Grilled Pesto Chicken with Tomato Basil
Cream Sauce / 226

Orange Coq Au Vin / 221

Patio Chicken / 219

Poulet a la Moutarde de Meaux / 223

Raspberry Cremé Poulet / 224

Slim Chicken / 228

Summer Grilled Chicken Paillards / 224

Taj Mahal Chicken / 227

Yum's the Word Chicken / 225

CHICKEN ITALIANO

A SIMPLE LO-CAL RECIPE THAT WILL BE ENJOYED BY ALL!

- In a large saucepan, combine all sauce ingredients. Bring to a boil, reduce heat and cook over low heat 20 minutes or until vegetables are tender-crisp.

- Pound chicken breasts to ¼ inch thickness.

- In a small bowl, combine ricotta, Parmesan, green onions, Italian seasoning and pepper.

- Place 1½ tablespoons cheese mixture on each chicken piece; roll up. Place seam side down in baking dish.

- Pour sauce over chicken and bake for 30 minutes.

- Place Mozzarella in a lattice design on top of chicken.

- Bake 5 minutes more or until cheese is melted.

Temperature: 375°

Time: 35 minutes

6 servings

SAUCE

¾ cup thinly sliced celery

½ cup thinly sliced carrots

¼ cup sliced fresh mushrooms

1 small onion, chopped

1 garlic clove, minced

1 can (8 ounces) tomato sauce

1 can (8 ounces) stewed tomatoes

1 teaspoon Italian seasoning

¾ teaspoon sugar

INGREDIENTS

6 boneless, skinless chicken breast halves

½ cup ricotta cheese

3 tablespoons grated Parmesan cheese

1 tablespoon chopped green onions

½ teaspoon Italian seasoning

Dash pepper

2 ounces Mozzarella cheese, cut into thin strips

Berried Chicken

INGREDIENTS

4 boneless, skinless chicken breast halves

Salt and pepper to taste

3 tablespoons margarine or butter

⅓ cup finely chopped onion

⅓ cup raspberry jam

¼ cup red wine vinegar

¼ cup dry sherry

¼ cup plain yogurt

Fresh berries

- Season chicken with salt and pepper.
- In skillet over medium heat, sauté chicken in melted butter until both sides are lightly browned.
- Add onion and cook until onion is transparent and chicken is done, but still moist.
- Remove chicken from skillet; keep warm.
- Stir jam, vinegar and sherry into pan juices. Boil, stirring often, until liquid is reduced by half.
- Gently stir in yogurt. Pour sauce over chicken, garnish with fresh berries and serve.

Hint: For a more piquant flavor, substitute red currant jelly for raspberry jam.

3 to 4 servings

Black Tie Chicken

INGREDIENTS

4 boneless, skinless chicken breast halves

1¼ cups shredded Monterey Jack cheese

1¼ cups shredded cheddar cheese

Freshly ground pepper to taste

¼ cup freshly minced parsley

½ teaspoon dried tarragon

4 tablespoons unsalted butter, softened

A VERY ELEGANT MEAL FOR THAT SPECIAL OCCASION

- Flatten chicken breasts to approximately ¼-inch thickness.
- In a bowl, combine cheeses, pepper, parsley, tarragon and butter. Form cheese mixture into four 3-inch ovals. Place one oval on each chicken breast. Roll up, tucking ends to seal.
- Lay one sheet of phyllo on work surface. Brush with melted butter. Top with second sheet of phyllo and brush again with butter. Center a chicken roll near narrower edge of phyllo. Fold dough over twice. Fold sides toward center and finish rolling.
- Place on foil-lined baking sheet and brush with butter.

- Continue with remaining breasts. (May be refrigerated at this point.)
- Bake 40 minutes or until golden brown. Baste with pan juices occasionally.

Temperature: 350°

Time: 40 minutes

4 servings

Wine Suggestions: French White Burgundy
French White Bordeaux
California Chardonnay

8 sheets phyllo dough

4 to 6 tablespoons melted butter

CHICKEN BREASTS WITH PECAN STUFFING

- In skillet over medium heat, brown sausage; drain, discarding fat. Wipe out skillet, then melt butter and sauté celery and onion. Stir in pecans, savory, salt and pepper. Sauté 3 minutes more.
- In a large bowl, combine pecan mixture, sausage and bread cubes; mix well. Stir in egg mixture.
- Using a ½ cup measure, form 12 mounds of stuffing. Arrange on a lightly oiled, foil-covered rack in a large roasting pan.
- Lightly sprinkle chicken with salt, then place a piece of chicken over each stuffing mound, tucking edges under stuffing.
- Brush chicken with melted butter and bake 25 to 30 minutes.

Temperature: 400°

Time: 25 to 30 minutes

12 servings

INGREDIENTS

1 pound bulk pork sausage

¾ cup butter

1 cup diced celery

1 large onion, chopped

1 cup pecans, chopped

½ teaspoon dried savory leaves

1 teaspoon salt

¼ teaspoon freshly ground pepper

8 cups dried bread cubes

*2 eggs beaten with
3 tablespoons milk*

*12 boneless, skinless chicken
breast halves*

Salt to taste

2 tablespoons melted butter

INGREDIENTS

½ cup raisins

2 medium apples, peeled, cored and finely chopped

½ cup sliced almonds

½ cup brown sugar

½ cup butter, melted

1½ teaspoons cinnamon

2½ teaspoons curry powder

8 boneless, skinless chicken breast halves

COUNTRY CINNAMON CHICKEN

- In small mixing bowl, mix all ingredients, except chicken.
- Place full tablespoon of apple mixture on each chicken breast.
- Roll and tuck corners; secure with a toothpick. Place seam side down in well-oiled baking dish.
- Spoon remaining apple mixture on top of chicken.
- Cover tightly with foil and bake.

Temperature: 350°

Time: 35 to 40 minutes

8 servings

INGREDIENTS

Juice of 1 lemon

1 cup butter, melted

8 boneless, skinless chicken breast halves

Salt and pepper to taste

1½ cups Dijon mustard

6 tablespoons freshly chopped chives

1 teaspoon basil

2 cups Italian seasoned breadcrumbs

BELLA'S SPECIAL CHICKEN

- Stir lemon juice and 1 tablespoon of water into melted butter. Set aside until slightly congealed.
- Sprinkle chicken with salt and pepper.
- In a bowl, mix mustard, chives and basil. With a pastry brush, coat both sides of chicken with mustard.
- Roll chicken in breadcrumbs; place pieces in an oiled, shallow pan.
- Pour butter mixture over chicken and bake 1 hour. After 30 minutes, baste chicken and turn over for even browning.

Temperature: 350°

Time: 1 hour

6 servings

Chicken Tarragon

INGREDIENTS

2 chicken breasts

1 cup white wine

1 tablespoon dried tarragon

4 tablespoons butter, divided

½ cup sliced fresh mushrooms

Salt and pepper to taste

1 cup heavy cream

- Remove meat from chicken breasts and cut into thick julienne strips.

- Add tarragon to wine; let stand 30 minutes.

- In skillet, melt 2 tablespoons butter over medium heat and sauté mushrooms. Remove mushrooms from skillet and set aside.

- In same skillet, quickly brown chicken in 2 tablespoons butter. Season with salt and pepper. Cover and cook on low heat 5 minutes or until juices run clear. Transfer chicken to a warm platter.

- Stir wine-tarragon mixture into juices remaining in skillet and cook over high heat until almost all of the wine evaporates.

- Stir in cream; simmer 5 minutes or until slightly thickened. If desired, whisk in 1 tablespoon flour to thicken sauce.

- Add chicken and mushrooms to sauce and heat through, approximately 2 to 3 minutes. Serve alone or over pasta.

Hint: For a bolder flavor, sauté ¼ cup minced green onions and 1 clove minced garlic with mushrooms.

4 servings

INGREDIENTS

2 cans (14 ounces each) artichoke
hearts, drained and quartered

1½ tablespoons lemon juice

4 cups cooked chicken, cubed

12 ounces fresh mushrooms sliced,
sautéed and drained

¼ cup margarine

¼ cup flour

½ teaspoon salt

½ teaspoon dried thyme

¼ teaspoon ground nutmeg

2 cups milk

1 chicken bouillon cube

1½ cups shredded cheddar cheese

⅓ cup crumbled blue cheese

CHEESY BLUE CHICKEN

- Place artichoke hearts in shallow baking dish; sprinkle with lemon juice.

- Add chicken and mushrooms.

- In saucepan, melt margarine; add flour and seasonings. Cook until frothy. Stir in milk and bouillon; cook until thickened. Stir in cheeses until melted.

- Pour over chicken. Bake 30 to 35 minutes.

Temperature: 350°

Time: 30 to 35 minutes

6 to 8 servings

INGREDIENTS

12 boneless, skinless chicken
breast halves

2 eggs

2 tablespoons minced fresh parsley

Salt and pepper to taste

½ cup flour

⅓ cup oil

4 tablespoons margarine, divided

CHICKEN FRENCH

- Lightly pound chicken breasts to flatten.

- Beat eggs with parsley, salt and pepper. Dip chicken first in egg mixture, then dredge in flour and again dip into egg mixture.

- In large skillet, heat oil and fry chicken, turning once, until golden brown. Remove from skillet to oiled baking dish.

- Wipe skillet clean and use same skillet to melt 2 tablespoons margarine. Stir in lemon juice and sherry. Pour over chicken.

- In same skillet, melt remaining 2 tablespoons margarine and sauté mushrooms. Pour mushrooms and pan juices over chicken.

- Top each chicken piece with a thin slice of lemon. Cover pan and cook just until heated through.

- Garnish with parsley and serve hot.

6 to 8 servings

½ cup lemon juice

2 tablespoons sherry

8 ounces sliced fresh mushrooms

1 lemon, thinly sliced

Minced fresh parsley

CHICKEN WITH ENDIVE

- In large skillet, melt 2 tablespoons butter over medium heat. Add bread crumbs and stir until lightly browned; remove from pan.

- Place chicken in same pan. Add lemon juice, salt, water and 2 tablespoons butter; heat to boiling, cover and simmer 10 minutes.

- Add endive, cut side down to skillet. Simmer an additional 5 minutes or until endive is tender.

- Remove chicken and endive to a warm platter and sprinkle with capers. Reserve liquid in skillet and keep platter warm.

- Blend flour and water; stir into pan juices remaining in skillet. Add cheese and heat until cheese melts.

- Pour sauce over chicken. Before serving, sprinkle with breadcrumbs.

4 to 6 servings

INGREDIENTS

4 tablespoons butter, divided

1 slice white bread, made into crumbs

8 boneless, skinless chicken breast halves

2 tablespoons lemon juice

1 teaspoon salt

½ cup water

2 medium Belgian endives, quartered lengthwise

2 tablespoons capers, drained

1 tablespoon flour

2 tablespoons water

¼ pound Swiss cheese, shredded

CHICKEN

3 chicken breasts, split

1 clove garlic, sliced

1 bay leaf

½ teaspoon dried rosemary

½ teaspoon dried thyme

¼ teaspoon dried tarragon

½ teaspoon salt

Freshly ground pepper

¼ cup white wine

3 medium carrots, diced

12 to 16 pearl onions, peeled

2 tablespoons butter

2 tablespoons flour

1 cup frozen peas

BISCUITS

2⅓ cups buttermilk baking mix

2 teaspoons ground sage

⅛ teaspoon nutmeg

⅔ cup water

CHICKEN WITH SAGE BISCUITS

- Cook chicken in water until tender; cool. Remove chicken from bones, shred and set aside.

- Return bones to pot along with seasonings and wine. Cook over medium heat about 15 to 20 minutes to reduce and enrich the stock. Strain.

- Cook onions and carrots in stock for approximately 10 minutes. Remove vegetables and reserve stock.

- In medium saucepan, melt butter. Stir in flour, then cook briefly but don't brown. Quickly stir in 2 cups stock and boil until sauce thickens.

- Add chicken and vegetables to sauce and pour into an ovenproof casserole.

(May be made ahead to this point and refrigerated.)

- Bake 10 minutes or until bubbling.

- Meanwhile, lightly combine biscuit ingredients.

- Stir peas into chicken mixture.

- Spoon biscuit batter around edge of casserole to form 10 to 12 drop biscuits.

- Bake 10 to 15 minutes until biscuits are golden brown.

Temperature: 450°

Time: 20 to 25 minutes

4 to 6 servings

Dill Chicken and Artichokes

- Pour salad dressing into 9 x 13-inch casserole. Add chicken breasts to pan.
- Sprinkle salt, pepper and dill weed over chicken. Refrigerate for at least one hour.
- Top chicken with mushrooms and artichokes.
- In small bowl, combine sour cream and chicken soup. Pour over chicken.
- Sprinkle with Parmesan cheese and bake for 1 hour.

Temperature: 350°
Time: 1 hour
6 to 8 servings

INGREDIENTS

8 ounces bottled Italian salad dressing

8 boneless, skinless chicken breast halves

1 teaspoon salt, optional

½ teaspoon pepper

1 teaspoon dill weed

1 pound fresh mushrooms, sliced

2 jars (6 ounces each) marinated artichoke hearts, drained and sliced

8 ounces sour cream

1 can (10¾ ounces) cream of chicken soup

¼ cup grated Parmesan cheese

Patio Chicken

- Place mustard in a medium bowl. Gradually whisk in lemon juice. Add olive oil, garlic, rosemary and generous amount of pepper. Coat chicken and zucchini with mustard mixture; cover and marinate two hours, refrigerated, turning chicken and zucchini occasionally.
- Drain chicken and zucchini; discard marinade. Grill chicken 10 minutes, then add zucchini to grill and cook both until chicken is done and zucchini is tender, turning often.

Hint: Chicken can be baked at 375° for 30 minutes, then add zucchini and bake 15 minutes more.

4 to 6 servings

INGREDIENTS

½ cup Dijon mustard

¼ cup fresh lemon juice

1 cup extra virgin olive oil

5 cloves garlic, minced

1½ tablespoons fresh rosemary, crumbled

Freshly ground pepper

12 bone-in chicken thighs

6 small zucchini, trimmed and halved lengthwise

INGREDIENTS

6 boneless, skinless chicken breast
halves

⅓ cup flour

3 tablespoons butter

½ cup sherry

2 teaspoons chicken bouillon
dissolved in ½ cup boiling water

¼ cup heavy cream

¼ cup sour cream

¼ teaspoon freshly ground pepper

½ cup walnuts, toasted and
coarsely chopped

4 strips bacon, crisply cooked and
crumbled

Fresh parsley

GREGOIRE'S FAVORITE CHICKEN

- Dredge chicken breasts in flour. Melt butter in skillet and sauté breasts until lightly browned and cooked through, turning once.

- Transfer chicken to warm platter; cover to keep warm. (May place in warm oven.)

- Add sherry and bouillon mixture to skillet, stirring to deglaze, approximately 3 to 4 minutes.

- Stir in heavy cream, sour cream, pepper, walnuts and bacon.

- Pour sauce over chicken on platter. Garnish with parsley and serve immediately.

4 to 6 servings

INGREDIENTS

4 boneless, skinless chicken breast
halves

2 tablespoons soy sauce

¼ cup dry sherry

½ teaspoon salt

1 teaspoon sugar

⅓ cup cornstarch

1 egg, beaten

¼ cup vegetable oil

½ cup coarsely chopped walnuts

CHINOIS CHICKEN

SERVE ON A SMALL MOUND OF RICE
WITH A SIDE DISH OF SNOW PEA PODS

- Cut chicken into 1-inch squares.

- Combine soy sauce, sherry, salt and sugar. Pour over chicken and marinate 30 minutes, turning chicken once or twice.

- Remove chicken from the marinade, dip in cornstarch, then in egg.

- In wok or skillet, heat oil and stir-fry walnuts until browned. Remove nuts, then brown chicken in same oil.

- Stir in garlic, ginger, water chestnuts, water and reserved marinade. Cook, covered, over low heat for 15 minutes.
- Add walnuts and heat only 1 minute longer. Serve immediately.

4 servings

1 clove garlic, minced

1 teaspoon powdered ginger

1 can (8 ounces) sliced water chestnuts, drained

½ cup boiling water

ORANGE COQ AU VIN

INGREDIENTS

- Combine flour, salt and pepper in a plastic bag. Shake chicken breasts, one at a time in flour mixture until lightly coated. Let stand on wax paper 5 to 10 minutes.

- Meanwhile, heat 3 tablespoons butter and 2 tablespoons oil in a large skillet over medium heat. When butter mixture is hot, sauté chicken breasts until golden. Turn and sauté other side. Remove to ovenproof pan as chicken browns. Season chicken with oregano and basil.

- Stir wine, orange juice and garlic into pan juices in skillet. Cook over medium heat, stirring frequently for 5 minutes. Pour sauce over chicken.

- In skillet, heat remaining butter and oil. Sauté mushrooms, onions, and green pepper just until softened.

- Top chicken pieces with vegetables. Bake, uncovered, 30 minutes, basting frequently. If desired, top with olives for the final 10 minutes baking.

Temperature: 375°

Time: 45 to 55 minutes

8 servings

½ cup flour

1 teaspoon salt

½ teaspoon pepper

8 boneless, skinless chicken breast halves

3 to 4 tablespoons butter, divided

2 to 3 tablespoons olive oil or salad oil, divided

1 teaspoon dried oregano

½ teaspoon dried basil

2 cups dry red wine

1 can (6 ounces) frozen orange juice concentrate

1 large clove garlic, minced

12 large mushroom caps

2 small red onions, sliced

2 green bell peppers, sliced into rings

Sliced black olives (optional)

INGREDIENTS

2 Cornish hens

Salt and pepper to taste

2 apple slices

1 onion

2 stalks of celery, coarsely chopped

4 bacon slices, uncooked

PURPLE PLUM SAUCE

1 can (17 ounces) purple plums

¼ cup margarine

3 tablespoons chopped onion

¼ cup lemon juice

¼ cup brown sugar

2 tablespoons chili sauce

1 teaspoon Worcestershire sauce

½ teaspoon ground ginger

CORNISH HENS WITH PURPLE PLUM SAUCE

- Rinse each bird, inside and out, with cold water; pat dry. Sprinkle cavities with salt and pepper. Place an apple slice, an onion half and ½ of the chopped celery in each cavity.

- Place birds on a rack in a shallow roasting pan, breast side up. Arrange 2 slices of bacon over each breast.

- Roast uncovered for 1½ to 2 hours. During final ½ hour, remove bacon and baste hens with purple plum sauce.

Purple Plum Sauce

- Drain plums and reserve juice. Discard any pits. In blender or food processor with steel blade, pureé plums. Add ¼ cup of reserved juice if purée is too thick.

- In a skillet, melt margarine over medium heat and sauté onion. Stir in remaining ingredients, including plum purée and reserved juice. Simmer over low heat for 30 minutes.

- Baste birds and serve remaining plum sauce at the table.

Temperature: 350°

Time: 1½ to 2 hours

3 to 4 servings

Hint: Pheasant, partridge or other small game birds are delicious substitutes for Cornish hens.

Poulet a la Moutarde de Meaux

INGREDIENTS

½ teaspoon salt

1 tablespoon cornstarch

2 egg whites, slightly beaten

1 cup plus 2 tablespoons dry white wine, divided

4 boneless, skinless chicken breast halves

¼ cup butter

5 shallots, minced

1 cup heavy cream

½ cup moutarde de Meaux

Fresh parsley

THE KEY TO THIS DELIGHT FOR THE PALATE IS THE MOUTARDE DE MEAUX. SUBSTITUTE MUSTARDS WILL NOT DO THE RECIPE JUSTICE!

- In a glass or ceramic dish, combine salt, cornstarch, egg whites and 2 tablespoons wine. Beat with fork until well blended. Add chicken and marinate, turning occasionally, for 1 to 2 hours.

- In a large heavy skillet over medium heat, melt butter and sauté shallots. Do not allow them to burn.

- Remove chicken from marinade, discarding marinade. Sauté chicken until lightly browned on both sides.

- Add 1 cup wine, reduce heat to low and simmer, covered for ten minutes. Remove chicken to serving platter; keep warm while preparing sauce.

- Turn heat to high and boil pan juices until they are about ⅓ of original volume.

- Stir in heavy cream and simmer, uncovered, until sauce is thickened.

- Over low heat, whisk in moutarde de Meaux. Simmer sauce for 1 to 2 minutes. Do not boil as sauce could curdle.

- Top chicken with some sauce; serve the rest separately. Garnish platter with fresh parsley.

3 to 4 servings

Wine Suggestions: French Beaujolaise
Red Burgundy
California Pinot Noir
White Burgundy
Chardonnay
Alsace Gewurtzraminer

RASPBERRY CREMÉ POULET

½ cup flour

8 boneless, skinless chicken breast halves

3 tablespoons butter

2 tablespoons oil

¾ cup raspberry vinegar

1¼ cups chicken stock

1¼ cups heavy cream

Fresh parsley

Fresh raspberries (if available)

- Dredge chicken in flour and sauté in butter and oil, browning well.
- Remove chicken, add raspberry vinegar to pan and bring to a boil.
- Reduce heat, add chicken stock and chicken to skillet. Cover and simmer 10 minutes.
- Remove chicken, set aside and keep warm.
- Boil liquid remaining in pan until reduced to consistency of cream.
- Add cream and cook over medium heat until thickened, but do not boil.
- Arrange warm chicken on warm platter. Pour cream sauce over chicken. Garnish with raspberries and parsley.

6 to 8 servings

SUMMER GRILLED CHICKEN PAILLARDS

INGREDIENTS

8 boneless, skinless chicken breast halves

2 teaspoons minced garlic

3 tablespoons lemon juice

¾ cup olive oil

½ teaspoon salt

- Pound and flatten chicken breasts until ¼ inch thick.
- Combine remaining ingredients in a shallow glass bowl.
- Add chicken to marinade, cover and refrigerate for at least two hours, turning occasionally.

- Grill about 3 inches over hot coals for 2 minutes each side. Do not overcook.
- If paillards are very thin, decrease cooking time. Serve immediately.

Cold leftover chicken makes a great chicken sandwich, served with lettuce and mayonnaise.

4 to 6 servings

¼ teaspoon pepper

2 teaspoons chopped fresh tarragon

YUM'S THE WORD CHICKEN

- In a large saucepan over medium heat, melt butter.
- Stir in flour and slowly add chicken broth, stirring constantly until thickened and smooth.
- Mix in garlic salt, white pepper, nutmeg, sour cream and vermouth.
- Add chicken and shrimp. Stir and heat 4 to 5 minutes.
- Serve over hot rice.

4 to 6 servings

INGREDIENTS

3 tablespoons butter

3 tablespoons flour

1 cup chicken broth

¾ teaspoon garlic salt

⅛ teaspoon white pepper

⅛ teaspoon nutmeg

1 cup sour cream

⅓ cup sweet vermouth

2 cups diced cooked chicken

1 pound cooked shrimp

2 cups cooked white rice

PESTO

2 cups fresh basil leaves, packed

1 clove garlic

½ cup pine nuts, lightly toasted

Freshly ground pepper

½ teaspoon seasoned salt

½ cup freshly grated Parmesan cheese

½ cup olive oil

CHICKEN

16 boneless, skinless chicken breast halves

4 thin slices ham

½ cup pesto

¼ cup olive oil

2 cloves garlic, minced

Freshly ground pepper to taste

2 tablespoons chopped fresh basil

1 tablespoon minced fresh parsley

TOMATO BASIL CREAM SAUCE

⅓ cup dry white wine

3 shallots, finely chopped

1½ cups heavy cream

¼ cup minced fresh basil

1 large ripe tomato, peeled, seeded and finely chopped

Freshly ground pepper to taste

Freshly ground nutmeg to taste

GRILLED PESTO CHICKEN WITH TOMATO BASIL CREAM SAUCE

Pesto

- In the bowl of a food processor fitted with a steel blade, mince basil and garlic with rapid on-off pulses.

- Add pine nuts, pepper, salt and cheese. Pulse until mixture is thoroughly minced.

- Add olive oil through feed tube and process 3 to 5 seconds more. Set aside. Leftover pesto can be frozen.

Chicken

- Pound chicken breasts slightly to flatten.

- Halve ham slices and top each piece of chicken with ham. Spread 1 tablespoon pesto over ham.

- Fold chicken in half and secure with a toothpick. (Chicken may be refrigerated at this point, covered, for 8 hours or overnight. Remove from refrigerator ½ hour prior to grilling.)

- For basting sauce, combine olive oil, garlic, pepper, basil and parsley in small bowl. Set aside.

- Grill chicken over medium coals, basting often. Grill 8 to 10 minutes on each side or until done. Serve immediately with Tomato Basil Cream Sauce.

Tomato Basil Cream Sauce

- In a small saucepan, boil wine and shallots until liquid is reduced to ¼ cup.

- Stir in cream and boil until liquid is reduced to about 1 cup.

- Stir in basil, tomato, pepper and nutmeg; simmer 3 to 4 minutes. Serve over grilled pesto chicken.

4 to 6 servings

TAJ MAHAL CHICKEN

- In large skillet over medium heat, heat oil and sauté chicken until browned. Remove from skillet. Sauté onion in skillet until golden brown. Add coriander, turmeric, cayenne, cinnamon, cloves, ginger, cardamon and garlic. Sauté 3 minutes.

- Stir in green pepper, coconut, salt, yogurt and broth.

- Add chicken; cover and simmer until chicken is tender, approximately 20 minutes.

- While chicken cooks, melt butter in a small saucepan. Add cashews and sauté for 5 to 8 minutes or until golden brown. Remove from heat and stir in lime juice.

- Place chicken in a serving dish, cover with cashews and garnish with mint leaves. Serve immediately.

6 servings

INGREDIENTS

¼ cup oil

8 boneless, skinless chicken breast halves

1 medium onion, finely chopped

1 teaspoon ground coriander

½ teaspoon turmeric

½ teaspoon cayenne

⅛ teaspoon ground cinnamon

⅛ teaspoon ground cloves

½ teaspoon grated fresh ginger

Pinch of ground cardamon

2 cloves garlic, minced

2 teaspoons chopped green pepper

½ cup grated unsweetened coconut

1 teaspoon salt

1 cup plain yogurt

1 cup chicken broth

2 tablespoons butter

⅔ pound cashews

Juice of one lime

Mint leaves

INGREDIENTS

6 boneless, skinless chicken breast halves

2 teaspoons minced fresh parsley

Salt to taste

1 onion, sliced

¼ cup chopped green pepper

1 cup sliced fresh mushrooms

SAUCE

1 tablespoon brown sugar

1 tablespoon flour

1 cup orange juice

¼ cup dry sherry

½ cup water

1 teaspoon salt

¼ teaspoon pepper

1 teaspoon orange rind

Paprika

Orange slices

SLIM CHICKEN

- Place chicken breasts in a shallow broiler pan. Sprinkle evenly with parsley and broil until brown. Sprinkle with salt.

- Combine onion, green pepper and mushrooms, and spread over chicken.

- In a saucepan, stir together brown sugar and flour, then add remaining ingredients, except paprika and oranges. Cook over medium heat, stirring constantly until thick and bubbly. Pour sauce over chicken.

- Bake for 45 minutes, basting frequently.

- Transfer chicken to serving dish. Baste with sauce and sprinkle with paprika. Garnish with orange slices.

Temperature: 375°

Time: 45 minutes

6 servings

FISH & SEAFOOD

Fish & Seafood / Index

Creole Shrimp Bake / 243

Florentine Roll with Shrimp Sauce / 242

Foiled Scallops / 241

Francoise's Seafood Sauce or Dip / 243

Grilled Jumbo Shrimp / 244

Grilled Nantucket Swordfish / 231

Hell-of-a-Halibut / 231

Kennebunkport Lobster / 232

Lasagne del Mar / 240

Ol' South Gumbo / 238

Orange Roughy with Tomato
   and Onions / 239

Salmon Fillet Amandine / 239

Saturday Night Scallops / 241

Seafood al Fresco / 237

Seafood Saffron Linguine / 236

Sensational Scallop Sauté / 236

Shrimp Casserole / 235

Shrimp Curry / 235

Shrimp in Velvet Sauce / 245

Skewered Swordfish / 233

Spicy Shrimp and Pasta / 233

Vegetable Stuffed Flounder / 234

Zesty Grilled Swordfish / 244

Zorba's Flaming Shrimp / 246

Grilled Nantucket Swordfish

INGREDIENTS

1½ cups mayonnaise

½ cup olive oil

2 teaspoons minced garlic

2 tablespoons minced fresh parsley

1 cup sour cream

4 pounds fresh swordfish steaks

- Mix all ingredients except fish in large shallow baking dish.
- Add swordfish and marinate, refrigerated, at least 2 hours, turning fish several times.
- Grill 4 to 5 inches from heat source, turning once, until fish flakes easily with fork.

Serve with Dilly Dijon Sauce

8 servings

Wine Suggestions: White Bordeaux
California Sauvignon Blanc
Italian White

Hell-of-a-Halibut

INGREDIENTS

½ cup margarine

¼ cup slivered almonds

2 tablespoons tarragon vinegar

2 teaspoons dry mustard

¼ cup sliced black olives

2 pounds halibut steaks

Freshly ground pepper

- In small saucepan over medium heat, melt margarine. Lightly sauté almonds. Stir in mustard, vinegar and olives.
- Arrange halibut steaks in a shallow oiled casserole. Pour sauce over the fish; season with pepper.
- Bake 20 minutes or until fish is opaque.

Temperature: 350°

Time: 20 to 30 minutes

4 servings

INGREDIENTS

6 tablespoons butter or margarine, divided

½ cup dry sherry

2 cups cubed cooked lobster

2 tablespoons flour

½ teaspoon salt

1½ cups half-and-half

4 egg yolks

½ cup cracker meal

3 tablespoons crushed potato chips

2 tablespoons grated Parmesan cheese

1 teaspoon paprika

KENNEBUNKPORT LOBSTER

- In a small saucepan over medium heat, melt 2 tablespoons butter or margarine. Add sherry and cook 1 minute. Remove from heat and add lobster; set aside.

- In another saucepan over low heat, melt 2 tablespoons butter. Stir in flour and salt. Gradually stir in half-and-half. Drain sherry mixture from reserved lobster and add to sauce. Cook and stir until thickened and smooth.

- In a bowl, beat yolks and gradually beat ½ cup hot sauce into the yolks, stirring vigorously. Immediately add yolks to the remaining sauce. Cook and stir until thickened and smooth. Do not boil.

- Add reserved lobster and turn into 4 individual baking dishes.

- In a small bowl, combine cracker meal, potato chips, cheese and paprika. Sprinkle evenly over lobster mixture.

- Melt remaining 2 tablespoons of butter and sprinkle on top of crumb mixture.

- Bake for 15 minutes or until bubbly. Serve immediately.

Temperature: 300°

Time: 15 minutes

4 servings

Spicy Shrimp and Pasta

- In a large skillet, sauté garlic and onion in oil. Add parsley, Italian seasoning, shrimp, and red pepper. Sauté 2 to 3 minutes more.

- Add tomatoes and heat to serving temperature.

- Season to taste with salt and pepper before serving over your favorite pasta.

4 servings

INGREDIENTS

1 medium onion, chopped

3 cloves garlic, minced

2 tablespoons olive oil

3 tablespoons minced fresh parsley

½ teaspoon Italian seasoning

1 pound shrimp, peeled and deveined

⅛ teaspoon crushed dried red pepper flakes

1 can (28 ounces) whole tomatoes in tomato puree, chopped

Salt and pepper to taste

Pasta

Skewered Swordfish

- Pour salad dressing over swordfish cubes; marinate, refrigerated for several hours.

- Alternate swordfish and hearts of palm, green and red peppers, mushrooms and onions on metal skewers.

- Grill or broil, turning occasionally, until swordfish is cooked through, approximately 10 minutes.

Hint: Instead of marinating, skewers can be basted with dressing while grilling.

4 servings

INGREDIENTS

1½ pounds swordfish cut into ¾-inch cubes

½ cup bottled ranch-style dressing

½ can (14 ounce can) hearts of palm, cut into ½-inch thick slices

1 green pepper, cut into ¾-inch pieces

1 red pepper, cut into ¾-inch pieces

½ pound mushrooms, cleaned

1 medium onion, cut into ¾-inch pieces

INGREDIENTS

2 teaspoons margarine

½ cup diced onion

1 clove garlic, minced

¼ cup chopped celery

¼ cup diced carrot

¼ cup chopped red bell pepper

1 cup thinly sliced mushrooms

Dash pepper, salt and thyme

2 tablespoons minced fresh
parsley, divided

4 flounder fillets (about 5
ounces each)

1 heaping tablespoon grated
Parmesan cheese

1 heaping tablespoon mayonnaise

½ teaspoon Dijon mustard

1 tablespoon lemon juice

Lemon slices and parsley

VEGETABLE STUFFED FLOUNDER

- In large saucepan, melt margarine. Sauté vegetables until tender and moisture has evaporated.

- Stir in salt, pepper, thyme and 1 tablespoon parsley.

- Place ¼ of vegetable mixture on each fillet; roll up. Place, seam-side down, in shallow baking dish.

- Combine cheese, mayonnaise, and mustard. Spread over fillet rolls.

- Sprinkle with lemon juice. Bake 20 minutes.

- Garnish with lemon slices and parsley.

Temperature: 400°

Time: 20 minutes

2 to 3 servings

SHRIMP CURRY

- In large saucepan over medium heat, melt butter.

- Gradually add flour, stirring constantly. Stir in salt, onion, curry powder, chicken stock and milk. Cook, stirring constantly, until sauce is thickened.

- Reduce heat to low. Stir in lemon juice and shrimp. Cook briefly until shrimp is warm.

- Serve curry over cooked rice with any of the following condiments: chutney, shredded coconut, chopped peanuts, pineapple and diced celery.

6 servings

Wine Suggestions: Chardonnay
White Burgundy

INGREDIENTS

¼ cup butter

⅓ cup flour

1 teaspoon salt

¼ cup chopped onion or
onion flakes

2 teaspoons curry powder

1 cup chicken stock

2 cups milk

1 teaspoon lemon juice

4 cups shrimp, cooked, shelled and
deveined

SHRIMP CASSEROLE

- In a skillet, melt butter and sauté green pepper, onion, and celery for 2 to 3 minutes.

- Add sliced mushrooms and sauté 2 minutes.

- Cook rice according to package directions.

- Combine vegetables, shrimp and rice. Add mayonnaise, sherry and seasonings. Place in casserole and bake 45 minutes.

Temperature: 350°

Time: 45 minutes

8 servings

INGREDIENTS

2 tablespoons butter or margarine

½ cup chopped green pepper

½ cup chopped onion

1 cup chopped celery

¾ pound mushrooms, sliced

¾ pound small raw shrimp,
cleaned and deveined

1 box (6 ounces) long-grain and
wild rice mix

1 cup mayonnaise

¼ cup sherry

1 teaspoon Worcestershire sauce

1 teaspoon curry powder

Salt and pepper to taste

INGREDIENTS

1 tablespoon butter or margarine

2 pounds sea scallops

2 tablespoons wine or water

1 teaspoon lemon juice

2 tablespoons olive oil

2 cloves garlic, chopped

1 onion, chopped

2 small zucchini, diced

*1 large red pepper, seeded
and diced*

16 mushrooms, thinly sliced

2 tablespoons minced fresh parsley

Pepper to taste

SENSATIONAL
SCALLOP SAUTÉ

SERVE THIS COLORFUL, LIGHT MEAL OVER BROWN RICE
WITH A SALAD FOR A COMPLETE QUICK MEAL

- In a very large skillet, melt butter over medium heat. Add scallops and sauté 1 minute. Stir in wine and heat just until scallops are firm but still raw in center. Remove scallops and liquid to a large bowl. Sprinkle with lemon juice.

- In skillet over medium heat, heat olive oil Quickly stir-fry garlic, onion, zucchini, red pepper, mushrooms and parsley.

- Add scallops and liquid to skillet. Season with pepper to taste and cook until scallops are cooked through, about 2 to 3 minutes. Remove and serve immediately.

8 servings

INGREDIENTS

1 cup bottled clam juice

½ cup dry white wine

¼ to ½ teaspoon saffron threads

*¾ pound large raw shrimp, peeled
and deveined*

½ pound sea scallops, quartered

3 tablespoons unsalted butter

1 tablespoon olive oil

2 cloves garlic, minced

SEAFOOD SAFFRON
LINGUINE

- In a medium skillet, simmer clam juice, wine and saffron for 10 minutes. Add shrimp and scallops. Poach until just opaque, 3 to 5 minutes. Remove skillet from heat. Remove seafood to a large bowl; reserve broth.

- In a small saucepan over moderate heat, melt 2 tablespoons butter in the olive oil. Add garlic, green onions and parsley. Cook, stirring constantly, for 10 seconds. Add ½ cup of the reserved broth and remove pan from heat. Season with pepper flakes and salt. Cover and keep warm.

- Cook pasta according to package directions until al dente; drain and place in large serving bowl.
- Toss pasta with remaining 1 tablespoon butter and ½ cup reserved broth. Top with seafood mixture. Pour warm sauce over all. Toss well and garnish with lemon wedges and parsley sprigs. Serve immediately.

4 servings

2 green onions, minced

1½ tablespoons minced fresh parsley

⅛ teaspoon red pepper flakes

Salt to taste

12 ounces fresh linguine

Lemon wedges

Parsley

SEAFOOD AL FRESCO

- In large mixing bowl, combine all ingredients except seafood and mushrooms; mix well.
- Add shrimp, scallops and mushrooms to marinade. Cover and refrigerate 1 hour, stirring the mixture occasionally.
- Thread seafood and mushrooms on skewers. (If bamboo skewers are used, first soak in water for 10 minutes.) Reserve marinade for basting.
- Grill approximately 8 minutes or until seafood is cooked, basting frequently.

6 servings

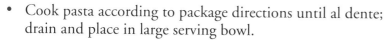

INGREDIENTS

⅔ cup soy sauce

4 teaspoons grated lime peel

½ cup fresh lime juice

3 cloves garlic, minced

2 tablespoons Dijon mustard

½ cup peanut oil

½ cup chopped green onions

½ teaspoon pepper

1 pound large, uncooked shrimp, peeled and deveined

½ pound sea scallops

12 to 16 ounces fresh mushrooms, stems removed

INGREDIENTS

¾ cup butter

¼ cup flour

1 pound okra, sliced

1 green pepper, chopped

1 red pepper, chopped

2 stalks celery, chopped

2 medium onions, chopped

2 cups fresh parsley leaves,
chopped

4 cups chicken stock

1 cup dry white wine

1 can (8-ounce) tomato sauce

1 can (16-ounce) tomatoes,
undrained

3 cloves garlic, minced

1 teaspoon salt

1 teaspoon pepper

1 teaspoon paprika

1 teaspoon sugar

1 bay leaf

1 teaspoon oregano

¼ teaspoon thyme

2 teaspoons Worcestershire sauce

¼ teaspoon hot pepper sauce

2 pounds cooked shrimp

1 pound crabmeat or other firm-
fleshed fish

OL' SOUTH GUMBO

FOR GOODNESS, A SURE TASTER'S CHOICE!

- In large saucepan over medium heat, melt ½ cup butter. Add flour and stir until butter and flour form a roux and are brown.

- Add okra and stir until okra is brown and no longer stringy, approximately 10 to 15 minutes.

- In a large saucepan over low heat, melt ¼ cup butter. Add chopped vegetables and sauté until tender-crisp.

- Add chicken stock, white wine, tomato sauce, tomatoes, garlic, salt, pepper, paprika, sugar, bay leaf, oregano, thyme, Worcestershire sauce, hot pepper sauce and sautéed vegetables to the okra. Simmer over low heat for 1 to 2 hours.

- Add shrimp and crabmeat or other seafood; simmer 30 minutes.

- Serve gumbo over rice in soup bowls or rimmed plates.

10 to 12 servings

Salmon Fillet Amandine

- Beat egg with milk.
- Season flour with salt and pepper.
- Dip salmon fillets in egg mixture. Drain and dredge with flour.
- In a large skillet, heat butter and olive oil. Sauté fillets for 10 minutes over medium high heat, turning fillets once.
- Transfer to platter and keep warm. Reserve cooking oils. Add almonds and sauté until lightly brown.
- Add Worcestershire sauce, lemon juice and parsley. Bring to boil. Pour over fish.
- Garnish with lemon slices and/or parsley. Serve immediately.

Hint: You may substitute trout fillets for salmon.

4 servings

INGREDIENTS

1 egg

1 cup milk

½ cup flour

Salt and freshly ground pepper to taste

4 fresh salmon fillets

¼ cup butter

¼ cup olive oil

⅓ cup slivered almonds

2 tablespoons Worcestershire sauce

Juice of 1 large lemon

1 tablespoon minced fresh parsley

Lemon slices and/or parsley sprigs

Orange Roughy with Tomato and Onions

- In large frying pan, melt margarine. Add fish and turn to coat both sides.
- Sprinkle onion, tomato and parsley on top of each fillet. Cover, reduce heat and cook for approximately 7 minutes.
- Sprinkle with cheese. Cover and heat until cheese is melted.

4 servings

INGREDIENTS

4 tablespoons margarine

3 orange roughy fillets (6 to 8 ounces each)

3 tablespoons chopped onion

3 tablespoons minced fresh parsley

3 tablespoons chopped tomato

½ cup grated cheddar cheese

INGREDIENTS

2 pounds bay or sea scallops

⅓ cup margarine, divided

1 cup chopped green onion

1 clove garlic, minced

¼ teaspoon dry thyme leaves, crushed

⅓ cup flour

1 cup chicken broth

1 cup half-and-half

½ cup dry white wine

½ pound uncooked lasagne noodles

½ pound (2 cups) shredded Jarlsberg or Swiss cheese

LASAGNE DEL MAR

- Rinse scallops well and drain. If scallops are large, cut into ½ inch pieces.

- Melt 1 tablespoon margarine in skillet. Add onion, garlic and thyme. Stir on medium heat for 1 minute.

- Add scallops and cook, stirring often, until they are opaque in the center (cut to test), approximately 2 to 3 minutes. Remove from heat and pour scallops into a large strainer positioned over a bowl; let drain 20 to 30 minutes, reserving juices.

- In the same frying pan, melt remaining margarine over medium heat. Add flour and stir until it turns a light golden color. Remove from heat and gradually mix in broth, half-and-half and wine. Return to high heat and bring to a boil, stirring. Set aside.

- Cook lasagne noodles according to package directions. Drain; rinse with cold water and drain again. Set aside.

- Pour scallop juices into saucepan and boil on high heat, uncovered, until reduced to about two tablespoons. Stir to prevent scorching. Mix juices with cream sauce.

- In well-oiled 9 x 13-inch baking dish, layer ⅓ noodles, ⅓ scallops, then ⅓ cheeses. Repeat layering, ending with cheese.

- Cover pan and bake 20 minutes. Uncover and bake 20 minutes longer or until cheese is golden. Let stand 15 minutes before serving.

Temperature: 350°

Time: 40 minutes

6 servings

SATURDAY NIGHT SCALLOPS

INGREDIENTS

1 pound large sea scallops

*½ pound mushrooms,
stems removed*

*1 can (20 ounces) pineapple
chunks, drained*

*½ pound partially cooked bacon,
cut into 2-inch pieces*

½ cup vegetable oil

¼ cup soy sauce

¼ cup lemon juice

¼ cup minced fresh parsley

1 clove garlic, minced

½ teaspoon salt

Dash freshly ground pepper

- In a large bowl, place scallops, mushrooms, pineapple and bacon.

- In a small bowl, combine remaining ingredients and pour over scallop mixture. Marinate 2 hours at room temperature.

- Alternate scallops, mushrooms, pineapple and bacon on skewers.

- Broil 4 inches from heat for 6 to 8 minutes, until bacon is crisp and scallops are done. Baste during cooking with reserved marinade.

Temperature: Broil

Time: 6 to 8 minutes

4 servings

FOILED SCALLOPS

INGREDIENTS

1½ pounds scallops

½ pound fresh mushrooms, sliced

1 pint cherry tomatoes, halved

1 medium zucchini, sliced

¼ teaspoon salt

½ teaspoon pepper

1½ teaspoons dried basil

½ teaspoon dried tarragon

Juice of ½ lemon

White wine, optional

- Line bottom and sides of jelly-roll pan with foil.

- Spread scallops and vegetables evenly in pan and season with salt, pepper, basil and tarragon.

- Squeeze lemon over scallops and vegetables and splash with white wine, if desired.

- Cover with foil and bake approximately 20 to 25 minutes.

Temperature: 450°

Time: 20 to 25 minutes

4 to 6 servings

2 tablespoons water

3 pounds fresh spinach

6 tablespoons melted butter

1½ teaspoons salt

½ teaspoon pepper

¼ teaspoon ground nutmeg

4 eggs, separated

¼ cup dried breadcrumbs

¼ cup grated Parmesan cheese

SAUCE

4 tablespoons butter

⅔ cup coarsely chopped
green onions

3 tablespoons flour

½ cup dry vermouth or
white wine

Salt and pepper to taste

⅛ to ¼ teaspoon hot pepper sauce

½ teaspoon dried tarragon or 1
tablespoon minced fresh tarragon

1½ cups half-and-half

½ cup minced fresh parsley

2 cups small cooked shrimp

FLORENTINE ROLL WITH SHRIMP SAUCE

- In a large covered saucepan, cook spinach with 2 tablespoons water just until spinach is wilted. Remove from heat, drain and chop spinach.

- In a large bowl, combine spinach, butter, salt, pepper and nutmeg. Beat in egg yolks, one at a time.

- In separate bowl, beat egg whites until soft peaks form. Gently fold spinach mixture into whites.

- Line an oiled jelly roll pan with wax paper. Oil the paper and sprinkle it with breadcrumbs.

- Gently spread spinach mixture evenly in pan. Sprinkle with Parmesan cheese. Bake 15 minutes or until firm.

- While roll is baking, melt butter in large frying pan over medium heat. Sauté green onions then blend in flour and cook for 2 minutes.

- Stir in vermouth or wine, salt, pepper, hot pepper sauce and tarragon.

- Gradually add half-and-half, parsley and shrimp. Stir constantly until shrimp are heated through. Remove from heat and keep warm.

- Remove baked roll from oven. Cover with a greased sheet of foil. Invert roll onto a pastry board. Peel off wax paper. Spread roll with ⅔ of sauce. Reserve balance.

- Roll as a jelly roll, lengthwise. Cut into serving pieces and place on individual plates. Spoon remaining sauce over each and serve immediately.

Temperature: 350°

Time: 15 minutes

6 servings

CREOLE SHRIMP BAKE

INGREDIENTS

3 slices bacon, chopped

½ pound butter

2 tablespoons Dijon mustard

1½ teaspoons chili powder

¼ teaspoon dried basil

¼ teaspoon dried thyme

1 teaspoon ground black pepper

½ teaspoon dried oregano

2 cloves garlic, minced

3 tablespoons shellfish seasoning

½ teaspoon hot pepper sauce

1½ pounds large shrimp, with or without shells

SERVE THIS SPICY SHRIMP ENTRÉE WITH FRESH, CRUSTY BREAD AND ENCOURAGE ALL TO DIP THE BREAD INTO THE SAUCE!

- In medium frying pan, fry the bacon until cooked,but not crisp. Drain excess fat and add butter. When butter is melted, add remaining ingredients except shrimp. Simmer 5 minutes.

- Put shrimp in baking dish, add hot sauce, stirring to coat all shrimp. Bake uncovered for 20 minutes, stirring twice while baking.

- Serve immediately. Peeling shrimp at table is part of the pleasure!

Temperature: 375°

Time: 20 minutes

4 servings

FRANÇOISE'S SEAFOOD SAUCE OR DIP

INGREDIENTS

2 tablespoons butter

½ cup heavy cream

2 tablespoons chopped fresh chives

Juice of ½ lemon

Black pepper to taste

THIS WARM, RICH, LEMONY SAUCE IS ACCENTED WITH CHIVES.

- In small saucepan over medium heat, melt butter and stir in cream; do not boil.

- Stir in chives and lemon juice; remove from heat and serve immediately with your favorite steamed seafood.

2 servings

INGREDIENTS

24 large raw jumbo shrimp,
    shelled and deveined

¼ cup minced shallots

2 tablespoons minced fresh ginger

¼ teaspoon crushed red pepper flakes

3 tablespoons minced fresh parsley

1 bay leaf

½ teaspoon thyme

2 tablespoons vegetable oil

Juice of 1 lemon

6 tablespoons unsalted butter, melted

1 clove garlic, minced

1 teaspoon Dijon mustard

GRILLED JUMBO SHRIMP

- In large mixing bowl, combine all ingredients, except shrimp. Add shrimp to marinade and refrigerate 30 minutes.

- Drain shrimp and grill over hot coals for 2 to 3 minutes, or until shrimp are firm and pink. Baste frequently with marinade. Be careful not to overcook.

- Remove shrimp to warm serving platter and baste again before serving.

Hint: Serve with rice for an entrée or arrange in individual ramekins or decorative scallop shells for appetizers.

4 servings

INGREDIENTS

1½ to 2 pounds fresh swordfish
steaks, approximately 1-inch thick

2 tablespoons soy sauce

2 tablespoons orange juice

1½ tablespoons olive oil

2 tablespoons ketchup

2 tablespoons minced fresh parsley

1 garlic clove, minced

2 teaspoons fresh lemon juice

½ teaspoon crumbled dried oregano

½ teaspoon freshly ground pepper

ZESTY GRILLED SWORDFISH

- Combine all ingredients, except swordfish. Pour over fish in shallow baking dish and marinate at room temperature 45 minutes, turning once after 20 minutes.

- Grill fish 4 inches from hot coals for approximately 8 minutes.

- Turn fish, baste with sauce and grill 7 to 10 minutes more or until fish flakes easily with a fork.

- Before serving, baste fish again. Serve with rice.

Hint: Sauce is excellent for grilled fish and chicken, too!

4 servings

SHRIMP IN VELVET SAUCE

INGREDIENTS

*1 pound large or jumbo
raw shrimp*

5 tablespoons butter, divided

2 teaspoons minced shallots

1½ cups bottled clam juice

¼ cup dry vermouth

1½ cups heavy cream

1 tablespoon flour

2 teaspoons minced fresh dill

2 teaspoons minced fresh chives

Salt to taste

Freshly ground pepper to taste

Fresh dill

STEAMED BROCCOLI FLORETS ARE THE PERFECT VEGETABLE
TO ACCOMPANY THIS STUNNING DISH

- Shell and devein shrimp, leaving tails attached. Split and butterfly shrimp up to tail section. Cover and refrigerate.

- In large saucepan, over medium heat, melt 2 tablespoons butter. Add shallots and sauté 2 minutes. Add clam juice and heat to boiling.

- Add shrimp and continue boiling for 2 minutes or until shrimp turn bright pink. Remove from heat. Using slotted spoon or skimmer, remove shrimp.

- Return pan to heat. When liquid boils, add vermouth and continue boiling until liquid is reduced by half. Add cream, stir, and again boil liquid until reduced by half.

- While sauce is reducing, prepare a buerre manié by mashing together 1 tablespoon butter and flour. Form into small ball and reserve.

- After final sauce reduction, add buerre manié and quickly stir to blend and slightly thicken sauce. Add remaining 2 tablespoons of butter, dill, chives, salt and pepper. Stir to blend.

- Gently fold reserved shrimp into sauce. Transfer and cook gently to reheat shrimp. To serve, garnish with dill sprigs.

4 servings

INGREDIENTS

4 cups chopped onions

6 cloves garlic, minced

¼ cup cooking oil

*4 cans (28 ounces each) whole
tomatoes, chopped and drained*

1 tablespoon basil

1 tablespoon ground cumin seed

2 teaspoons sugar

Freshly ground pepper to taste

6 tablespoons unsalted butter

2½ pounds shelled shrimp

3 tablespoons Ouzo

5 tablespoons cognac

½ pound feta cheese, crumbled

Parsley

ZORBA'S FLAMING SHRIMP

- Sauté onion and garlic in oil until soft, but not brown. Add tomatoes, basil, cumin, sugar and pepper. Cook, uncovered, about 30 minutes.

- In large skillet, sauté shrimp in melted butter until just pink.

- Gently warm Ouzo. Carefully ignite and pour over shrimp. Repeat with cognac.

- Arrange shrimp and pan juices in shallow casserole. Pour tomato sauce over shrimp. Top with feta cheese.*

- Bake for 20 minutes until hot and bubbly, but do not let shrimp overcook. Garnish with fresh parsley.

Temperature: 375°

Time: 30 minutes

8 to 10 servings

Hint: May be made ahead to this point. If so, remove from refrigerator 30 minutes before reheating.

DESSERTS

Desserts / Index

Cakes

Apple-Mince Torte / 274
Baker's Choice Carrot Cake / 278
Blue Ribbon Chocolate
    Cake / 279
Chocolate Mirror / 280
Chocolate Raspberry Torte / 281
Chocolate Rum Torte with
    Chocolate Ganache / 282
Double Encore / 284
Fresh Apple Cake with Caramel
    Glaze / 289
Gâteau au Chocolat / 286
Lemon Charlotte with Blueberry
    Sauce / 285
Maple Walnut Cake / 276
Mint Chocolate Mousse
    Cake / 283
Quaker Cake / 277
Regal Cheesecake / 291
Spiced Yogurt Pound Cake / 275
Sponge Cake with Orange
    Sauce / 288
Strawberry Ginger Bliss / 290
Swedish Tosca Cake / 287
Thanksgiving Cake / 275
Whimsy Cakes / 290
Wonderful Walnut Torte / 292

Candies

"Bacon and Eggs" / 316
Chocolate Haystacks / 316
Fancy Fudge / 317
Sugar-and-Spice Nuts / 317
Truffles For Your Valentine / 318

Cookies

Almond Dreams / 300
Babe Ruth Bars: A Real "Hit" /
    300
Brag About Brownies / 301

Brown-eyed Susans / 302
Butter Fingers / 303
Caramel Delights / 302
Cashew Capers / 304
Catch a Husband Squares / 305
Chinese Sweet Sesames / 306
Chocolate Chippies Deluxe / 307
Chocolate Intrigues / 306
Date Nut Crunchies / 298
Glazed Apple Cookies / 299
Graham Glories / 309
Holiday Jewels / 298
Lebanese Nut Cookies / 296
Lots O' Chocolate Drops / 311
Macadamia Shortbread / 310
Melt-in-Your-Mouth Walnut
    Cookies / 312
Nana's Sugar Cookies / 313
Nut Horn Crescents / 312
Orange Brandy Chews / 314
P. B. O. Colossals / 296
Peanutties / 295
Pecan Tassies / 294
Pucker-Up Lemon Kisses / 294
Raisin Puffs / 293
Raspberry Chocolate Supremes /
    314
Rocky Road Brownies / 315
Strawberry Starlights / 308
The Ultimate Toffee
    Cookie / 297
Whirligigs / 310

Pies

Aloha Pie / 263
Chocaroon Pie / 264
Chocolate Velvet Pie / 266
Creamsicle Pie / 265
Eggnog Pie / 266
Freshest Blueberry Pie / 267
Fruit on a Cloud / 268

Island Pie / 270
Limelight Pie / 268
Mocha Cloud / 269
Old-Fashioned Currant
    Tarts / 273
PBIF Pie Peanut Butter Ice Cream
    Fudge Pie / 271
Peach Melba Ice Cream Pie / 272
A Peach of a Blueberry Pie / 264
Peachy Cream Pie / 272
Raspberry Glacé Pie / 262
Winter Apple Pie / 263

Et cetera

Butterscotch Heavenly
    Delight / 253
Cherry-Peach Flambé / 260
The Chocolate Chill / 258
Classic Pavlova / 256
English Blueberry Pudding / 256
Foamy Sauce / 260
Frosted Honeydew / 249
Frosty Strawberry Squares / 261
Frozen Toffee Surprise / 251
Grand Finalé / 252
Hazelnut Heaven Sundae / 257
Luscious Lemon Mousse with
    Raspberry Sauce / 250
Mocha Magic / 259
No-Stress Chocolate Soufflé / 252
Par Excellence / 254
Plantation Deep-Dish Apple
    Crunch / 262
Pôts de Créme Parisienne / 254
Pumpkin Mousse / 249
Sassy Lemon Curd / 259
Sumptuous Chocolate
    Mousse / 251
Tally Ho Trifle / 255

Frosted Honeydew

- In small bowl, stir cornstarch into water until smooth.

- In a large saucepan over medium heat, combine berries and sugar. Stir in cornstarch mixture and cook, stirring constantly, until mixture boils and sauce thickens.

- When sauce is cool, stir in creme de cassis, lemon juice and cinnamon. Refrigerate until ready to use.

- To serve, place honeydew wedges onto individual serving plates. Top with sherbet and blueberry sauce.

4 servings

INGREDIENTS

½ cup cold water

1 tablespoon cornstarch

1½ cups fresh blueberries

¼ cup sugar

2 tablespoons creme de cassis

1 tablespoon lemon juice

¼ teaspoon ground cinnamon

1 medium honeydew, seeded and quartered

4 scoops lemon sherbet

Pumpkin Mousse

A LIGHT ALTERNATIVE TO PUMPKIN PIE

- In a large bowl, combine pumpkin, brown sugar, cinnamon, and nutmeg.

- In a separate bowl, whip heavy cream to soft peaks. Fold whipped cream into pumpkin mixture; blend well.

- Spoon into custard cups. Refrigerate until serving.

- Serve garnished with whipped cream, cinnamon sticks or sprig of mint.

8 servings

INGREDIENTS

1 can (16 ounces) pumpkin

¾ cup brown sugar

1 teaspoon cinnamon

¼ teaspoon nutmeg

1½ cups heavy cream

Whipped cream

Cinnamon sticks (optional)

Fresh mint (optional)

CRUST

½ cup almonds

1 cup flour

¼ cup brown sugar

½ cup margarine, melted

FILLING

4 eggs, separated

1½ tablespoons grated lemon zest

½ cup fresh lemon juice

1 cup sugar

⅛ teaspoon cream of tartar

1½ cups heavy cream, whipped

2 to 3 drops yellow food coloring
(optional)

RASPBERRY SAUCE

1 package (10 ounces) frozen
raspberries, undrained

Orange liqueur to taste

LUSCIOUS LEMON MOUSSE WITH RASPBERRY SAUCE*

THIS LUSCIOUS FROZEN DESSERT
CAN BE FROZEN TWO WEEKS BEFORE YOUR PARTY!

- In food processor fitted with a steel blade, finely chop almonds. Add flour, brown sugar and melted margarine. Pulse mixture until blended.

- Pour mixture into jelly roll pan and bake for 8 to 10 minutes until golden brown, stirring every 3 minutes. Remove from oven and press mixture onto bottom of 9-inch springform pan. Set aside to cool.

- Combine egg yolks, lemon zest, lemon juice and ¼ cup sugar. Blend well, using a wire whisk.

- In a large bowl, beat egg whites until foamy. Add cream of tartar and continue beating until soft peaks form. Gradually add remaining ¾ cup of sugar, beating constantly until peaks are stiff and glossy.

- Gently fold stiff egg whites and whipped cream into egg yolk mixture. Pour mousse into pan. Cover with foil and freeze at least 8 hours.

- Transfer mousse to refrigerator 30 to 60 minutes before serving.

- To prepare raspberry sauce, purée berries in food processor. Add orange liqueur to taste. Serve sauce over mousse or pass separately.

Temperature: 375°

Time: 8 to 10 minutes

12 servings

* This recipe contains uncooked egg yolks/whites. See SPECIAL NOTE page 7.

FROZEN TOFFEE SURPRISE*

- In a mixing bowl, combine crushed cookies and pecans. Spread ⅔ of the crumbs into a 9 x 13-inch pan.
- In a large saucepan over medium heat, melt butter and chocolate together, stirring constantly. Remove from heat.
- Add confectioners' sugar to chocolate mixture and beat until smooth. Stir in egg yolks and vanilla, beating until well blended.
- In a medium bowl, beat egg whites until stiff peaks form. Fold egg whites into chocolate mixture.
- Spread the chocolate mixture into the crumb-lined pan. Freeze for at least two hours.
- Spread softened ice cream over frozen chocolate. Top with reserved crumbs. Sprinkle with crushed candy.
- Refreeze for at least two hours. Cut into squares to serve.

12 to 15 servings

*This recipe contains uncooked egg yolks/whites. See SPECIAL NOTE page 7.

INGREDIENTS

8 to 9 ounces pecan shortbread cookies, crushed

½ cup pecans, crushed

⅔ cup butter

3 ounces unsweetened chocolate

1½ cups confectioners' sugar

3 eggs, separated

1 teaspoon vanilla

½ gallon vanilla ice cream, softened

4 to 5 (1.2-ounce) English-style toffee candy bars, crushed

SUMPTUOUS CHOCOLATE MOUSSE*

- In a small saucepan over medium heat, melt chocolate with vanilla and liqueurs.
- Place eggs, egg yolks and sugar in blender. Blend well, approximately 2 minutes.
- Add chocolate mixture to blender; blend 2 minutes. Slowly add cream and blend 3 minutes or until mixture is thick.
- Pour into small serving dishes. Chill 4 hours before serving.
- Serve with a dollop of whipped cream.

4 servings

* This recipe contains uncooked egg yolks/whites. See SPECIAL NOTE page 7.

INGREDIENTS

6 ounces semi-sweet chocolate chips

1 teaspoon vanilla

2 tablespoons coffee liqueur

2 tablespoons orange liqueur or orange juice

2 eggs

2 egg yolks

¼ cup sugar

1 cup heavy cream

Additional whipped cream

GRAND FINALÉ*

INGREDIENTS

1 egg white

1 tablespoon powdered instant coffee

Pinch of salt

¼ cup plus 2 tablespoons sugar

1 cup heavy cream

1 teaspoon vanilla

¾ cup shredded coconut, toasted

Chocolate shells (optional)

- In a small bowl, beat egg white until stiff. Stir in coffee, salt and 2 tablespoons sugar.
- In a large bowl, whip cream, adding ¼ cup sugar and vanilla.
- Fold egg white into cream. Add ½ cup coconut.
- Line muffin tins with fluted paper or foil cups. Fill each three-fourths full with mixture.
- Sprinkle with remaining coconut. Freeze for 24 hours.
- Before serving, transfer desserts to refrigerator for 45 minutes. Peel off liners and serve. For elegance, set each mousse into a chocolate shell.

6 to 8 servings

* This recipe contains uncooked egg yolks/whites. See SPECIAL NOTE page 7.

NO-STRESS CHOCOLATE SOUFFLÉ

INGREDIENTS

8 ounces semi-sweet chocolate

8 ounces fine quality bittersweet chocolate

1 cup butter

3 tablespoons orange liqueur

9 large eggs, separated

1⅔ cups sugar

Whipped cream

Strawberries

- In a double boiler over hot water, melt chocolate and butter. Remove from heat. When chocolate reaches room temperature, stir in liqueur.
- In a large bowl, beat egg yolks and sugar for 10 minutes or until ribbons form when beaters are lifted.
- In another large bowl, beat egg whites until they barely hold stiff peaks.
- Fold in ⅓ of the chocolate mixture into the yolks. Then fold ⅓ of egg whites into the egg yolks. Add remaining chocolate and whites in the same manner.

- Pour into a greased and floured 9 to 10-inch springform pan. Bake 25 to 30 minutes or until edge has puffed. Center will not be set. Let soufflé cool in pan on a rack.

- Cover pan loosely and refrigerate for at least 4 hours.

- Prior to serving, run a thin knife around the edge of the pan and remove the sides.

- To serve, remove sides of pan and slice. Garnish each serving with whipped cream and strawberries.

Temperature: 350°

Time: 25 to 30 minutes

12 servings

Hint: Soufflé slices more easily if sharp knife is dipped into hot water before cutting.

BUTTERSCOTCH HEAVENLY DELIGHT

- In a large bowl, whip cream until it begins to thicken. Slowly add butterscotch syrup and vanilla and continue beating until mixture is thick.

- Slice cake into 3 equal horizontal layers. Place bottom layer onto cake plate and spread with about 1½ cups of the whipped topping.

- Sprinkle with ¼ of the crushed toffee.

- Repeat layers, frosting sides as well as top of completed dessert. Sprinkle toffee bars over top and sides.

- Refrigerate at least 6 hours before serving.

12 servings

INGREDIENTS

Angel food cake (9½-inch diameter)

2 cups heavy cream

¾ cup butterscotch syrup or ice cream topping

½ teaspoon vanilla

¾ pound toffee bars, crushed

INGREDIENTS

1 cup graham cracker crumbs

¼ cup brown sugar, firmly packed

6 tablespoons unsalted butter, divided

2 cups creamy peanut butter

2 cups sugar

2 packages (8 ounces each) cream cheese

2 teaspoons vanilla

1½ cups heavy cream, whipped

1 cup chopped, unsalted, dry roasted peanuts

4 ounces semi-sweet chocolate

3 tablespoons plus 2 teaspoons hot coffee

PAR EXCELLENCE

FOR CHOCOLATE AND PEANUT BUTTER LOVERS ONLY!

- In a medium bowl combine crumbs, brown sugar, and 4 tablespoons melted butter. Press into 9-inch springform pan.

- In a large bowl, combine peanut butter, sugar, cream cheese, remaining butter, and vanilla until smooth and creamy.

- Fold in whip cream and peanuts. Spoon filling into crust. Refrigerate 6 hours.

- In a double boiler over hot water, melt chocolate and coffee. Spread over filling. Refrigerate until firm.

16 servings

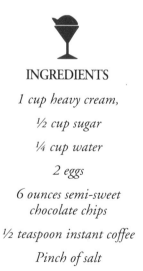

INGREDIENTS

1 cup heavy cream,

½ cup sugar

¼ cup water

2 eggs

6 ounces semi-sweet chocolate chips

½ teaspoon instant coffee

Pinch of salt

PÔTS DE CRÉME PARISIENNE*

AN IRRESISTIBLE COMBINATION OF ORANGE AND CHOCOLATE

- In food processor fitted with a steel blade, process cream until thickened (about 30 seconds). Transfer cream into a bowl. (No need to wash processor bowl).

- In a saucepan over medium heat, bring sugar and water to a boil. Remove from heat.

- In food processor, process eggs, chocolate chips, coffee and salt for several seconds. With machine running, pour sugar syrup carefully through feed tube and process until smooth, approximately 20 seconds. Add extract and brandy and process an additional 20 seconds. Add whipped cream. "Pulse" processor on and off until cream is combined.

- Place in serving dish or dishes and chill several hours or overnight.

- Serve with a dollop of whipped cream and a candied orange peel or chocolate shavings.

6 servings

* This recipe contains uncooked egg yolks/whites. See SPECIAL NOTE page 7.

1 teaspoon orange extract

1 tablespoon brandy

Whipped cream (optional)

Candied orange peel (optional)

Chocolate shavings (optional)

TALLY HO TRIFLE

- Separate ladyfingers and spread cut surfaces with preserves.

- Arrange preserve side up, on bottom of a trifle dish or straight-sided glass bowl. Break ladyfingers to fit area, if necessary.

- Spread berries evenly over the ladyfingers. Sprinkle with sherry.

- Place banana slices onto the berries and spread with custard to form the next layer.

- Spread whipped cream over custard; decorate with almonds. Refrigerate.

Hint: Strawberries coupled with strawberry preserves are a nice variation of this traditional Thames treat.

6 to 8 servings

INGREDIENTS

1 package (3 ounces) ladyfingers

½ cup raspberry preserves, at room temperature

1 pint fresh raspberries

¼ cup sherry

3 bananas, sliced

2 cups prepared vanilla custard, cooled

1 cup heavy cream, whipped

¼ cup thinly sliced toasted almonds

ENGLISH BLUEBERRY PUDDING

INGREDIENTS

1 pint fresh blueberries

1 tablespoon lemon juice

1¾ cups sugar, divided

4 tablespoons butter, softened

½ cup milk

1 cup flour

1 teaspoon baking powder

½ teaspoon salt

1 tablespoon cornstarch

¼ teaspoon salt

1 cup boiling water

- Pour blueberries in well-oiled 8-inch square pan. Sprinkle with lemon juice.
- In a large bowl, cream butter and ¾ cup sugar. Stir in milk.
- Sift together flour, baking powder and salt. Add dry ingredients to batter and mix well. Spread the batter over berries.
- In a small bowl, combine 1 cup sugar, cornstarch and salt. Sprinkle the mixture evenly over the batter.
- Gradually pour boiling water over top surface but do not stir.
- Bake for 45 to 60 minutes or until toothpick inserted into the top cake-like layer "comes clean".
- Serve slightly warm with vanilla ice cream or whipped cream.

Temperature: 375°

Time: 45 to 60 minutes

8 servings

CLASSIC PAVLOVA

INGREDIENTS

6 egg whites, room temperature

Pinch of salt

2 cups sugar

1½ teaspoons white vinegar

1½ teaspoons vanilla

THIS AUSTRALIAN CLASSIC IS STUNNING SERVED WITH STRAWBERRIES AND KIWI.

- Preheat oven to 450°.
- In a large bowl, beat egg whites with salt at high speed until soft peaks form. Add sugar gradually, beating until stiff peaks form.
- Fold in vinegar and vanilla.

- Line a baking sheet with wax paper. Lightly grease the paper. Mound meringue into a circle, depressing the center slightly to form a cup shape.

- As soon as Pavlova is placed in oven, reduce temperature to lowest setting. Bake 1 to 1½ hours or until crisp and pale straw color.

- Turn oven off and leave Pavlova in oven to cool.

- Whip cream and fold in fruit.

- Once cooled, gently remove Pavlova to serving plate. When ready to serve, fill with whipped cream and fruit.

Temperature: 450°, then 250° or less

Time: 1 to 1½ hours

8 to 10 servings

2 cups heavy cream

2 cups fresh fruit

Hazelnut Heaven Sundae

- In a heavy-bottomed medium saucepan, heat butter and water to boiling, stirring constantly.

- Stir in chocolate. When chocolate is melted, add sugar, corn syrup and salt. Simmer for 5 minutes, stirring frequently.

- Remove from heat and stir in vanilla. Cool slightly before assembling sundaes.

- In tulip-shaped goblet, put a serving of sauce. Top with ice cream. Drizzle Frangelico over ice cream; sprinkle with hazelnuts and garnish with whipped cream.

8 servings

INGREDIENTS

6 tablespoons unsalted butter

½ cup water

4 ounces unsweetened chocolate

1 cup sugar

3 tablespoons light corn syrup

Dash salt

2 teaspoons vanilla

SUNDAE

½ gallon coffee ice cream

Frangelico liqueur to taste

1 cup chopped, toasted hazelnuts

Whipped cream

INGREDIENTS

½ cup sugar

½ cup water

4 egg yolks, room temperature

8 ounces semi-sweet chocolate chips, melted and cooled

1 cup fresh raspberries

1 cup heavy cream, whipped

THE CHOCOLATE CHILL

BRING OUT YOUR ICE CREAM MAKER FOR THIS TREAT

- In a heavy saucepan, heat sugar and water until sugar dissolves and mixture comes to a boil.

- In bowl, beat egg yolks with a mixer until yolks turn thick and pale yellow. Slowly beat in hot sugar water.

- Return mixture to saucepan. Stir over low heat until mixture thickens, about 4 to 5 minutes. Do not boil mixture because it will curdle.

- Pour mixture into a large bowl; cover and refrigerate for ½ hour.

- Whisk chocolate into egg mixture. Fold in berries and whipped cream.

- Process in ice cream maker following manufacturer's directions. Note: This mixture will not freeze solid; it remains custard-like.

- Transfer mixture to freezer container. Cover and freeze for 3 to 4 hours before serving.

Hint: If frozen berries are substituted for fresh, drain well and reserve the juice to drizzle over individual servings.

1 quart

Mocha Magic

A SUPERB DESSERT SAUCE
TO SERVE OVER ICE CREAM OR POUND CAKE

- In heavy saucepan, combine sugar, corn syrup and espresso powder.

- Over medium heat, boil mixture 5 minutes, stirring constantly.

- Remove from heat and stir in chocolate until melted. Stir in cream and Kahlua.

- Serve immediately over ice cream or pound cake.

Hint: Leftover sauce keeps refrigerated up to 2 weeks.

2 cups

INGREDIENTS

1 cup dark brown sugar

½ cup light corn syrup

5 teaspoons instant espresso powder

3 ounces semi-sweet chocolate, coarsely chopped

½ cup heavy cream

2 tablespoons Kahlua

Sassy Lemon Curd

SERVE THIS VERSATILE LEMON CUSTARD OVER
OLD-FASHIONED GINGERBREAD IN *APPLEHOOD AND MOTHERPIE,*
IN TART SHELLS, OR ON TOAST OR MUFFINS.

- In a medium bowl, cream butter and sugar together. Stir in lemon juice and egg yolks.

- Transfer mixture to a double boiler and simmer 15 minutes or until thickened, stirring constantly.

2 cups

INGREDIENTS

½ cup butter

¾ cup sugar

Juice of 3 lemons

4 egg yolks

INGREDIENTS

1 cup currant jelly

2 cans (16 ounces each) peach halves, drained

2 cans (16 ounces each) pitted black cherries, drained

½ cup brandy

½ gallon coffee ice cream

CHERRY-PEACH FLAMBÉ

- In a shallow 1½-quart microwavable dish, melt jelly on high, approximately 1½ minutes.

- Add cherries and peach halves, cut side down. Mix fruits with melted jelly. Microwave 3½ minutes. Turn peaches cut side up.

- Into a small microwavable bowl, heat brandy on high for 1 minute.

- To serve, bring fruit and brandy to the table. Gently pour hot brandy over fruit mixture and ignite. When flames subside, spoon brandied fruit over ice cream.

8 servings

INGREDIENTS

¾ cup heavy cream

2 eggs, separated, at room temperature

2 tablespoons sugar

FOAMY SAUCE*

A GLORIOUS SUBSTITUTE FOR WHIPPED CREAM. TRY THIS UNIQUE SAUCE WITH QUAKER CAKE INSTEAD OF ICING.

- In a large bowl, whip heavy cream until soft peaks form.

- In a small bowl, beat egg whites until stiff peaks form. Fold into cream. Add sugar and blend.

- In another small bowl, beat egg yolks and add to cream mixture.

- Whisk sauce before serving.

1 cup

* This recipe contains uncooked egg yolks/whites. See SPECIAL NOTE page 7.

FROSTY STRAWBERRY SQUARES

- In a medium bowl, combine flour, brown sugar, nuts and butter. Mix well until crumbly.

- Sprinkle mixture in an ungreased 9 x 13-inch baking pan. Bake for 20 minutes, stirring occasionally. Cool thoroughly. Remove about ⅓ of crumbs for garnish; spread remainder evenly in pan.

- In a very large bowl, combine egg whites, sugar, berries and lemon juice. Using an electric mixer, beat at high speed to stiff peaks, about 10 minutes.

- Fold in whipped cream. Spoon over nut mixture. Top with remaining nut mixture.

- Freeze for 6 hours or overnight.

- Remove from freezer 20 minutes before serving. While still partially frozen, cut into squares. Garnish with fresh whole berries.

Temperature: 350°

Time: 20 minutes

10 to 12 servings

* Or use 10 ounces sweetened frozen strawberries, partially thawed and drained. Reduce sugar to ⅔ cup.

INGREDIENTS

1 cup sifted flour

¼ cup brown sugar

½ cup chopped walnuts or pecans

½ cup butter, melted

2 egg whites, beaten but not stiff

1 cup sugar

2 cups sliced fresh strawberries*

2 tablespoons fresh lemon juice

½ pint heavy cream, whipped

Fresh whole berries for garnish

INGREDIENTS

6 cooking apples, cored, thinly sliced, and cut in half

½ cup sugar

½ teaspoon cinnamon

½ teaspoon ground nutmeg

½ teaspoon salt

¾ cup unsalted butter, softened

1¼ cups flour

1¼ cups dark brown sugar

PLANTATION DEEP-DISH APPLE CRUNCH

- Place sliced apples in a buttered 9 x 13-inch baking dish and sprinkle with sugar, cinnamon, nutmeg and salt.

- In a medium bowl combine butter, flour and brown sugar. Spread mixture evenly over the apples.

- Bake 40 to 50 minutes.

- Serve immediately.

Temperature: 350°

Time: 40 to 50 minutes

6 to 8 servings

INGREDIENTS

3 tablespoons raspberry-flavored gelatin

3 tablespoons cornstarch

¾ cup sugar

1 cup water

2 pints fresh raspberries

1 9-inch pie shell, baked and cooled

Whipped cream

RASPBERRY GLACÉ PIE

AN ELEGANTLY PRESENTED SUMMER DELIGHT!

- In heavy saucepan, combine gelatin, cornstarch, sugar and water. Cook over medium heat, stirring constantly just until mixture thickens and boils.

- Place half the raspberries in the pie shell and top with half the gelatin mixture. Repeat layers. Chill.

- Before serving, garnish with whipped cream.

8 servings

Winter Apple Pie

- In a medium mixing bowl combine 1¼ cups flour, salt, sugar and baking powder. Cut in ½ cup butter until dough mixture is crumbly.
- In a small bowl, combine egg yolk and milk. Stir yolk mixture into dough until thoroughly blended.
- Shape dough into a ball. Press into the bottom and 1-inch up sides of 9-inch round cake pan.
- Core and cut each apple into 12 wedges. Arrange on pastry.
- Top with raisins and nuts.
- In a small bowl combine sugar, 2 tablespoons flour, cinnamon, ginger, nutmeg and cloves. Cut in 2 tablespoons butter until crumbly. Sprinkle topping over pie.
- Bake 45 minutes or until apples are tender.
- Serve warm. Delicious with ice cream or whipped cream.

Temperature: 350°
Time: 45 minutes
6 to 8 servings

INGREDIENTS

1¼ cups plus 2 tablespoons flour, divided

¼ teaspoon salt

1 tablespoon brown sugar

1 teaspoon baking powder

½ cup plus 2 tablespoons butter or margarine

1 egg yolk

2 tablespoons milk

2 Granny Smith, Crispin or "20-Ounce" apples

¼ cup raisins

¼ cup walnuts or pecans (optional)

½ cup sugar

½ teaspoon cinnamon

⅛ teaspoon ground ginger

⅛ teaspoon ground nutmeg

⅛ teaspoon ground cloves

Aloha Pie

- Beat cream cheese and sugar until very smooth.
- Add pineapple, mixing well.
- Gently fold in whipped cream and spoon into crust.
- Chill for at least 2 hours before serving.
- Garnish with fruit (such as mandarin oranges).

6 to 8 servings

INGREDIENTS

1 package (8 ounces) cream cheese

¼ cup sugar

1 can (20 ounces) crushed pineapple, drained

1 cup heavy cream, whipped

1 prepared 9-inch graham cracker crust

Fruits for garnish

INGREDIENTS

2¼ cups plus ⅓ cup flour, divided

2 teaspoons sugar

1 teaspoon salt

½ cup vegetable oil

2 tablespoons milk

½ cup confectioners' sugar

2 cups fresh blueberries

*2 cups fresh peaches, peeled and
sliced*

½ cup firmly packed brown sugar

½ teaspoon cinnamon

⅓ cup butter, softened

Whipped cream (optional)

A PEACH OF A BLUEBERRY PIE

- Combine 1½ cups flour, sugar, salt, oil and milk to form a soft pastry dough.

- Press dough evenly in 9-inch pie pan.

- Combine confectioners' sugar, ⅓ cup flour and fruit. Spoon over pastry.

- Combine ¾ cup flour, brown sugar and cinnamon. Cut in butter until crumbly. Spread topping over fruit.

- Bake 40 to 45 minutes until topping is golden brown. Serve with whipped cream, if desired.

Temperature: 375°

Time: 40 to 45 minutes

8 servings

INGREDIENTS

3 ounces unsweetened chocolate

½ cup butter

3 eggs, slightly beaten

¾ cup sugar

½ cup flour

1 teaspoon vanilla

2⅔ cups coconut

⅔ cup sweetened condensed milk

CHOCAROON PIE

- In a saucepan, melt chocolate and butter over very low heat.

- Whisk in eggs, sugar, flour and vanilla. Pour mixture into an oiled 9-inch pie pan.

- Combine coconut and condensed milk and spoon over filling leaving a ½ inch border around edge.

- Bake for 30 to 35 minutes or until center is set.

- Cool before serving. For added decadence, serve with ice cream.

Temperature: 350°

Time: 30 to 35 minutes

8 servings

CREAMSICLE PIE

INGREDIENTS

2 egg whites

2 teaspoons vanilla

⅛ teaspoon salt

½ cup plus 2 teaspoons sugar

1 pint orange sherbet, softened

1 pint vanilla ice cream, softened

4 ounces vanilla wafers

1 cup heavy cream

2 teaspoons vanilla

Orange slices, optional

THIS PIE WILL BE SURE TO BRING BACK CHILDHOOD MEMORIES OF REFRESHING CREAMSICLES ON HOT SUMMER DAYS!

- In large bowl, beat egg whites, vanilla and salt until foamy. Gradually add ½ cup sugar, beating until stiff peaks form.

- Spread meringue onto bottom and sides of pie pan. Bake for 1 hour.

- Turn off heat and let stand 4 hours or overnight to dry.

- Spread sherbet over meringue shell; top with ice cream.

- Coarsely crush cookies in plastic bag with rolling pin. Sprinkle over ice cream. Freeze until firm.

- Thaw pie 10 minutes before serving.

- Whip cream with 2 teaspoons sugar and vanilla. Spread over pie. Garnish with orange slices, if desired.

Temperature: 250°

Time: 1 hour

8 to 10 servings

INGREDIENTS

3 eggs, separated

¼ teaspoon cream of tartar

1½ teaspoons vanilla, divided

1½ cups sugar, divided

⅓ cup finely chopped walnuts

½ cup butter, softened

1 square unsweetened chocolate, melted

1 cup heavy cream, whipped

INGREDIENTS

¼ cup cold water

1 tablespoon gelatin

2 cups milk

¾ cup sugar

1 tablespoon cornstarch

¼ teaspoon salt

4 eggs, separated

1 tablespoon vanilla

CHOCOLATE VELVET PIE*

- In a large mixing bowl, beat egg whites and cream of tartar until foamy. Stir in ½ teaspoon vanilla. Gradually add ¾ cup sugar, beating until stiff peaks form.

- Spread meringue onto bottom and sides of a well-oiled 9-inch pie pan. Sprinkle with nuts.

- Bake for 1 hour. Cool completely, (at least 4 hours) before adding filling.

- In a large mixing bowl, beat butter until fluffy. Gradually add remaining ¾ cup sugar, beating until smooth. Stir in chocolate and remaining 1 teaspoon vanilla. Add egg yolks, one at a time, and beat for 3 to 4 minutes.

- Pour filling into meringue shell. Refrigerate until serving.

- Before serving, swirl whipped cream over pie.

Temperature: 275°

Time: 1 hour

6 to 8 servings

* This recipe contains uncooked egg yolks/whites. See SPECIAL NOTE page 7.

EGGNOG PIE*

A WONDERFUL DESSERT FOR THE HOLIDAYS!

- Place water in a cup or bowl and sprinkle with gelatin.

- In a double boiler, heat milk. Stir but do not boil.

- In a small bowl, combine sugar, cornstarch and salt. Stir into hot milk.

- In a medium bowl, beat egg yolks until creamy. Add yolks to milk and cook until thickened, about 10 minutes, beating occasionally with a rotary beater or whisk.

- Remove from heat and add vanilla and gelatin; cool.
- In a large bowl, beat egg whites until foamy. Gradually add sugar and beat until stiff peaks form.
- Fold the yolk mixture into the egg whites.
- Pour filling into pie shell; sprinkle with nutmeg; refrigerate.
- Serve with whipped cream.

8 servings

* This recipe contains uncooked egg yolks/whites. See SPECIAL NOTE page 7.

4 tablespoons sugar

2 teaspoons freshly grated nutmeg

1 cup heavy cream, whipped

1 8 to 9-inch baked pie shell

FRESHEST BLUEBERRY PIE

FRESH IS THE KEY TO THIS SCRUMPTIOUS BLUEBERRY PIE

- In saucepan, cook 1 cup blueberries and water until boiling, then simmer for 4 minutes.
- Remove from heat; stir in butter.
- In small bowl, combine sugar, cornstarch, salt and cinnamon. Add to hot berries and cook slowly.
- Remove from heat; stir in lemon juice.
- Combine sauce and remaining 3 cups of berries. Pour into pastry shell. Refrigerate.
- To serve, pipe a border of whipped cream around perimeter of pie.

6 to 8 servings

INGREDIENTS

4 cups fresh blueberries, divided

¾ cup water

1 tablespoon butter

1 cup sugar

5 tablespoons cornstarch

⅛ teaspoon salt

⅛ teaspoon cinnamon

1 teaspoon fresh lemon juice

1 9-inch baked pie shell

1 cup heavy cream, whipped

Fruit on a Cloud

INGREDIENTS

¾ cup sugar

½ teaspoon baking powder

⅛ teaspoon salt

3 egg whites

½ teaspoon vanilla

19 round butter crackers, coarsely crushed

½ cup chopped pecans

½ pint heavy cream, whipped

2 cups sliced fresh strawberries, whole raspberries, blueberries or other favorite bite-sized fruit pieces

Whipped cream for garnish

- In a small bowl, combine sugar, baking powder and salt.

- In a large bowl, beat egg whites until foamy. Gradually add sugar mixture and continue to beat until stiff peaks form and sugar has dissolved.

- Fold in vanilla, crackers and nuts.

- Spread over bottom and 1-inch up the sides of a well-oiled 9-inch pie pan. Bake for 30 minutes.

- Set on a rack to cool away from drafts. (Shell may sag in center.)

- When shell is cooled, place whipped cream in shell, leaving a ½-inch border of shell showing around the outside edge. Arrange fruit on top.

- Refrigerate pie at least 8 hours before serving. Garnish with whipped cream.

Temperature: 325°

Time: 30 minutes

8 servings

Note: Substitute 1 bag (16 ounces) of frozen fruit, thawed and drained, if fresh fruit is not available.

Limelight Pie*

INGREDIENTS

4 eggs, separated

1 can (14 ounces) sweetened condensed milk

½ cup fresh lime juice

Baked 9-inch graham cracker crust

- In large bowl, use whisk or rotary beater to beat egg yolks.

- Add milk and beat until well blended. Stir in lime juice. Beat slowly until thick.

- Pour into cooled pie shell.

- In large bowl, beat egg whites until foamy. Gradually add sugar and vanilla. Continue to beat until stiff peaks form.

- Spread meringue on pie. Bake approximately 5 to 7 minutes or until top browns.
- Refrigerate until serving time.

Hint: This pie is best made one day in advance.

Temperature: 375°
Time: 5 to 7 minutes
8 servings

* This recipe contains uncooked egg yolks/whites. See SPECIAL NOTE page 7.

MOCHA CLOUD

- In large bowl, beat egg whites and cream of tartar, until foamy. Gradually add 1 cup sugar, beating until stiff peaks form.
- Spread meringue on bottom and sides of 9-inch pie pan.
- Bake for 1 hour. Cool.
- Fill meringue shell with coffee ice cream; freeze.
- For sauce, melt butter and chocolate together.
- Stir in remaining ¾ cup sugar, cocoa and half-and-half. Cook, stirring constantly and boil 1 minute or until sugar is dissolved.
- Remove from heat, add vanilla.
- Remove pie from freezer 15 minutes before serving. Pass hot chocolate sauce.

Temperature: 275°
Time: 1 hour
6 to 8 servings

Hint: Chocolate sauce may be made ahead and refrigerated. Reheat before serving. Other ice cream flavors may be substituted.

¼ cup confectioners' sugar
½ teaspoon vanilla

INGREDIENTS

3 egg whites
¼ teaspoon cream of tartar
1¾ cups sugar, divided
½ gallon coffee ice cream, softened
¼ cup butter
1 square unsweetened chocolate
¼ cup cocoa
½ cup half-and-half
1 teaspoon vanilla

ISLAND PIE*

INGREDIENTS

3 cups finely shredded coconut

5 tablespoons melted butter
or margarine

½ cup lime juice

1 envelope unflavored gelatin

5 eggs, separated

1 cup sugar, divided

3 tablespoons light rum

1 tablespoon Cointreau or
Triple Sec

Grated peel of 2 limes

Green food coloring, optional

2 cups heavy cream, divided

Lime slices

- Toast coconut on a baking sheet until golden, approximately 7 minutes. Stir frequently. Reserve half for garnish.

- In a medium bowl, combine half the coconut and butter. Toss with two forks until coated.

- Press coconut into bottom and sides of 9-inch pie pan. Cover and refrigerate until firm, about 2 to 3 hours.

- In a small bowl, sprinkle gelatin over lime juice. Place bowl in simmering water; heat until gelatin is completely dissolved.

- In top of a double boiler, beat egg yolks; stir in ½ cup sugar and gelatin; beat well.

- Place double boiler over water on medium heat and cook, stirring often until thickened (about 10 minutes).

- Remove from heat; when cool, stir in rum, Cointreau and lime peel.

- In a large bowl, beat egg whites until soft peaks form. Add remaining green food coloring, if desired. Gradually add ½ cup sugar and continue to beat until stiff peaks form.

- First fold 1 heaping tablespoon of egg white into custard, then gently fold custard into egg whites to create a marblelized effect.

- Whip 1 cup cream and fold into custard.

- Mound filling into crust, swirling to create a domed shape. Refrigerate until firm.

- Before serving, whip 1 cup cream and dollop in center of pie. Garnish with lime slices and sprinkle with reserved toasted coconut.

Temperature: 325°

Time: 7 to 10 minutes

8 servings

* This recipe contains uncooked egg yolks/whites. See SPECIAL NOTE page 7.

PBIF Pie
Peanut Butter Ice Cream Fudge Pie

INGREDIENTS

½ cup peanut butter

½ cup light corn syrup

2¼ cups crispy rice cereal

2 pints vanilla or coffee ice cream

¾ cup sugar

½ cup cocoa

½ cup heavy cream

4 tablespoons margarine

1 teaspoon vanilla

- Mix peanut butter and corn syrup until blended. Add crispy rice cereal and stir until coated.

- Press into bottom and sides of a 9-inch pie pan.

- Top with 1 pint ice cream which has been softened slightly. Freeze until firm.

- In saucepan, heat sugar, cocoa, cream and margarine, stirring constantly, until boiling.

- Remove from heat and stir in vanilla. Cool.

- Pour 1½ cups sauce over ice cream. Freeze until hardened, about 20 minutes.

- Soften remaining ice cream and spread over frozen pie. Drizzle with remaining sauce. Freeze until firm, approximately 3 hours.

- Remove from freezer approximately 10 minutes before serving.

Hint: For a tasty variation, add ½ cup mini chocolate chips to the crust.

8 servings

INGREDIENTS

1 package (7 ounces) flaked coconut

1 cup chopped walnuts

4 tablespoons butter, melted

1 quart peach ice cream or frozen yogurt, softened

1 pint vanilla ice cream or frozen yogurt, softened

1 package (12 ounces) frozen raspberries, thawed

1 tablespoon cornstarch

½ cup sugar

2 peaches, thinly sliced

PEACH MELBA ICE CREAM PIE

- Combine coconut, walnuts and butter. Press into bottom and sides of a 9-inch pie pan.

- Bake for 10 to 15 minutes until golden brown. Cool.

- Spoon peach ice cream into crust; freeze until firm.

- Spoon vanilla ice cream over the peach layer; freeze.

- Drain raspberries. In small saucepan, cook raspberry juices, cornstarch and sugar over medium heat, stirring constantly until thickened.

- Remove from heat and stir in berries. Cool.

- Garnish pie with peaches. Spoon raspberry sauce over each serving.

Temperature: 325°

Time: 10 to 15 minutes

8 servings

INGREDIENTS

1 unbaked 9-inch pie crust

4 to 6 fresh peaches, peeled and sliced

½ cup sour cream

1 cup sugar

2 tablespoons flour

2 eggs, beaten

Nutmeg

PEACHY CREAM PIE

REMEMBER THIS WHEN HOMEGROWN PEACHES ARE AT THEIR PEAK OF FLAVOR

- Place peaches in pastry.

- Combine sour cream, sugar, flour and eggs. Pour over peaches.

- Sprinkle with nutmeg and bake 45 minutes.

Temperature: 400°

Time: 45 minutes

6 servings

OLD-FASHIONED CURRANT TARTS

INGREDIENTS

Pastry for 2 9-inch crusts

½ cup butter, softened

1 cup sugar

1 egg

2 teaspoons vanilla

1 cup currants

A TASTY ADDITION TO ANY DESSERT TRAY

- Roll out dough on floured surface; cut out 4-inch circles and press into muffin tins.
- Cream butter, sugar, egg and vanilla.
- Stir in currants.
- Place one heaping teaspoon of filling in each unbaked tart shell.
- Bake 20 to 25 minutes.

Hint: Mini muffin tins are too small for this recipe.

Temperature: 350°

Time: 20 to 25 minutes

3 dozen

CRUST

1½ cups sifted flour

⅓ cup confectioners' sugar

½ cup butter, melted

FILLING

5 cups peeled and thinly sliced tart apples

Juice of one large orange (scant ¼ cup)

½ cup brown sugar

½ teaspoon salt

¼ teaspoon nutmeg

1 teaspoon cinnamon

⅛ teaspoon rum extract, optional

TOPPING

1 cup regular or quick cooking rolled oats

1½ cups prepared mincemeat filling

APPLE-MINCE TORTE

- In a medium bowl, combine flour and sugar. Add melted butter and mix thoroughly, until mixture resembles coarse meal.

- Press mixture smoothly onto bottom only of a 10 or 12-inch ovenproof flan dish. Bake at 350° for 20 minutes or until slightly golden. Cool on rack.

- In a large bowl, combine all filling ingredients. Use a slotted spoon to transfer apples to crust. Reserve juice mixture.

- Combine topping ingredients and reserved juices. Spread evenly over apples.

- Bake at for 30 minutes.

Temperature: 350° – 20 minutes
                     375° – 30 minutes

8 servings

Thanksgiving Cake

- In a large mixing bowl, combine eggs and sugar. Beat well. Stir in oil and pumpkin.

- In a medium bowl, combine flour, baking powder, baking soda, salt and cinnamon. Add this to pumpkin mixture; mix well.

- Stir in nuts and chocolate chips. Pour batter into an oiled Bundt or tube pan.

- Bake for 75 minutes.

- Remove pan from oven and invert onto a cooling rack. Cake will fall from pan as it cools.

Temperature: 350°
Time: 75 minutes
12 to 15 servings

INGREDIENTS

4 eggs

2 cups sugar

1 cup oil

2 cups canned pumpkin

3 cups flour

2 teaspoons baking powder

2 teaspoons baking soda

½ teaspoon salt

½ teaspoon cinnamon

1 cup chopped nuts

1 cup chocolate chips

Spiced Yogurt Pound Cake

- In a large bowl, cream sugar and butter until light and fluffy.

- Using low speed, add remaining ingredients.

- Beat at high speed approximately 4 minutes or until well mixed.

- Bake 45 to 55 minutes in well-oiled Bundt pan.

- Cool 20 minutes before removing from pan.

Temperature: 325°
Time: 45 to 55 minutes
14 to 16 servings

INGREDIENTS

2 cups sugar

1 cup butter or margarine, softened

2¼ cups flour

1 cup plain yogurt

3 eggs

1 teaspoon vanilla

1 teaspoon ground cinnamon

1 teaspoon ground allspice

½ teaspoon ground nutmeg

½ teaspoon salt

1½ teaspoons baking soda

¼ teaspoon ground cloves

INGREDIENTS

⅓ cup butter or margarine

¾ cup light brown sugar

¼ cup white sugar

2 eggs, separated

1½ cups flour

½ teaspoon salt

2 teaspoons baking soda powder

¾ cup milk

½ cup chopped walnuts

1¼ teaspoons maple flavoring

GLAZE

1 cup confectioners' sugar

1½ tablespoons margarine

2 tablespoons warm milk

¾ teaspoon maple flavoring

¼ cup chopped walnuts

MAPLE WALNUT CAKE

- In large bowl, cream together butter and sugars.

- Beat egg yolks and add to mixture.

- Sift flour, salt and baking powder. Alternately add milk and flour mixture. Blend thoroughly.

- Stir in nuts and maple flavoring.

- Beat egg whites until stiff peaks form and fold into batter.

- Spread batter into a well-oiled 8 x 8-inch pan.

- Bake 35 to 40 minutes.

- For glaze, cream together sugar and margarine. Stir in milk and maple flavoring.

- Frost cooled cake and sprinkle with chopped nuts.

Temperature: 350°

Time: 35 to 40 minutes

6 to 8 servings

Quaker Cake

- In a small bowl, combine oatmeal and water.

- In a large bowl, cream together butter and sugars. Add eggs, one at a time, and beat well.

- In a medium bowl, combine flour, baking soda, salt and cinnamon.

- Alternately add dry ingredients and cooled oatmeal to butter mixture. Stir in vanilla. Pour batter into a well-oiled 9 x 13-inch pan and bake 35 to 40 minutes.

- For icing, in a saucepan over medium heat, melt butter. Add milk, sugar and nuts.

- Remove from heat and stir in vanilla. Frost cake as soon as it is removed from oven.

- Broil cake 2 minutes, watching carefully. Cool cake on rack.

Temperature: 350°

Time: 35 to 40 minutes

16 to 18 servings

Hint: For a tasty variation, try Foamy Sauce instead of icing.

INGREDIENTS

1 cup oatmeal

1½ cups boiling water

½ cup butter

1 cup brown sugar

1 cup sugar

2 eggs

1½ cups flour

1 teaspoon baking soda

½ teaspoon salt

2 teaspoons cinnamon

1 teaspoon vanilla

ICING

4 tablespoons butter

¼ cup milk

1 cup brown sugar

1 cup chopped nuts

1 teaspoon vanilla

INGREDIENTS

3 cups flour

2¾ cups sugar

1 teaspoon salt

1 tablespoon baking soda

2½ teaspoons cinnamon

½ cup unsalted butter, melted

4 large eggs

1 cup vegetable oil

1 tablespoon vanilla

2 cups chopped walnuts or pecans

1 cup shredded coconut

1½ cup carrots, steamed, mashed

1 cup crushed pineapple, drained

ICING

2 packages (8 ounces each) cream cheese, softened

⅔ cup butter, softened

6 cups confectioners' sugar

2½ teaspoons vanilla

Rind of 1 lemon, finely grated

Juice of 1 lemon, strained

BAKER'S CHOICE CARROT CAKE

- Sift flour, sugar, salt, baking soda and cinnamon together into a large bowl.

- Add butter, eggs, oil and vanilla. Beat well.

- Stir in nuts, coconut, carrots and pineapple.

- Divide batter among 3 well-oiled 9-inch pans.

- Bake 35 minutes or until edges pull slightly away from pan. Cool.

- For icing, beat cream cheese and butter together. Add confectioners' sugar, vanilla, lemon rind and juice. Beat 5 minutes.

- Chill 30 minutes or until spreading consistency.

- Use to frost between cake layers, as well as top and sides.

Temperature: 350°

Time: 35 minutes

20 to 25 servings

Blue Ribbon Chocolate Cake

- Melt chocolate in a double boiler.
- In a large bowl, combine flour, baking powder, baking soda, and salt.
- Beat in egg; stir in melted chocolate.
- Beat in sugar and oil, then add zucchini and walnuts.
- Pour batter into well-oiled 8-inch cake pan. Bake 30 minutes or until cake pulls away from sides of pan.
- Cool 10 minutes before removing from pan.
- For frosting, beat cream cheese and butter until smooth.
- Add sugar, vanilla and cocoa. Beat until smooth. Spread frosting on cake.

Temperature: 350°

Time: 30 minutes

10 servings

INGREDIENTS

1 ounce unsweetened chocolate

¾ cup flour

½ teaspoon baking powder

½ teaspoon baking soda

¼ teaspoon salt

1 egg, slightly beaten

¾ cup sugar

½ cup vegetable oil

¾ cup grated zucchini, loosely packed

¼ cup chopped walnuts

FROSTING

3 ounces cream cheese

¼ cup unsalted butter, softened

½ pound confectioners' sugar

½ teaspoon vanilla

⅓ cup cocoa

INGREDIENTS

2 cups sugar

1¾ cups all purpose flour

1 cup unsweetened cocoa

2 teaspoons baking soda

1 teaspoon baking powder

3 eggs, beaten

1 cup buttermilk

1 cup strong coffee, at room temperature

½ cup butter or margarine, softened

2 teaspoons vanilla

GLAZE

1 cup heavy cream

1 tablespoon honey or corn syrup

1 cup sugar

1 cup unsweetened cocoa powder

2 tablespoons butter or margarine

1½ tablespoons vanilla

CHOCOLATE MIRROR

- Grease a 12 cup non-stick Bundt pan; "dust" with cocoa powder, tapping out excess.

- In a large bowl, sift together sugar, flour, cocoa, baking soda and baking powder.

- In a small bowl, combine eggs, buttermilk, coffee, butter and vanilla.

- Add egg mixture to dry ingredients. Beat with electric mixer on low until blended, about 30 seconds, then beat on medium for 2 minutes.

- Pour batter into prepared pan and bake for 40 to 50 minutes. Center of cake will be moist, but sides will pull away from pan and top will spring back lightly to touch.

- Cool pan on a rack for 15 minutes, then remove from pan and cool completely.

- In a heavy saucepan, combine all glaze ingredients except vanilla. Cook and stir over low heat until smooth; do not boil.

- Remove from heat. Stir in vanilla. Pour glaze through a fine strainer.

- Place cake on wire rack over plate or baking sheet. Pour warm glaze over cake to cover completely.

- Refrigerate cake 30 minutes before serving.

Hint: Leftover glaze can be stored in the refrigerator and used as a dessert sauce.

Temperature: 350°

Time: 40 to 50 minutes

10 to 12 servings

CHOCOLATE RASPBERRY TORTE

- Melt chocolate chips in microwave or double boiler. Use approximately ¼ cup chocolate to "paint" underside of real leaves for garnish. Refrigerate leaves.

- Add butter to remaining melted chocolate.

- Beat egg yolks until thick and pale yellow. Gradually beat in ½ cup sugar.

- Stir in chocolate mixture, nuts, 1 tablespoon liqueur and vanilla.

- Beat egg whites with cream of tartar until foamy. Gradually add ½ cup sugar and beat until stiff peaks form.

- Gently fold half the egg whites into the chocolate, then fold mixture back into the remaining whites. Pour into greased and floured 10-inch springform pan.

- Bake 30 minutes at 350°, then reduce heat to 275° and bake an additional 30 minutes.

- Remove from oven. Top with raspberry jam.

- When completely cool, refrigerate at least 6 hours.

- Whip cream and add confectioners' sugar and 2 tablespoons liqueur. Spread smoothly over top of cake.

- Let stand at room temperature for 30 minutes before serving. Garnish with fresh raspberries and chocolate leaves.

Temperature: 350° - 30 minutes
                275° - 30 minutes

10 servings

1 package (12 ounces) semi-sweet chocolate chips

½ cup butter

6 eggs, separated, room temperature

1 cup sugar, divided

½ cup chopped walnuts or hazelnuts

3 tablespoons Chambord liqueur

½ teaspoon vanilla

Pinch of cream of tartar

½ cup seedless raspberry jam

2 cups heavy cream

½ cup confectioners' sugar

Fresh raspberries

INGREDIENTS

¾ cup plus 2 tablespoons flour

½ teaspoon baking powder

¼ teaspoon baking soda

½ teaspoon salt

*2 ounces unsweetened chocolate,
in pieces*

1¼ cups sugar

1 tablespoon cocoa

⅓ cup boiling water

*¾ cup unsalted butter, softened,
cut in pieces*

2 eggs

½ cup sour cream

1 tablespoon dark rum

GANACHE

*8 ounces bittersweet or semi-sweet
chocolate*

½ cup heavy cream

2 tablespoons light corn syrup

1 tablespoon dark rum

Candied violets

VANILLA CUSTARD SAUCE

2 cups half-and-half

⅔ cup whole milk

1 vanilla bean, split

5 egg yolks

CHOCOLATE RUM TORTE WITH CHOCOLATE GANACHE

- Butter bottom of a 9½-inch or 10-inch springform pan. Cut circle of wax paper to fit bottom of pan. Butter paper and flour.

- Combine flour, baking powder, baking soda and salt in a food processor. Process for 5 seconds. Transfer to wax paper.

- Combine chocolate, sugar, and cocoa in processor. Process 1 minute. With motor still running, add boiling water then butter. Process 1 minute. Add eggs. Process 1 minute.

- Scrape down sides of processor. Add sour cream and rum. Process 5 seconds. Add flour and process using 5 on/off pulses. Do not over process. Batter will be thin.

- Pour into prepared pan. Bake 40 minutes or until cake pulls away from sides of pan.

- Cool cake. Remove side of pan; peel wax paper from bottom of cake, then place cake right side up on plate.

- For ganache, chop chocolate in small chunks in food processor.

- Heat cream to boiling and pour in processor while motor is running.

- Add corn syrup and rum. Pulse to process.

- Refrigerate for 10 minutes or until spreading consistency.

- Spread on cooled cake; decorate with candied violets.

- For custard sauce, combine half-and-half and milk in saucepan. Scrape vanilla bean seeds into milk and add pod. Bring mixture just to a simmer. Cover, remove from heat and let steep 1 hour.

- Whisk egg yolks, sugar and salt.

- Bring half-and-half mixture back to a boil. Whisk a little into the egg yolks then whisk yolks into pan with half-and-half. Cook over low heat until custard thickens slightly, and leaves a path on the back of a wooden spoon when finger is drawn across, (about 8 to 10 minutes). Do not boil.

- Cover and refrigerate until well chilled.
- Serve torte on a pool of custard sauce.

Temperature: 325°

Time: 40 minutes

10 to 12 servings

⅔ cup sugar

Dash salt

MINT CHOCOLATE MOUSSE CAKE*

INGREDIENTS

12 ounces mint chocolate chips

6 eggs, separated

4 tablespoons sugar

3 cups heavy cream, divided

2 tablespoons chocolate mint liqueur

3 packages (3 ounces each) plain ladyfingers

Shaved chocolate

Chocolate leaves

- In a double boiler over hot water, melt chocolate. Cool to room temperature.
- In a large bowl, beat egg yolks. Stir in cooled chocolate.
- In a medium bowl, whip egg whites with 2 tablespoons sugar until stiff peaks form. Fold whites into chocolate mixture.
- In another large bowl, whip 2 cups heavy cream with 2 tablespoons sugar. Fold into chocolate mixture.
- Layer a 10-inch springform pan with ladyfingers on bottom and around edges, with rounded sides facing outside.
- Pour ⅓ of chocolate mixture into pan on bottom layer of ladyfingers. Repeat with 2 more layers of ladyfingers and chocolate.
- Refrigerate overnight.
- Before serving, whip 1 cup heavy cream and spread on top of cake. Sprinkle with shaved chocolate or chocolate leaves.

12 to 16 servings

* This recipe contains uncooked egg yolks/whites. See SPECIAL NOTE page 7.

DOUBLE ENCORE

INGREDIENTS

4 eggs, separated

1½ cups sugar, divided

½ cup butter or margarine

6 tablespoons milk

1 cup flour

1 teaspoon baking powder

1 teaspoon vanilla

*½ cup coarsely ground walnuts
or pecans*

1 cup heavy cream

1 cup fresh fruit, sliced

- In a medium bowl beat egg whites until foamy. Gradually add 1 cup sugar, beating until stiff peaks form.

- In a large bowl, cream ½ cup butter or margarine, ½ cup sugar and egg yolks.

- Stir in milk, flour, baking powder and vanilla.

- Pour cake batter into 2 well-greased, 9-inch cake pans. Spread ½ of the meringue into each pan. Sprinkle with nuts.

- Bake 30 minutes or until delicately browned.

- Cool pans on rack.

- Flip 1 cake, meringue side down, onto cake plate.

- In a medium bowl, whip heavy cream. Fold in fruit and spread entire amount of cream onto first layer.

- Remove remaining cake from pan and carefully place on top of whipped cream filling, meringue-side up.

- Refrigerate up to 8 hours before serving.

Temperature: 350°

Time: 30 minutes

8 to 10 servings

Hint: If fresh fruit is unavailable, substitute 1 cup frozen fruit, thawed and drained.

LEMON CHARLOTTE WITH BLUEBERRY SAUCE*

- Line bottom and sides of a 9-inch or 9½-inch springform pan with ladyfingers.

- In a medium saucepan, whisk together gelatin, pudding, sugar, egg yolks and water. Cook over medium heat until mixture comes to a full boil, stirring constantly.

- Remove from heat. Stir in lemon juice and rind.

- Place the pan into a large bowl partially filled with ice water; stir until cool.

- In a medium bowl, beat egg whites with an electric mixer until stiff. Set aside.

- In a large bowl, whip heavy cream with confectioners' sugar.

- Fold ⅔ of the whipped cream and all of the beaten egg whites into the cooled lemon mixture. Spoon filling into pan. Chill at least 3 hours or until set.

- Place reserved whipped cream into a pastry bag and decorate cake top, or dollop the whipped cream with a spoon.

- When ready to serve, place charlotte on a serving platter and remove springform ring.

- For sauce, crush 1 cup of the blueberries in saucepan. Add water, sugar and cornstarch. Stir and cook 1 minute.

- Remove saucepan from heat. Stir in lemon juice.

- Refrigerate and serve with the charlotte.

12 to 14 servings

* This recipe contains uncooked egg yolks/whites. See SPECIAL NOTE page 7.

INGREDIENTS

2 packages (3 ounces each) ladyfingers, split

1 package (3½-ounces) lemon flavored gelatin

1 package (3½-ounces) lemon pudding-and-pie-filling

⅓ cup sugar

2 eggs, separated

2½ cups water

Juice of 1 lemon

Grated rind of 1 lemon

1½ cups heavy cream, whipped

2 tablespoons confectioners' sugar

SAUCE

2 cups fresh blueberries

⅓ cup water

¼ cup sugar

1 tablespoon corn starch

1 tablespoon fresh lemon juice

INGREDIENTS

¾ cup blanched whole almonds

5 ounces semi-sweet chocolate

⅔ cup unsalted butter

¾ cup sugar

3 eggs, separated

⅔ cup flour

¼ cup milk

½ teaspoon vanilla

½ teaspoon salt

FROSTING

5 ounces semi-sweet chocolate

3 tablespoons milk

¼ cup unsalted butter

1 cup confectioners' sugar

¼ teaspoon almond extract

⅔ cup sliced almonds

GÂTEAU AU CHOCOLAT

- In a food processor fitted with metal blade, finely grind almonds. Set aside.

- In a double boiler over hot water, melt chocolate. Remove from heat.

- Using an electric mixer, cream butter until smooth. Beat in sugar, 2 tablespoons at a time, until fluffy.

- Mix in egg yolks, beating until light. Stir in melted chocolate. At low speed, beat in the flour and milk alternately, beginning and ending with flour. Stir in vanilla and ½ cup ground almonds.

- In a medium bowl, beat egg whites with salt at high speed until stiff peaks form. With wire whisk, gently fold whites into batter until combined. Turn batter into lightly greased and floured 9-inch springform pan, spreading evenly.

- Bake for 25 to 30 minutes. Remove from oven and cool in pan on wire rack for 10 minutes. Remove cake from pan and continue cooling over rack. Frost when cooled.

- For frosting, in double boiler over hot water, melt semi-sweet chocolate with milk and butter. Remove from heat. Add confectioners' sugar and almond extract. Beat until thin and smooth.

- To frost cake, set the cake on the serving plate. Pour the warm frosting onto the center of the cake and spread the frosting thinly toward the edge. Create a ridge at the edge with the excess frosting. As the frosting begins to set, bring it down over the top edge and frost the sides.

- While the frosting is still moist, sprinkle the reserved

ground almonds over the top and press the sliced almonds into the sides. Refrigerate cake.

Temperature: 350°
Time: 25 to 30 minutes
12 servings

SWEDISH TOSCA CAKE

- Butter sides and bottom of a 9-inch round or springform pan. Coat lightly with crumbs.

- In a medium bowl, mix flour, baking powder and salt. Set aside.

- In a large bowl with an electric mixer, beat eggs slightly. Gradually add sugar and continue beating until thick and pale yellow. Add butter and vanilla. Fold in dry ingredients alternately with cream.

- Spread batter into pan and bake for 25 to 30 minutes. Remove cake from oven and set on a rack to cool for 10 minutes.

- In a small saucepan, combine all the topping ingredients. Bring to a boil, stirring constantly.

- Spread mixture evenly on top of slightly cooled cake. Broil 3 to 4 inches from heat until golden color. Remove and serve either warm or at room temperature.

Temperature: 350°
Time: 25 to 30 minutes
6 to 8 servings

INGREDIENTS

1 tablespoon butter

¼ cup graham cracker crumbs

¾ cup flour

1 teaspoon baking powder

½ teaspoon salt

2 eggs

¾ cup sugar

¼ cup butter, melted and cooled

½ teaspoon vanilla

¼ cup heavy cream or half-and-half

TOPPING

¼ cup sugar

¼ cup butter

1 tablespoon flour

1 tablespoon heavy or light cream

½ cup slivered almonds

INGREDIENTS

1 cup sifted cake flour

¼ teaspoon salt

5 eggs, separated

Juice of ½ lemon

1 cup sugar

SAUCE

2 egg whites

¾ cup sugar

Juice of one lemon

2 cups orange juice

Whipped cream

SPONGE CAKE WITH ORANGE SAUCE*

- In a large mixing bowl, combine flour and salt. Sift together four times. Set aside.

- In a medium bowl, beat yolks until thick and lemon colored. Add lemon juice and blend.

- In a medium bowl, beat whites until foamy, then gradually add sugar, beating until stiff peaks form. Fold in yolks then fold the batter into flour.

- Pour batter into an ungreased 8½-inch tube pan. Bake 55 to 65 minutes or until tester is removed clean.

- Remove from oven and invert pan for one hour over a narrow neck bottle. While cake is cooling, prepare sauce.

- For sauce, beat egg whites until stiff. Add sugar, lemon juice and orange juice. Blend.

- When cake is cool, pour sauce over entire cake. Refrigerate at least 8 hours or overnight.

- Serve with a dollop of whipped cream.

Temperature: 325°

Time: 55 to 65 minutes

10 to 12 servings

* This recipe contains uncooked egg yolks/whites. See SPECIAL NOTE page 7.

288 / DESSERTS

Fresh Apple Cake with Caramel Glaze

- In a large bowl, cream together butter and sugar until light and fluffy.

- Add eggs, one at a time, beating well after each addition.

- Combine dry ingredients and add to creamed mixture. Stir in vanilla, apples and walnuts.

- Spoon batter into a greased and floured 10-inch tube pan. Bake 70 to 75 minutes or until tester comes out clean.

- Cool on rack for 20 to 30 minutes then remove cake from pan and cool completely on rack.

- For glaze, combine all ingredients in a saucepan; bring to a boil, stirring occasionally.

- Boil 3 minutes without stirring, over medium high heat.

- Remove from heat. Let cool 3 to 4 minutes and spoon over cake.

Temperature: 325°

Time: 70 to 75 minutes

14 to 16 servings

INGREDIENTS

1 cup butter

2 cups sugar

3 eggs

3 cups flour

1½ teaspoons baking soda

½ teaspoon salt

1 heaping teaspoon cinnamon

⅛ teaspoon nutmeg

2 teaspoons vanilla

3 cups chopped, peeled apples

1 to 1½ cups chopped walnuts

CARAMEL GLAZE

½ cup brown sugar

¼ cup butter (do not substitute margarine)

¼ cup heavy cream

INGREDIENTS

1½ cups gingersnap crumbs

¼ cup butter, melted

FILLING

½ cup butter, softened

2½ cups confectioners' sugar

2 eggs

1 cup heavy cream

¼ cup sugar

2½ cups sliced strawberries

½ cup chopped pecans

STRAWBERRY GINGER BLISS

- In medium bowl, combine gingersnap crumbs and butter. Press crumbs into a 9 x 9-inch pan, reserving ½ cup for topping.

- In a large bowl, cream butter and confectioners' sugar until mixture is light and fluffy. Add eggs, one at a time, and continue beating until fluffy.

- Spoon mixture into crust in pan. Refrigerate.

- In another large bowl, whip cream and sugar together. Fold in strawberries and pecans.

- Spread topping over mixture in pan. Top with remaining crumbs.

- Cover and refrigerate 8 hours or overnight.

12 servings

INGREDIENTS

3 cups flour

2 cups sugar

½ cup cocoa

2 teaspoons baking soda

2 cups water

⅔ cup oil

3 tablespoons vinegar

2 teaspoons vanilla

WHIMSY CAKES

- In a large mixing bowl, sift together flour, sugar, cocoa and baking soda.

- Add water, oil, vinegar and vanilla. Beat with an electric mixer on high, 3 to 4 minutes.

- Using a food processor fitted with a metal blade, process cream cheese, egg, sugar and salt.

- Stir in chocolate chips.

- Either grease muffin pans or use fluted cupcake liners. Fill each ⅔ full with batter. Gently spoon 1½ teaspoons cream cheese mixture into center of each cake.
- Bake 20 to 25 minutes. The centers will still be moist.
- Serve either warm or at room temperature.

Temperature: 350°
Time: 20 to 25 minutes
12 servings

1 package (8 ounces) cream cheese

1 egg

⅓ cup sugar

Dash of salt

6 ounces semi-sweet chocolate chips

REGAL CHEESECAKE

- Combine graham cracker crumbs, sugar and butter. Press into bottom of 9-inch springform pan.
- Bake at 325° for 10 minutes. Remove from oven.
- Combine cream cheese, sugar, juice and rind. Mix well.
- Beat in egg whites, one at a time.
- Pour into crust and bake at 300° for 55 minutes.
- Combine sour cream, sugar and vanilla. Pour over cheesecake and spread to cover. Bake for additional 10 minutes.
- Cool and refrigerate at least 8 hours before removing from pan or serving.

Temperature: 325° – 10 minutes
                    300° – 65 minutes

12 servings

INGREDIENTS

1 cup graham cracker crumbs

2 tablespoons sugar

3 tablespoons butter, melted

3 packages (8 ounces each) cream cheese, softened

¾ cup sugar

1 tablespoon lemon juice

½ tablespoon grated lemon rind

3 large egg whites

1 cup sour cream

2 tablespoons sugar

1 teaspoon vanilla

INGREDIENTS

1 cup shortening

1½ cups sugar, divided

½ teaspoon vanilla

4 egg yolks

1 cup cake flour

1 teaspoon baking powder

Pinch of salt

⅓ cup milk

5 egg whites, stiffly beaten

½ teaspoon cream of tartar

¾ cup chopped walnuts

FROSTING

⅓ cup cocoa

¾ cup sugar

1½ cups heavy cream

½ cup whole walnuts

WONDERFUL WALNUT TORTE

- In large bowl, cream shortening and ½ cup sugar. Add vanilla and egg yolks, one at a time, beating until fluffy.

- Sift together flour, baking powder and salt.

- Alternately add dry ingredients and milk to egg mixture.

- Pour batter into two 8½-inch greased round pans.

- Beat egg whites and cream of tartar until foamy. Continue beating, and gradually add remaining 1 cup sugar until stiff peaks form. Fold in walnuts.

- Spread over top of cake and bake 45 minutes or until tester comes out clean.

- For frosting, combine cocoa, sugar and cream in a mixing bowl. Refrigerate at least 1 hour.

- Before serving, whip frosting and frost between layers and on top. Garnish with whole walnuts.

Temperature: 300°

Time: 45 minutes

12 servings

Raisin Puffs

INGREDIENTS

1 cup dark raisins

½ cup golden raisins

2½ cups sugar, divided

1 cup butter

2 eggs

1 tablespoon vanilla

3½ cups flour

1 teaspoon baking soda

½ teaspoon salt

- In a medium saucepan, bring 1 cup water to a boil. Add raisins, reduce heat to low, and simmer until all water is absorbed. Remove from heat.

- In a large bowl, cream 1½ cups sugar and butter until fluffy. Add eggs, one at a time, mixing well. Stir in vanilla.

- In a large bowl, sift together flour, baking soda and salt. Gradually add dry ingredients to the butter mixture.

- Gently fold in cooked raisins and refrigerate dough for about one hour.

- Roll dough into 1 to 1½-inch balls and roll in remaining granulated sugar. Place on greased baking sheet and bake for 15 minutes.

Temperature: 350°

Time: 15 minutes

6 dozen

Hint: For richer flavor, heat raisins in rum or brandy instead of water.

INGREDIENTS

2 packages (3 ounces each) cream cheese, softened

2 cups flour

1 cup butter, softened

1 cup chopped pecans

2 eggs

1½ cups brown sugar

2 tablespoons butter

¼ teaspoon vanilla

Dash of salt

PECAN TASSIES

- In a large bowl, combine cream cheese, flour and butter until creamy.

- Form dough into 1-inch diameter balls and press each into mini-muffin tins to resemble petite pie crusts.

- Sprinkle nuts over pastry.

- In a medium saucepan, beat together eggs, brown sugar, butter, vanilla and salt. Cook over low heat until mixture turns dark brown and is blended thoroughly. Do not boil.

- Spoon filling over nuts and bake 15 to 18 minutes, or until pastry is light brown.

- Cool slightly and remove from pans. Tassies must be removed while they are warm or they will stick to the pan.

Temperature: 350°
Time: 15 to 18 minutes
12 servings

INGREDIENTS

1½ cups butter or margarine, softened

¾ cup sugar

1 tablespoon lemon extract

2⅔ cups flour

1½ cups finely chopped almonds

1 package (14 ounces) milk chocolate "kisses"

PUCKER-UP LEMON KISSES

A TRULY SPECIAL COOKIE, WORTH THE EFFORT!

- Using an electric mixer, beat butter, sugar and lemon extract until light and fluffy.

- Add flour and almonds and beat at low speed until well blended.

- Refrigerate, covered, at least 1 hour for easier handling.

- Shape scant tablespoonful of dough around each un-wrapped candy kiss, covering completely. Roll in hands to form a ball. Place on ungreased cookie sheet.

- Bake for 8 to 12 minutes, or until set and bottom edges are slightly brown. Cool 1 minute. Remove from baking sheet and cool completely.

- Lightly sprinkle cooled cookies with confectioners' sugar.

- In small saucepan over low heat, melt chocolate pieces and shortening, stirring until smooth. Drizzle over each cookie.

Temperature: 375°
Time: 8 to 12 minutes
6 dozen

¼ cup confectioners' sugar

½ cup semi-sweet chocolate pieces

1 tablespoon shortening

PEANUTTIES

THE FULL FLAVOR OF NATURAL PEANUT BUTTER DISTINGUISH THESE FROM THE STANDARD PEANUT BUTTER COOKIE.

- In a large bowl, cream together butter, sugars, peanut butter and egg.
- Add flour, salt, baking soda and vanilla, mixing well.
- Stir in chopped peanuts.
- Drop by generous teaspoonfuls onto greased baking sheet. Flatten with fork tines.
- Bake for 10 to 12 minutes, or until slightly brown.

Temperature: 350°
Time: 10 to 12 minutes
2 dozen

INGREDIENTS

½ cup butter or margarine

½ cup brown sugar

½ cup sugar

½ cup chunky natural-style peanut butter

1 egg

1 cup flour

¼ teaspoon salt

½ teaspoon baking soda

Drop of vanilla

½ cup chopped unsalted peanuts

INGREDIENTS

½ cup butter or margarine, softened

1 cup sugar

1 cup plus 2 tablespoons brown sugar, firmly packed

3 eggs

2 cups peanut butter

¼ teaspoon vanilla

¾ teaspoon light corn syrup

4½ cups uncooked rolled oats

2 teaspoons baking soda

¼ teaspoon salt

1 cup miniature semi-sweet chocolate chips

P. B. O. COLOSSALS

THESE COLOSSAL COOKIES ARE SO INCREDIBLE, THEY'RE WORTH THE CALORIES!

- In a large bowl, cream butter. Gradually add sugars, beating until fluffy.

- Add eggs, peanut butter, vanilla and corn syrup, mixing well.

- Stir in oats, baking soda, salt and chips. Batter will be stiff.

- Spoon ¼ cup of dough onto a lightly oiled baking sheet. Pat each in a 3-inch circle. Space cookies 4 inches apart.

- Bake for 12 to 15 minutes. Cool slightly on pan, then finish cooling on rack.

Temperature: 350°

Time: 12 to 15 minutes

2½ dozen

INGREDIENTS

2 cups butter

4 cups flour

⅓ cup sugar

1 teaspoon cinnamon

1¼ cups sliced almonds, chopped

4 cups confectioners' sugar

¼ to ½ cup milk

LEBANESE NUT COOKIES

- In food processor using the steel blade, process butter and flour until it forms a ball.

- Form dough into 1-inch balls and place on ungreased baking sheet. Use your knuckle to make a nest-like indentation in each cookie. Combine sugar, cinnamon and almonds; spoon mixture into indentations.

- Bake for 20 to 30 minutes or until slightly browned.

- Gradually add milk to confectioners' sugar to form a glaze.

- Drizzle glaze over cookie to partially fill the indentations.
- Cool before serving.

Temperature: 350°
Time: 20 to 30 minutes
3 dozen

THE ULTIMATE TOFFEE COOKIE

INGREDIENTS

¾ cup dark brown sugar, packed

½ cup sugar

¾ cup unsalted butter, softened

1 large egg

1 teaspoon vanilla

1 cup flour

½ teaspoon baking soda

⅛ teaspoon salt

1¾ cups uncooked rolled oats

¾ cup coarsely chopped pecans

4 English-style toffee bars (1.2 ounces each), chopped coarsely

- In a large mixing bowl, beat sugars, butter, egg and vanilla. When smooth, add flour, baking soda, salt and rolled oats, mixing well.
- Use a wooden spoon to stir in pecans and candy.
- Use ¼ cup measure, drop dough on lightly-oiled baking sheet. Flatten each cookie slightly leaving 2 inches between cookies.
- Bake until set, about 15 minutes. Leave on baking sheet on rack 3 minutes, then transfer cookies to racks to cool completely.
- Store in an airtight container up to four days or freeze for longer storage.

Temperature: 350°
Time: 15 minutes
16 cookies

INGREDIENTS

4 cups flour

1 teaspoon baking soda

1 teaspoon salt

1 cup shortening

2 cups brown sugar, firmly packed

2 eggs

⅔ cup buttermilk or plain yogurt

1 cup pecans, chopped

1 cup candied cherries, quartered

2 cups chopped dates

1 cup candied fruit and peels

HOLIDAY JEWELS

- Sift together flour, baking soda and salt; set aside.

- In a large bowl, cream shortening and sugar until fluffy. Beat in eggs.

- Alternately add buttermilk and flour to the egg mixture. Stir in nuts and fruit.

- Chill dough at least one hour, then drop by rounded teaspoonfuls onto ungreased baking sheets.

- Bake for 10 to 12 minutes.

Temperature: 375°

Time: 10 to 12 minutes

6 dozen

INGREDIENTS

½ cup butter

1 egg

½ cup sugar

½ pound dates, chopped

1 teaspoon vanilla

½ cup chopped walnuts or pecans

2½ cups crisp rice cereal

1 cup confectioners' sugar

DATE NUT CRUNCHIES

- In a large saucepan, melt butter. Add egg and sugar, stir until well blended.

- Stir in chopped dates and cook over low heat, stirring constantly, until mixture is thick and almost pasty.

- Remove from heat and stir in vanilla, nuts and cereal.

- When cool, roll into ¾-inch balls and roll in confectioners' sugar.

- Store in airtight containers.

5 dozen

Glazed Apple Cookies

- In a large mixing bowl, cream butter, brown sugar and vanilla. Add egg and mix well.
- Sift dry ingredients and stir into creamed mixture along with milk.
- Stir in apple, nuts and raisins.
- Drop by rounded teaspoonfuls onto a greased baking sheet.
- Bake for 11 to 12 minutes.
- Combine all icing ingredients, adding just enough milk for a thin glaze.
- Glaze cookies with icing while still warm.
- Cool on wire racks. Store in airtight container.

Temperature: 375°

Time: 11 to 12 minutes

3 to 4 dozen

INGREDIENTS

½ cup butter or margarine

1⅓ cups brown sugar

1 teaspoon vanilla

1 egg

2 cups flour

1 teaspoon baking soda

½ teaspoon salt

1 teaspoon cinnamon

¼ teaspoon nutmeg

¼ cup milk

1 cup finely chopped, peeled apple

1 cup raisins

1 cup chopped walnuts

ICING

1½ cups confectioners' sugar

1 tablespoon softened butter or margarine

½ teaspoon vanilla

1 to 2 teaspoons milk

1¼ cups sugar, divided

½ cup confectioners' sugar

½ cup flour

½ teaspoon salt

1 pound almond paste

4 egg whites

⅔ cup sliced almonds

ALMOND DREAMS

- In food processor fitted with a metal blade, process ½ cup sugar, confectioners' sugar, flour, salt, and almond paste until blended.

- Add egg whites and process until blended.

- Refrigerate dough, then roll 1 teaspoon dough into fat finger shapes.

- Combine almonds and remaining ¾ cup sugar. Roll cookies in mixture.

- Bake for 20 to 30 minutes.

Temperature: 350°

Time: 20 to 30 minutes

6 dozen

Note: Look for almond paste where speciality ingredients are sold.

INGREDIENTS

6 cups cornflakes

1 cup light corn syrup

½ cup sugar

½ cup brown sugar

1 cup smooth peanut butter

1 cup salted peanuts

1 cup semi-sweet chocolate chips

BABE RUTH BARS: A REAL "HIT"

- Crush cornflakes in a large mixing bowl and set aside.

- In a large saucepan, combine syrup and sugars. Bring to a boil, stirring often.

- Remove from heat and stir in peanut butter and peanuts, mixing well.

- Pour the syrup mixture over the crushed cornflakes. Blend thoroughly.

- Spread the mixture evenly in an well-oiled 9 x 13-inch pan.
- Sprinkle chocolate chips over surface.
- Bake for 10 minutes. Remove pan from oven and smooth the melted chips to form an even glaze. Cool and cut into 1-inch squares.

Temperature: 250°
Time: 10 minutes
24 bars

Brag About Brownies

INGREDIENTS

1 cup butter

4 ounces unsweetened chocolate

2 cups sugar

½ teaspoon salt

4 eggs

1 teaspoon vanilla

1 cup flour

2 cups coarsely chopped walnuts

- In the top of a double boiler over hot water, melt butter and chocolate, stirring frequently.
- In a large mixing bowl combine sugar and salt. Add melted chocolate mixture and beat slightly.
- Add eggs one at a time until blended. Stir in vanilla, flour and nuts.
- Pour into well-oiled 9 x 13-inch pan.
- Bake 35 to 40 minutes or until tester comes out clean.
- For frosting, in the top of a double boiler over hot water, melt butter and chocolate, stirring frequently. Add vanilla and beaten egg.
- In a large bowl, combine confectioners' sugar and the chocolate mixture, mixing well. Frost cooled brownies.

FROSTING

¼ cup butter

1 ounce unsweetened chocolate

1 teaspoon vanilla

1 egg beaten

2¼ cups confectioners' sugar

Temperature: 325°
Time: 35 to 40 minutes
48 brownies

INGREDIENTS

½ cup peanut butter

½ cup margarine

½ cup brown sugar

½ cup sugar

1 egg

1¼ cups flour

1 teaspoon baking powder

½ teaspoon vanilla

1½ packages (14 ounces each) miniature peanut butter cups

BROWN-EYED SUSANS

- In a large bowl, cream together peanut butter, margarine, sugars and egg.

- Sift together flour and baking powder and add to the creamed mixture. Blend thoroughly and stir in vanilla.

- Roll ½ tablespoon dough into a ball. Place each ball in an ungreased mini-muffin tin. Press the top of each ball slightly with thumb.

- Bake for 8 to 10 minutes.

- Lightly press an unwrapped peanut butter cup into the center of each cookie. Allow to set 15 minutes and remove from pan.

Temperature: 350°

Time: 8 to 10 minutes

4 dozen

INGREDIENTS

1 cup flour

1¼ cups quick or regular rolled oats

¾ cup brown sugar

½ teaspoon baking soda

¼ teaspoon salt

¾ cup margarine, melted

CARAMEL DELIGHTS

- In a medium bowl, combine flour, oats, brown sugar, baking soda, salt and margarine. Reserve ¾ cup. In an ungreased 9 x 9-inch glass baking dish, pat remainder to form a crust. Bake for 10 minutes.

- Remove from oven and sprinkle with chocolate chips and walnuts.

- In a small bowl, combine caramel or butterscotch sauce with the flour. Drizzle sauce evenly on top of chip layer.

- Sprinkle reserved ¾ cup oat mixture over all.
- Return to oven for 15 to 20 minutes, until golden brown. Cut into squares when cool.

Temperature: 350°
Time: 10 minutes
 15 to 20 minutes

3 dozen

8 ounces semi-sweet chocolate chips

½ cup chopped walnuts

¾ cup caramel or butterscotch sauce

3 tablespoons flour

BUTTER FINGERS

- In a large bowl, cream butter and sugar.
- Add flour and nuts.
- Roll into short "fingers" or ¾-inch balls.
- Place on ungreased baking sheet and bake for 15 to 20 minutes.
- While warm, roll in confectioners' sugar.

Hint: For a richer cookie, melt ½ cup semi-sweet chocolate chips. Dip one end of each cooled cookie into the chocolate. Let chocolate set before serving.

Temperature: 350°
Time: 15 to 20 minutes
2 dozen

INGREDIENTS

1 cup butter

6 tablespoons confectioners' sugar

2 cups flour

¾ cup chopped walnuts

Confectioners' sugar

INGREDIENTS

½ cup butter

1 cup packed brown sugar

1 egg

½ teaspoon vanilla

2 cups flour

¾ teaspoon baking soda

¾ teaspoon baking powder

¼ teaspoon salt

½ teaspoon cinnamon

¼ teaspoon nutmeg

⅓ cup sour cream

1 cup salted cashews,
coarsely chopped

FROSTING

3 tablespoons butter

2 cups confectioners' sugar

2 tablespoons milk

1 teaspoon vanilla

CASHEW CAPERS

BAKE THESE WHEN YOU WANT A COOKIE THAT'S NOT TOO SWEET

- In a large bowl, cream butter and sugar. Beat in egg and vanilla.

- Sift dry ingredients together, then alternately add dry ingredients and sour cream to butter mixture. Blend well; stir in nuts.

- Roll into ¾-inch balls and put onto greased baking sheet. Flatten each cookie slightly with bottom of a glass.

- Bake for 8 to 10 minutes until slightly browned.

- For frosting, in a small saucepan, heat butter until browned.

- Remove from heat and slowly beat in confectioners' sugar, milk and vanilla. Frost cooled cookies.

Temperature: 375°
Time: 8 to 10 minutes
4 dozen

CATCH A HUSBAND SQUARES

- Sift together flour, cocoa and salt.
- In a small bowl, mix dates, boiling water and baking soda; cool.
- In a large bowl, cream butter, shortening and sugar until fluffy. Add eggs and beat 1 minute.
- Alternately stir flour mixture and date mixture into butter mixture, blending well. Stir in vanilla and beat 1 more minute.
- Spread in well-oiled 9 x 13-inch pan. Sprinkle with nuts and chocolate chips.
- Bake for 40 minutes; cool.

Hint: For cookies, cut into 2-inch squares. For dessert, cut into 3-inch squares and top with a dollop of whipped cream.

Temperature: 350°
Time: 40 minutes
2 dozen

INGREDIENTS

1¾ cups flour

2 tablespoons cocoa

½ teaspoon salt

1 cup dates, finely chopped

1 cup boiling water

1 teaspoon baking soda

½ cup butter or margarine

½ cup shortening

1 cup sugar

2 eggs

1 teaspoon vanilla

1 cup chopped nuts

1 package (6 ounces) chocolate chips

Whipped cream

INGREDIENTS

2 cups softened butter

1½ cups sugar

3 cups flour

1 cup untoasted sesame seeds

2 cups shredded coconut

½ cup finely chopped almonds

CHINESE SWEET SESAMES

A PERFECT COOKIE FOR TEA — NOT TOO SWEET

- In a large bowl, cream butter and sugar until mixture is light and fluffy. Add flour and mix until just combined. Stir in sesame seeds, coconut and almonds, mixing well.

- Divide dough into three equal parts. Place each piece on a sheet of wax paper and shape it into a long roll, 2 inches in diameter. Wrap in wax paper and refrigerate until firm, 3 to 4 hours or overnight.

- Unwrap the dough and slice ¼-inch thick. Bake on ungreased baking sheet for 30 minutes, until cookies are slightly puffed but not yet golden brown. Do not overbake. Cool on rack.

Hint: To add a festive look, press ½ red or green candied cherry into center of each cookie before baking.

Temperature: 300°

Time: 30 minutes

5 to 6 dozen

INGREDIENTS

1½ cups flour

½ cup cocoa

¼ teaspoon salt

¼ teaspoon baking powder

¼ teaspoon baking soda

½ cup butter or margarine, softened

CHOCOLATE INTRIGUES

- In a medium bowl, stir together flour, cocoa, salt, baking powder and baking soda.

- In a large bowl, cream butter and sugar until fluffy. Beat in egg and vanilla.

- Gradually add dry ingredients, mixing well.

- Shape dough into 1-inch balls and place on ungreased baking sheet. Make an indentation with thumb in center of each cookie. Drain maraschino cherries, reserving juice. Halve cherries and place a well-drained cherry half in the center of each cookie.

- In a small saucepan, melt chocolate chips with condensed milk, stirring often. Stir in 4 teaspoons of the reserved cherry juice.

- Spoon about 1 teaspoon of chocolate over each cherry, spreading to cover cherry.

- Bake for about 10 minutes, but do not overbake. Cool on wire rack.

Temperature: 350°
Time: 10 minutes
4 dozen

1 cup sugar

1 egg

1½ teaspoons vanilla

1 jar (10 ounces) maraschino cherries

6 ounces semi-sweet chocolate chips

½ cup sweetened condensed milk

CHOCOLATE CHIPPIES DELUXE

- Combine flour, cinnamon, baking soda, salt and grated chocolate, mixing well.

- Beat sugars, vanilla and butter together.

- Stir in eggs, one at a time.

- Stir in flour mixture and chocolate chips.

- Drop by rounded teaspoonfuls onto ungreased cookie sheet. Bake for 8 to 10 minutes.

Temperature: 375°
Time: 8 to 10 minutes
4 dozen

INGREDIENTS

2 cups sifted flour

¼ teaspoon cinnamon

1 teaspoon baking soda

1 teaspoon salt

1 square bittersweet chocolate, grated

¾ cup light brown sugar

¾ cup sugar

1 teaspoon vanilla

1 cup unsalted butter

2 eggs

1 package (12 ounces) mini-chocolate chips

STRAWBERRY STARLIGHTS

COOKIE-SIZE CLASSIC MERINGUES ARE PERFECT
FOR BRIDAL SHOWERS AND SPECIAL PARTIES

INGREDIENTS

4 egg whites

Pinch salt

¼ teaspoon cream of tartar

1¼ cups confectioners' sugar

BUTTER CREAM

*1 pint strawberries, washed
and hulled*

¼ cup light corn syrup

¼ cup sugar

2 egg yolks

1 cup unsalted butter, softened

2 teaspoons vanilla

2 drops red food coloring

- Cover baking sheets with parchment paper. Draw 18 2-inch circles on each sheet.

- Using an electric mixer, beat egg whites on high until foamy. Add salt and cream of tartar. When soft peaks form, add confectioners' sugar ¼ cup at a time. Beat 1 minute after each addition.

- Fit pastry tube with a #20 star tip. Fill bag with mixture. Fill circles on baking sheets by spiralling circles from circle outline to center. Cookies will be approximately ¼-inch thick.

- Bake 1 hour, switching position of baking sheets once during baking. Turn oven off and leave in oven 1 hour longer.

- Cool briefly and remove from paper to finish cooling on racks. Store in airtight container.

- For buttercream filling, purée berries in blender. Set aside.

- In a saucepan over medium heat, cook corn syrup and sugar until it begins to boil. Set aside, but keep hot.

- Beat egg yolks with electric mixer until light.

- With mixer on high, add sugar syrup to yolks. Beat until cool, approximately 7 to 10 minutes.

- With mixer on medium, add butter, 1 tablespoon at a time.

- Add strawberry purée slowly. Add vanilla and food coloring. Beat well to blend.

- Fit pastry tube with a #20 star tip. Fill the bag with butter cream. Chill 30 minutes. If buttercream is hard, let it soften before using.

- Pipe filling over cookie, following the same spiral pattern as the meringue.

- Top with slice of strawberry or strawberry half.

- Serve immediately as after one hour, the buttercream will begin to melt the cookie.

Temperature: 225°

Time: 1 hour

3 dozen

Hint: Meringues can be made weeks ahead and stored in airtight containers. Buttercream can be made several days ahead and then refrigerated.

GRAHAM GLORIES

A SURPRISING TREAT FOR KIDS OF ALL AGES!

- Place graham crackers on a baking sheet, side by side.

- In a saucepan over medium heat, melt butter and brown sugar. Bring to a boil, stirring constantly. Cook for 5 minutes.

- Gently pour caramel over crackers. Sprinkle with nuts.

- Bake for 10 minutes.

- Cool for 10 minutes. Divide crackers into 24 squares, then cut each square in half on the diagonal.

Temperature: 350°

Time: 10 minutes

4 dozen

INGREDIENTS

12 whole graham crackers

1 cup butter or margarine

1 cup brown sugar, firmly packed

1½ cups chopped pecans, almonds or walnuts

WHIRLIGIGS

INGREDIENTS

½ cup butter

½ cup sugar

½ cup dark brown sugar

½ cup creamy peanut butter

1 egg

1¼ cups sifted flour

½ teaspoon salt

½ teaspoon baking soda

1 package (6 ounces) semi-sweet
chocolate chips

- In a large bowl, combine butter, sugars, peanut butter and egg; beat until smooth.

- Stir in flour, salt and baking soda.

- Refrigerate dough 20 minutes, then place chilled dough on wax paper. With palm of hand, pat dough into a rectangle about 6 x 10-inches.

- In a double boiler over boiling water, melt chocolate. Spread chocolate over dough.

- Pick up edge of wax paper and gently roll dough lengthwise jelly roll fashion. Secure ends. Refrigerate for 30 minutes.

- Slice chilled dough into ¼-inch cookies. Bake on an ungreased baking sheet for 8 to 10 minutes. Allow cookies to set for a few minutes before transferring to cooling rack.

Temperature: 375°

Time: 8 to 10 minutes

2 dozen

MACADAMIA SHORTBREAD

INGREDIENTS

½ cup butter, room temperature

½ cup confectioners' sugar, sifted

½ teaspoon vanilla

1 cup flour

2 tablespoons cornstarch

- In a large bowl, cream butter and sugar until fluffy. Stir in vanilla.

- In a small bowl, sift together flour and cornstarch. Add to butter mixture, using pastry blender or 2 knives to cut in until mixture is crumbly. Stir in nuts.

- Form dough into a ball, then roll between 2 sheets of plastic wrap to ¼-inch thickness.

- Cut into squares and place cookies onto ungreased baking sheet. Sprinkle with sugar, if desired.

- Bake on center rack in oven for 15 to 20 minutes, or until cookies just begin to turn golden. Do not overbake.

- Set cookie sheet on wire rack to cool.

Temperature: 325°

Time: 15 to 20 minutes

2 dozen

¼ cup finely chopped macadamia nuts

¼ cup sugar, optional

LOTS O' CHOCOLATE DROPS

- In a large bowl, cream sugar, butter, chocolate, eggs and vanilla until smooth.

- In a medium bowl, combine flour, baking soda and salt.

- Add dry ingredients alternately with milk to the creamed mixture. Stir in walnuts.

- Drop by teaspoonful onto ungreased baking sheet. Bake for 12 to 15 minutes.

- Frost while warm with icing made by blending cocoa and butter until smooth. Beat in 2 tablespoons milk, vanilla, salt and confectioners' sugar. Add additional milk, if needed to achieve a spreadable icing.

Temperature: 350°

Time: 12 to 15 minutes

3 to 4 dozen

INGREDIENTS

1 cup brown sugar

½ cup butter

3 ounces unsweetened chocolate, melted

2 eggs

½ teaspoon vanilla

1⅔ cups flour

½ teaspoon baking soda

¼ teaspoon salt

½ cup milk

1 cup chopped walnuts

CHOCOLATE ICING

¼ cup cocoa

2 tablespoons butter, melted

2 to 4 tablespoons milk

1 teaspoon vanilla

⅛ teaspoon salt

1½ cups sifted confectioners' sugar

INGREDIENTS

1 cup butter or margarine

1 scant cup corn or vegetable oil

1 cup sugar

1 cup confectioners' sugar

2 eggs

1 teaspoon vanilla

4 cups flour

1 teaspoon baking soda

1 teaspoon salt

1 teaspoon cream of tartar

Walnut halves (about 48)

Confectioners' sugar

Melt-in-Your-Mouth Walnut Cookies

- In a large bowl, cream together butter, oil, and sugars.

- Add all other ingredients, except walnuts and additional confectioners' sugar, mixing well.

- Refrigerate dough at least one hour or overnight.

- Form dough into ¾-inch diameter balls and arrange on well-oiled baking sheet. Press a walnut half into each cookie.

- Bake for 10 to 13 minutes until golden brown.

- Sprinkle cookies with confectioners' sugar. Best served warm.

Temperature: 350°

Time: 10 to 13 minutes

3 to 4 dozen

INGREDIENTS

2 cups flour

1 cup butter or margarine, softened

1 egg yolk

¾ cup sour cream

Nut Horn Crescents

- In a large bowl, mix flour and butter.

- Add egg yolk and sour cream, mixing well.

- Cover and refrigerate dough overnight.

- Next day, combine filling ingredients. Divide dough into 4 balls.

- Roll one at a time, on a floured board to ⅛-inch thickness. Sprinkle each with ¼ of the nut filling.

- Cut each circle into 12 wedges.

- Roll crescents from wide end toward point and place, point down, on well-oiled baking sheet.
- Bake for 15 to 20 minutes until golden brown.
- These cookies must be refrigerated.

Temperature: 375°
Time: 15 to 20 minutes
4 dozen

FILLING

½ cup sugar

½ to 1 teaspoon cinnamon

½ cup walnuts, finely chopped

NANA'S SUGAR COOKIES

THIS RECIPE IS FROM A 1910 RIT
HOME ECONOMICS GRADUATE!

- In a large bowl, cream butter and sugar until fluffy. Add egg and milk, mixing well.
- In a medium bowl, sift flour, salt, baking soda and nutmeg. Combine dry ingredients with butter mixture.
- Drop by tablespoonfuls onto an ungreased baking sheet, spacing cookies 2-inches apart.
- Bake for 8 to 10 minutes, or until golden brown.
- Sprinkle with sugar while still warm.

Temperature: 350°
Time: 8 to 10 minutes
2 dozen

INGREDIENTS

¼ cup butter or margarine

1 cup sugar

1 egg, slightly beaten

½ cup buttermilk or sour cream

2 heaping cups flour

Dash of salt

¾ teaspoon baking soda

1 teaspoon nutmeg

Sugar

 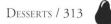

ORANGE BRANDY CHEWS

INGREDIENTS

¾ cup butter

½ cup sugar

¼ cup dark brown sugar

½ cup molasses

⅜ teaspoon ground ginger

¾ teaspoon grated orange rind

¾ teaspoon cinnamon

1½ cups flour

1 tablespoon brandy

- In a large saucepan over medium heat, melt butter.

- Immediately stir in sugars, molasses, ginger, orange rind and cinnamon. Reduce heat to low and simmer until sugars are dissolved, stirring frequently.

- Remove from heat and add flour. Mix well, using a wire whisk. Stir in brandy.

- Drop by tablespoonfuls, several inches apart, onto an ungreased baking sheet.

- Bake for 12 to 15 minutes or until golden brown. During baking, cookies will spread and become thin and crisp.

- Let stand for a minute before removing from baking sheet. Cool on a flat surface.

Temperature: 300°

Time: 12 to 15 minutes

2½ dozen

RASPBERRY CHOCOLATE SUPREMES

INGREDIENTS

1 cup flour

¼ cup confectioners' sugar

½ cup butter or margarine

½ cup raspberry jam or preserves

1 cup vanilla milk chips (4 ounces white chocolate)

- In medium bowl, combine flour and sugar. Using pastry blender, cut in butter until crumbly. Press mixture into an ungreased 9-inch square pan. Bake for 15 to 17 minutes, or until lightly browned.

- Spread jam evenly over baked crust.

- Melt vanilla chips or white chocolate and allow to cool slightly.

- In medium bowl, beat cream cheese and milk until smooth. Stir in melted vanilla chips and spread cheese mixture over jam, covering entire surface. Refrigerate until set.

- In a small saucepan, melt semi-sweet chocolate with shortening, stirring constantly. Gently spread over white chocolate layer. Cool completely. Cut into bars. Store in refrigerator.

Temperature: 375°
Time: 15 to 17 minutes
25 bars

1 package (3 ounces) cream cheese, softened

2 tablespoons milk

2 ounces semi-sweet chocolate, cut into pieces

1 tablespoon shortening

ROCKY ROAD BROWNIES

A SINFULLY RICH TREAT!

- In a large saucepan, combine chocolate and butter. Over low heat, stir until melted and smooth. Remove from heat.

- Beat in eggs, sugar and vanilla.

- Add flour, mixing well. Stir in nuts, if desired.

- Spread in well-oiled 9 x 13-inch pan and bake for 25 minutes. Be careful not to overbake.

- For frosting, cook butter and chocolate over low heat, stirring constantly, until mixture is smooth. Remove from heat.

- Add eggs, vanilla and confectioners' sugar. Beat until smooth.

- Stir in marshmallows and immediately spread frosting over brownies.

- Refrigerate overnight. Cut into bars. Keep leftovers refrigerated.

Temperature: 350°
Time: 25 minutes
40 brownies

INGREDIENTS

4 ounces unsweetened chocolate

1 cup butter or margarine

4 eggs

1¾ cups sugar

1 tablespoon vanilla

1 cup flour

½ to 1 cup chopped pecans or walnuts, optional

FROSTING

1 cup butter

4 ounces unsweetened chocolate

2 eggs

1 tablespoon vanilla

3¾ cups confectioners' sugar

4 cups miniature marshmallows

INGREDIENTS

48 3-inch pretzel rods

48 white chocolate melting wafers

48 yellow-colored candy-coated chocolates

"Bacon and Eggs"

THE GOURMET TASTE OF CHOCOLATE-COVERED PRETZELS!

- On a microwave safe plate, arrange parallel pairs of pretzel rods.

- Top each pair with 2 melting wafers, leaving a ½ inch space between the wafers.

- Microwave on High for 1 to 1½ minutes or until wafers begin to melt.

- Place an individual chocolate candy in the center of each wafer. Set aside to let harden.

2 dozen

INGREDIENTS

12 ounces semi-sweet chocolate chips

1 teaspoon peanut butter, smooth or crunchy

1 can (1 to 2 ounces) shoestring potatoes, broken up

½ cup chopped pecans

Chocolate Haystacks

KEEP KIDS OF ALL AGES GUESSING WHAT THE SECRET INGREDIENT IS!

- In a small saucepan over medium heat, melt chocolate chips with peanut butter, stirring frequently.

- Remove from heat and add shoestring potatoes and pecans.

- Drop the mixture by teaspoonful into lightly-oiled 9 x 13-inch pan. Refrigerate 2 to 3 hours.

2 to 2½ dozen

Fancy Fudge

THE PERFECT HOMEMADE HOSTESS GIFT.

- Line an 8 x 8-inch pan with foil or waxed paper.

- In saucepan over low heat, cook chocolate with milk and salt. When chocolate is melted, remove from heat.

- Stir in vanilla, nuts and cherries. Pour mixture into pan. Refrigerate 2 hours or until firm. Cut into small pieces.

5 dozen

INGREDIENTS

18 ounces semi-sweet chocolate chips

1 can (14 ounces) sweetened condensed milk

Pinch of salt

1½ teaspoons vanilla

1½ cups chopped walnuts

¼ cup chopped red candied cherries

¼ cup chopped green candied cherries

Sugar-and-Spice Nuts

A GIFT GIVER'S DREAM! GREAT FOR NIBBLES OR OVER ICE CREAM.

- In medium saucepan, cook sugar, salt, cinnamon and milk until mixture comes to boil, stirring constantly.

- Remove from heat and stir in vanilla and nuts.

- Spread mixture on baking sheets. Leave uncovered for at least 24 hours to dry. When most of the nuts are dry, remove and store in airtight containers.

3 cups

INGREDIENTS

1½ cups sugar

¾ teaspoon salt

1½ teaspoons cinnamon

½ cup evaporated milk

2 tablespoons vanilla

2 cups walnut halves

INGREDIENTS

*6 ounces semi-sweet
chocolate chips*

6 ounces milk chocolate chips

¼ cup heavy cream

*¼ cup liqueur (raspberry, orange
or Irish cream)*

4 dozen 1-inch foil candy cups

TRUFFLES
FOR YOUR VALENTINE

VARY THIS LAVISH TREAT WITH OTHER LIQUEURS

- In food processor fitted with steel blade, chop both chocolates until fine.

- In a small saucepan, cook cream and liqueur until mixture boils, stirring constantly.

- With processor running, pour hot cream mixture through feed tube. Process until chocolate is melted.

- Using a ladle or spoon, pour candy into foil cups. Refrigerate until set, about 30 minutes.

4 dozen

APPENDIX

FOLLOWING IS A COMPREHENSIVE LIST OF DELICIOUS,
BUT REASONABLY-PRICED WINES TO ENHANCE YOUR DINING EXPERIENCES.
SPECIFIC WINES WERE CHOSEN BECAUSE OF THEIR WIDESPEAD AVAILABILITY.
THE SYMBOL $ DENOTES MODERATELY-PRICED WINES,
WHILE $$ SUGGESTS WINES THAT ARE MORE SPECIAL.

WHITE WINES $

Glen Ellen Chardonnay (California)

M.G. Vallejo Chardonnay (California)

Napa Ridge Chardonnay (California)

Sebastiani Chardonnay (California)

Fetzer "Sundial" Chardonnay (California)

Monterey Classic Chardonnay (California)

Robert Mondavi "Woodbridge" Chardonnay (California)

Columbia Crest Chardonnay (Washington State)

Fetzer Sauvignon Blanc (California)

Groth Sauvignon Blanc (California)

Parducci Sauvignon Blanc (California)

Kenwood Sauvignon Blanc (California)

Robert Mondavi Sauvignon Blanc (California)

Macon Village by Joseph Drouhin (French Burgundy)

Macon Village by Debeouf (French Burgundy)

Patriarche Chardonnay (French Burgundy)

Chardonnay by "B & G" (French Burgundy)

Macon Lugny by Cave D'Lugny (French Burgundy)

St. Veran by Debeouf (French Burgundy)

Macon Village by Bouchard Pere & Fils
(French Burgundy)

Pinot Blanc (French Alsace) by Hugel or Trimbach or
William

Riesling (French Alsace)

Lacour Pavillon (Bordeaux, France)

Chateau Lauretan (Bordeaux, France)

Maitre D'Estournel (Bordeaux, France)

Chateau Timberlay (Bordeaux, France)

Mouton Cadet (Bordeaux, France)

Seppelt Chardonnay (Australia)

Lindeman Chardonnay (Australia)

Montrose Chardonnay (Australia)

Muscadet (Loire Valley, France)

Vouvray (Loire Valley, France)

Pinot Grigio (Italy)

Frascati (Italy)

Soave (Italy)

Orvietto (Italy)

Corvo (Italy)

J. Lohr Riesling (California)

Beringer Riesling (California)

Chateau St. Jean Riesling (California)

Rieslings form Germany: Kabinett or Spatleseo

Riesling wines from Alsace, France

Riesling by Widmer (New York State)

Riesling by Glenora (New York State)

Riesling by Dr. Frank (New York State)

Riesling by Heron Hill (New York State)

WHITE WINES $$

Kendall Jackson Chardonnay (California)

Beringer Chardonnay (California)

La Crema Chardonnay (California)

Callaway Chardonnay (California)

J. Lohr Chardonnay (California)

Parducci Chardonnay (California)

Sonoma Cutrer Chardonnay (California)

Wente Brothers Chardonnay (California)

William Hill Chardonnay (California)

Robert Mondavi Chardonnay (California)

Franciscan Chardonnay (California)

St. Francis Chardonnay (California)

St. Michelle Chardonnay (Washington State)

St. Veran by Louis Latour (French Burgundy)

St. Veran by Louis Jadot (French Burgundy)

Pouilly Fuisse by Debeouf (French Burgundy)

Pouilly Fuisse by Louis Latour (French Burgundy)

Bourgogne Blanc by Louis Latour (French Burgundy)

La Foret Chardonnay by Drouhin (French Burgundy)

Chardonnay by Louis Jadot (French Burgundy)

Chablis Domaine Maladiere (French Burgundy)

Sancerre (Loire Valley, France)

Gewürztraminer (Alsace, France)

White Graves from France

Wolf Blass Chardonnay (Australia)

Penfolds Chardonnay (Australia)

Brown Brothers Chardonnay (Australia)

RED WINES $

Bourgogne Rouge by Louis Latour (French Burgundy)

Beaujolais Villages by Bouchard, Dubeouf, Drouhin, Jadot, by Latour, etc. (French Burgundy)

Cotes Du Rhone (France)

Torres Coronas (Spain)

Marques De Caceras (Spain)

Jean Leon Cabernet Sauvignon (Spain)

Chianti Classico (Italy)

Bardolino (Italy)

Valpolicella (Italy)

Spanna (Italy)

Montepulcrana D'Abruzzo (Italy)

Dolcetto (Italy)

Barbera (Italy)

Corvo (Italy)

Salice Salentino (Italy)

La Vieille Ferme (France)

Mouton Cadet (French Bordeaux)

Lacour Pavillon (French Bordeaux)

Chateau Timberaly (French Bordeaux)

Chateau Greysac (French Bordeaux)

Chateau Larose Trintaudon (French Bordeaux)

Los Vascos Cabernet Sauvignon (Chile)

Santa Rita Cabernet Sauvignon (Chile)

St. Morillon Cabernet (Chile)

Walnet Crest Cabernet (Chile)

Undurraga Cabernet (Chile)

Penfolds Koonunga Hill Cabernet-Shiraz (Australia)

Jacobs Creek Cabernet (Australia)

Seppelt Cabernet (Australia)

Beaulieu Vineyard "Beautor" Cabernet Sauvignon (California)

Fetzer Cabernet Sauvignon (California)

Glen Ellen Cabernet Sauvignon (California)

Hawkcrest Cabernet Sauvignon (California)

Vallejo Cabernet Sauvignon (California)

Mondavi "Woodbridge" Cabernet Sauvignon (California)

Zinfandel by Seghesio (California)

Red Wines $$

La Foret Pinot Noir (French Burgundy)

Brouilly (French Beaujolais)

Fleurie (French Beaujolais)

Julienas (French Beaujolais)

Morgon (French Beaujolais)

Moulin A Vent (French Beaujolais)

Pinot Noir by Louis Jadot (French Burgundy)

Cote De Beaune (French Burgundy)

Cote De Nuits (French Burgundy)

French Chateaux from the Medoc or Haut-Medoc or St. Emilion Pomerol, or Graves

Chateauneuf Du Pape (French Cotes Du Rhone)

Robert Mondavi Pinot Noir (California)

Beaulieu Vineyard Rutherford Cabernet Sauvignon (California)

Franciscan Cabernet Sauvignon (California)

Parducci Cabernet Sauvignon (California)

Zinfandel from Ridge Vineyards (California)

Clos Du Boi Cabernet Sauvignon (California)

Vino Nobile De Monte Pulciano

Champagnes $

Saint Michelle (Washington State)

Tott's (California)

Cook's (California)

Sutter Home Sparkling White Zinfandel

Le Domaine (California)

Freixenet (Spain)

Codorniu (Spain)

Asti Spumante (Sweet Italian Sparkling)

Kriter (France)

Great Western (New York State)

Taylor (New York State)

Champagnes $$

Korbel (California)

Chateau St. Jean (California)

Charbaut Methode Champenoise (France)

Bouvet (France)

Henkell (Germany)

Domaine Chandon (California)

Domaine Mumm (California)

Piper Sonoma (California)

ACKNOWLEDGEMENTS

THE JUNIOR LEAGUE OF ROCHESTER DEDICATES THE SUCCESS OF FOR GOODNESS TASTE
TO THE MEMBERS, FAMILIES AND FRIENDS WHO HAVE CONTRIBUTED RECIPES TO MAKE THIS BOOK
POSSIBLE. WE SINCERELY HOPE THAT NO ONE HAS BEEN INADVERTENTLY OMITTED.

Cheryl Abelson
Betty Ackerman
Judith Ackerman
Kathy Adler-Zimmer
Neal Albright
Nancy Alderman
Liz Aldridge
Susan Aldridge
James Alesi
Bonnie J. Allen
Fred Allen
Lee S. Allen
Sallie Allen
Kathleen Allison
Colleen S. Altavela
Jennifer P. Anderson
Judy A. Anibal
Jaime Porter Armstrong
Beth Aten
Ruth W. Bagg
Pamela Baker
Sandy Baker
Mary Ellen Ballard
Robbie Baltzer
Suzanne Barbee
Julia Barnum
Nancy Barrett
Richelle Beach
Ann D. Beckerman
Joyce Beckerman
Susan J. Beimler
J. Charmaine Bennett
Susan A. Bensman
Kathy Benson
John S. Bereman
Gretchen Berger
Kathy Berry
Nancy Bertino
Diane Betts
Susan Bickel

Gail Hutchison Biemiller
Ann M. Blauvelt
Lisa Bodensteiner
Marti Bowen
Leslie L. Brackett
Mary Lou Branch
Mary Jo Brandt
Paula Briggs
Carolyn A. Brigham
Elizabeth Brisbin
Nancy Brown
Lynne Brubaker
Jeanne Burgdorf
Stephen Burgdorf
Linda D. Burns
Linda W. Buttrill
Terry Butwid
Barbara Cain
Debbie Cain
Tobie Calkins
Mary Callaway
Sian G. Cameron
Nancy J. Cameros
Natalie Campbell
Patty Campbell
Florence Carrington
Jeanne V. Casares
Caroline Centner
Dorothy G. Centner
Elizabeth Chase
Cassandra Chomo
Victoria G. Clark
Charlotte Boyle Clune
Charlotte B. Cohen
Donna Cohen
Beryl O. Cole
Connie Colleran
Katie Colleran
Carol L. Confer
Mary Jo Coniglio

Loyola N. Connolly
Marie Connolly
Ruth M. Connor
Lucy W. Cook
Elizabeth Corrigan
Nella Z. Corryn
Margie Cowgill
Susan V. R. Crego
Charlotte Creighton
Ann Crerand
Chris Culp
Judith Curry
Mary Beth Curtin
Jane M. Dalba
Linda Wells Davey
Susan C. DeBlase
Elizabeth Young DeBruyne
Gill R. Dechario
Mary Q. De Ciantis
Linda C. Degan
Joyce Ann Deihl
Steven Dejoy
Stephany DeMetsenaere
Susan N. Denaro
Jeanne DesMarteau
James DiBella
Rose DiBella
Jean R. Dingerson
Beth Anne Dobrzynski
Judy Dollinger
Marilyn Dollinger
Linnea Donahower
Nicki Doolittle
Tex Doolittle
Nancy Dorschel
Laurene Douglas
Ellen Todd Drew
Nancy Duffus
Lisa Dunn
Bev Dyminski

Barbara B. Echter
Dorothy F. Echter
Marjorie O. Echter
Susan Eddy
Kathy Edelman
Donna Edelstein
Betty Edgerton
Robert Edgerton
Molly Efron
Phyllis Ehmann
Deborah Eisenberg
Anne C. Endler
Linda M. Enochson
Dorothy L. Evans
Martha Every
Candy Falk
Roberta E. Faloon
Virginia Farmer
Jane Fassett
Gayle Fehlmann
Dale G. Fennie
Marge Fergusson
Emilia Fierro
Malinda Berry Fischer
Toni Flaherty
Gerry Fleckenstein
Pamela T. Flynn
DeMille Foreman
Laureen Burke Forsythe
Regie Foster
Pamela T. Foye
Nancy Mott Frank
Sandra L. Frankel
Jan Fugler
Lillian Futran
Margaret M. Futran
Neal Futran
Nancy Gaden
Sarah Todd Gallagher
Jana Gandy

ACKNOWLEDGEMENTS CONTINUED

Libby Gandy
Rhonda Gardner
Ann S. Garrett
Lindsay Garrett
Anneliese Garver
Julia Garver
Nora Gates
Tania G. George
Joanne Gianniny
Mark Gianniny
Sandy Gianniny
Kandy Giblin
Peggi Godwin
Sherry Goldman
Sally R. Green
Gloria J. Griffin
Michele G. Griffin
Marian Gutowski
Denise Hadley
Pat Hainen
Joan Hallenbeck
Lynne Hambleton-Magee
Nancy S. Hammond
Alice S. Hanford
Jane R. Hanford
Ann C. Hanley
Suzanne Hanson
Norma Hardwick
Nancy Evans Hargrave
Louise B. Harris
Elizabeth Hart
Samantha Hayes
Larry Hayman
Diane Heald
Chris Heisman
Margaret W. Hellebush
Diane Henderson
Emily Henderson
Jeanne R. Henderson
Susan W. Henderson
Suzy Hengerer
Susan Herrman
Sabra Hickam
Janice Martin Hickey

Pamela E. Hill
Tanya B. Hill-Boyd
Kathleen Hoch
Margaret B. Hoffower
Audrey Lee Holmes
Mary Anne Hoppe
Patricia Hopwood
Christina Howard
Jane Crowley Howe
Ginger & Dick Howell
Paula S. Howk
Deena Banks Hucko
Mary Inkley
Deforest Inkley
Lois M. Inman
Karen E. Jensen
Betty Jepson
Mary Jo Jepson
Dorothy E. Johnson
Sandra Johnson
Christina Jones
Nancy Jones
V.E. Kapusta
Judith Karsten
Lynn Keegan
Beth H. Keigher
Michelle Requa Keller
Sharon Kelly
Abigail S. Kennedy
Nancy Kennedy
Patricia Kerper
Barbara Kerr
Marilyn S. Kessler
Liz Koch
Kirsten O. Koenig
Jack Koerner
Nancy Koris
Doey Kane Krachenko
Nancy Kratzert
Chris Kreutziger
Robyn Kunz
Susan Kusak
Amy Kutner
Hazel M. LaForte

Susan R. LaForte
Anne C. Lambert
Gail Landon
Donna Lauricella
Susan Lednar
Jody Lehr
Cheryl Leisner
Virginia E. Leonard
Amy Flatley Levine
Gail A. Lewis
Judy L. Lewis
Marilyn E. Lewis
Mary L. Lewis
Robert L. Lewis
Stephanie Lindner
Maryjane K. Link
Barb Lipari
Jane Littell
Donette Loehr
Laurie Long
Mary Ellen Lopata
Ann Love
Sandra P. Lovell
Barbara Lovenheim
Carol S. Lutterbein
Carol K. MacDonald
Beth Howe Madden
Cheri L. Magin
Susan Maher
Lucille M. Mahoney
Debra L. Maier
Anita Malone
Judy Malone
Barbara M. Manson
Sandra Mason
Cathy Maxwell
Judie Mayo
Hildy Mazur
Mary Liz McCahill
Monica M. McConville
Mary McCramer-Wojdylo
Linda L. McGarry
Judith McKelvey
Gayle S. Medill

Jeannie Mercurio
Lorraine Merrall
Karla Linn Merrifield-Smith
Caroll Meyers
Victoria Meyers
Betty Middleton
Peter Millick
Priscilla L. Minster
Cecily Molak
Nina Moore
Queen Moore
Sally S. Moore
Patsy Moran
Karen B. Morphy
Barbara Morris
Patricia Morris
Sue A. Moscato
Marilyn Mossien
Ann Mott
Carole J. Mulgrew
Mary Kay Mullin
Lynn Natapow
Susan Navarra
Marge Nelson
Anthony A. Nero
Suzanne W. Neumer
Lynda B. Newman
Diana Nielsen
Holly Nielsen
Kathleen Nojay
Linda Novak
Linda Obourn
Peter W. Odenbach
Sandra Odenbach
Diane Okel
L. Devens Osborne
Barbara Oski
Debra Osowski
Carol C. Panzer
Louise Paolino
Ann Parker
Pat Pascucci
Barbara Pasley
Betsy Patterson

ACKNOWLEDGEMENTS CONTINUED

Peggy Patterson
Linda Peglow
Susan Perkins
Susanne Perrone
Marsha Peskin
Devon Pfeif
Lynne Phelps
Joyce Poleshuck
Dianna Porter
Susan Powell
Cindy Pownall
Susan Prophet
Mary R. Quandt
Elinor W. Quinn
Judy Randall
Mary Recco
June Reeder
Mary Rees
Lucy Regna
Alison Reidy
Julie D. Reynolds
Gloria M. Ricco
Renee M. Ricco
Maryann Rinas
Susan W. Robbins
Cheryl Robinson
Marion Robinson
Margaret L. Roddy
Janet E. Rogers
Janice S. Rogers

Nancy M. Rubery
Jane Ruch
Jennifer Ruggeri
Jo Anne Clair St. John
Suzanne Salsbury
Carolyn H. Saum
Marilyn Schaefer
Frances Hubbard Schenck
June Schirmer
Christine Schlageter
David P. Schlageter
Diane Schneider
Lori Schott
Cathy Schramm
Kathryn Schuster
Katy Jacobson Serr
Nan Sharp
Lucia H. Shaw
Joann Sicilla
Christine Simonson
Elizabeth Skic
Alice K. Smith
Florence C. Smith
Anne Sorensen
Susan Sotendahl
Suzanne Spencer
Patricia W. St. Clair
Cathy Steffen
Jane W. Steinhausen
June Clair Stephens

Carole Stepinski
Laura N. Stern
Dorothy Sterner
Jane K. Stevens
Natalie B. Stewart
Gayle Stiles
Mary Ann Stone
Isabel M. Stoutenburg
Lisa M. Strasenburgh
Carol Sweeney
Sarah Sweeney
Laura A. Swett
Brenda B. Tartaglia
Patricia Taylor
Abbe A. Tegzes
Sally Thomas
Nancy Thompson
Sherry Timms
Nancy J. Tonucci
Nancy J. Tosch
Anne C. Townsend
Pamela Turnbloom
Hether Turner
Sally Turner
Joyce W. Underberg
Patricia Utz
Lori Van Dusen
Elizabeth Van Ranst
Sue van der Stricht
Anne Vilas

Judy von Bucher
Judy Waldert
Catherine S. Ward
Sally Ward
Lois I. Watts
J.M. Webber
Wanda G. Webster
Kathryn P. Weider
Margot Weismiller
Beverly West
Elizabeth White
Barbara Whitney
Dana Widmer-Quiel
Edna C. Wilcher
Helen Williams
Debbie S. Willsea
Macie Willsea
Roberta L. Winner
Ellen K. Wheeler Winter
Steve Wirth
Georgia Woodring
Sarah Woodward
Arlene A. Wright
Carol B. Wright
Eileen Y. Wright
Gertrude Yager
Carmen M. Yargeau
Anne S. Young

THE JUNIOR LEAGUE OF ROCHESTER WISHES TO ACKNOWLEDGE
THOSE WHO HAVE GENEROUSLY SUPPORTED THE CREATION OF FOR GOODNESS TASTE.

Adele Kent, The Marble Room
Businessland, Inc.
Classic Travel
Cooks World
Creme de la Creme
Diana Leach, Longaberger
  Baskets
Digital Image & Sound Corp.
East Avenue Gift Shop
Elmwood Inn
Food in Concert

Genesee Country Museum
Habersham
The Harro East Appearance
  Center
Howard Kaplan Associates
Las Vegas Discount Golf and
  Tennis
Lock, Stock & Barrel
Marcie Ver Ploeg
Mary Mary

Mary Mullard Young
Onnie's Closet
Our Front Porch
The Paper Store
Parkleigh
Pierce Brown Associates, Inc.
Polliwogs & Pigtails
Remingtons
Seasonal Kitchen
Shadow Lake

Sherwood I. Deutsch, Century
  Liquor and Wine
Silo
Stanley's Flowers
Table Toppers of Rochester
The Stouffer Rochester Plaza
  Hotel
Tucker Printers
Village Green
Water Street Grill

INDEX

A Peach of a Blueberry Pie / 264
A+ Apricots / 126
Addicting Munchies / 30
Adirondack Chicken Salad / 73
Alcoholic Beverages
for complete listing see page 20
Almond Dreams / 300
Almonds
    Graham Glories / 309
    Lebanese Nut Cookies / 296
Aloha Pie / 263
Angel Biscuits / 110
Antipasto Medley / 76
Appetizers
for complete listing see page 20
Apple-Kraut Pork Chops / 186
Apple-Mince Torte / 274
Apples
    Baked Apple Pecan Pancake / 122
    Cinnamon Apple Treasures / 99
    Clubhouse Chicken Salad / 74
    Country Cinnamon Chicken / 214
    Fresh Apple Cake / 289
    Glazed Apple Cookies / 299
    Harvest Soup with Brandy Cream / 55
    Medieval Apple Fritters / 107
    Plantation Deep Dish Apple
        Crunch / 262
    Winter Apple Pie / 263
Applesauce
    What's-the-Secret Salad / 91
Apres Ski Shrimp / 43
Apricot Daiquiri Blush / 47
Apricot Nut Bread / 103
Ariste Con Carne / 188
Arrivederci Veal / 197
Artichokes
    Artichokes Dijon / 32
    Broccoli and Artichoke Stir-Fry / 157
    Cheesy Blue Chicken / 216

    Dill Chicken and Artichokes / 219
    Elegant Artichoke Canapes / 33
    Spinach-Artichoke Bake / 161
Artichokes Dijon / 32
Asparagus
    Baked Asparagus / 149
    Ham Asparagus Tetrazzini / 188
    Vegetable Vinaigrette / 90
Asparagus Napoli / 150
Babe Ruth Bars / 300
Back Country Cookout / 190
Bacon
    Breakfast Extraordinaire / 115
    Creamy Bacon Combo / 25
    Eggs in Bacon Baskets / 116
    Pasta Carbonara / 139
Bacon and Eggs / 316
Bacon-Cheese Toasties / 33
Baked Aloha / 127
Baked Apple Pecan Pancake / 122
Baked Asparagus / 149
Baked in a Pie / 185
Baked Steak / 179
Baker's Choice Carrot Cake / 278
Banana Blueberry Bread / 100
Basil
    Grilled Zucchini with Basil
        Butter / 147
Batter Up French Toast / 123
Beans
    Couscous Marrakesh / 81
    Potluck Beans / 170
    Sweet and Sour Beans / 169
Beef
for complete listing see page 178
    Hearty Sicilian Soup / 68
    Potluck Beans / 170
    Roast Beef Nicoise / 77
    Tavern Beef Soup / 66
Beijing Beef / 182

Bella's Special Chicken / 214
Berried Chicken / 212
Berry Wassail / 52
Beverages
for complete listing see page 20
Biscuits
for complete listing see page 98
    Chicken with Sage Biscuits / 218
Bistro Tomato Soup / 64
Black Tie Chicken / 212
Blintz Souffle / 114
Blue Ribbon Chocolate Cake / 279
Blue Ribbon Pork Marinade / 206
Blueberries
    A Peach of a Blueberry Pie / 264
    Banana Blueberry Bread / 100
    English Blueberry Pudding / 256
    Freshest Blueberry Pie / 267
    Lemon Charlotte / 285
Blueberry Hill Muffins / 101
Bourbon Slush / 49
Brag About Brownies / 301
Brandy
    Apricot Daiquiri Blush / 47
    Open House Golden Punch / 49
Bread
for complete listing see page 98
Breakfast Extraordinaire / 115
Breakfast Pizza / 114
Bristol Mulled Wine / 52
Broccoli
    Baked in a Pie / 185
    Crispy Broccoli with Zesty Lime
        Dip / 29
    Fresh Cream of Broccoli Soup / 63
    Ham and Sauerkraut Puff / 116
    Sunny Broccoli Salad / 80
    Swiss Brunch / 120
Broccoli and Artichoke Stir-Fry / 157
Broccoli Forest / 156

Broccoli with Lemon Cream Sauce / 157
Brown-eyed Susans / 302
Brownies
   Brag About Brownies / 301
   Rocky Road Brownies / 315
Brussels Sprouts
   Les Petits Choux / 29
Bulgur Pilaf / 176
Butter Fingers / 303
Butterhorns / 109
Buttermilk Blue Dressing / 95
Butterscotch
   Caramel Delights / 302
Butterscotch Heavenly Delight / 253
Cabbage
   Carolina Coleslaw / 79
   Oktoberfest Rolt Kraut / 168
Cajun Cream of Tomato Soup / 57
Cakes
for complete listing see page 248
Candy
for complete listing see page 248
Caramel
see also Butterscotch
Caramel Delights / 302
Caramelized Carrots with Grand
    Marnier / 152
Carolina Coleslaw / 79
Carrot Cheddar Bake / 149
Carrot Ginger Melody / 152
Carrot Souffle / 153
Carrot Vichyssoise / 56
Carrots
   An Excuse to Eat Carrot Cake for
    Breakfast / 100
   Baker's Choice Carrot Cake / 278
   Caramelized Carrots with Grand
    Marnier / 152
   Hawaiian Bread / 102
Cashew Capers / 304
Casino Linguine / 133
Catch a Husband Squares / 305
Cauliflower Gratine / 153

Cauliflower
   Cheesy Cheddar Cauliflower Soup / 58
   Red, White and Green Salad / 81
Cauliflower Bon Vivant / 154
Caviar
   Elegant Caviar Pie / 22
Caviar Pate / 24
Celery
   Cottage Celery Soup / 58
Chalupa / 34
Cheese
   Bacon-Cheese Toasties / 33
   Black Tie Chicken / 212
   Buttermilk Blue Dressing / 95
   Creamy Bacon Combo / 25
   Devilicious Cheese / 24
   Herbed Brie en Croute / 34
   Linguine with Brie and Fresh Tomato
    Sauce / 133
   My Bleu Heaven Sauce / 208
   Say Cheese...Zucchini / 148
   Three Cheese Fettucini / 134
Cheese Royale / 23
Cheesecake
   Regal Cheesecake / 291
Cheesy Blue Chicken / 216
Cheesy Cheddar Cauliflower Soup / 58
Cherries
   Chocolate Intrigues / 306
Cherry Blossom Coffee Cake / 105
Cherry-Peach Flambe / 260
Chicken
   Adirondack Chicken Salad / 73
   Party Poulet / 21
   Pizza with Pizzazz / 142
   Rochester Wings / 39
   Tomato Chicken Enchiladas / 143
   Vineyard Chicken Salad / 74
   Wonton Chicken Salad / 76
   Clubhouse Chicken Salad / 74
   Summer Night Chicken Salad / 75
Chicken French / 216
Chicken Italiano / 211
Chicken Nips / 35

Chicken Salad Oriental / 72
Chicken Tarragon / 215
Chicken with Endive / 217
Chicken with Pecan Stuffing / 213
Chicken with Sage Biscuits / 218
Chinese Sweet Sesames / 306
Chinois Chicken / 220
Chocaroon Pie / 264
Chocolate
   Babe Ruth Bars / 300
   Bacon and Eggs / 316
   Blue Ribbon Chocolate Cake / 279
   Brag About Brownies / 301
   Brown-eyed Susans / 302
   Butter Fingers / 303
   Caramel Delights / 302
   Catch a Husband Squares / 305
   Chocaroon Pie / 264
   Fancy Fudge / 317
   Gateau au Chocolate / 286
   Lots o' Chocolate Drops / 311
   Mint Chocolate Mousse Cake / 283
   P. B. O. Colossals / 296
   Par Excellence / 254
   PBIF Pie / 271
   Pots de Creme Parisienne / 254
   Raspberry Chocolate Supremes / 314
   Rocky Road Brownies / 315
   The Chocolate Chill / 258
   Truffles for Your Valentine / 318
   Whimsy Cakes / 290
   Whirligigs / 310
   No Stress Chocolate Souffle / 252
   Sumptuous Chocolate Mousse / 251
Chocolate Chippies Deluxe / 307
Chocolate Haystacks / 316
Chocolate Intrigues / 306
Chocolate Mirror / 280
Chocolate Raspberry Torte / 281
Chocolate Rum Torte / 282
Chocolate Velvet Pie / 266
Cinnamon Apple Treasures / 99
Cinnamon Sensations / 104
Citrus Dressing / 93

Clams
for complete listing see page 230
    Casino Linguine / 133
Clams Rock / 41
Clubhouse Chicken Salad / 74

Coconut
    Chinese Sweet Sesames / 306
    Chocaroon Pie / 264
    French Coconut-Battered Shrimp / 42
    Grand Finale / 252
    Island Pie / 270
Company's Coming Potatoes / 171
Confetti Pasta / 131
Consomme Rice / 175

Cookies
for complete listing see page 248

Corn
    Back Country Cookout / 190
    Fiesta Corn Flan / 158
    Winter Sunshine Salad / 89
Cornish Hens with Purple Plum
    Sauce / 222
Cottage Celery Soup / 58
Country Cinnamon Chicken / 214
Couscous Marrakesh / 81
Coye Point Salad / 80

Crab
for complete listing see page 230
    Polynesian Crabmeat Bites / 39

Cranberry
    Fruity Cranberry Relish / 95
Cranberry Bow Daiquiri / 48
Cranberry Molded Salad / 91
Cream of Vidalia Onion Soup / 61
Creamsicle Pie / 265
Creamy Bacon Combo / 25
Creamy Mustard Dressing / 94
Creamy Salmon Soup / 64
Creamy Tarragon Dressing / 92
Creole Shrimp Bake / 243
Crispy Broccoli with Zesty Lime Dip / 29
Crunchy Calico Peas / 159
Crunchy Cracked Wheat Bread / 112

Currants
    Old-Fashioned Currant Tarts / 273
Curried Tomato Bisque / 60
Date Nut Crunchies / 298

Dates
    Catch a Husband Squares / 305
    Holiday Jewels / 298

Desserts
for complete listing see page 248
Devilicious Cheese / 24
Dijon Baked Tomatoes / 163
Dill Chicken and Artichokes / 219
Dilly Dijon Sauce / 203

Dips and Spreads
for complete listing see page 20
Double Encore / 284
Dramatic Crown Roast / 189

Dressings
for complete listing see page 70
Dynamite Cocktail Sauce / 203
Eastman House Rolls / 110
Egg Nog Pie / 266

Eggplant
    Hunan Eggplant / 154

Eggs
for complete listing see page 98
    Snowlight Eggnog / 50
Eggs in Bacon Baskets / 116
Elegant Artichoke Canapes / 33
Elegant Caviar Pie / 22
Elegant Wild Rice / 175
The Emperor's Wontons / 36

Enchiladas
for complete listing see page 130

Endive
    Chicken with Endive / 217
    Raspberry Endive Salad / 83
English Blueberry Pudding / 256
Estofado / 183
An Excuse to Eat Carrot Cake for
    Breakfast / 100
Family Swedish Rye / 113
Fancy Fudge / 317
Feather-Light Cheese Souffle / 117

Fennel Salad with Sesame Dressing / 88
Festival of Greens / 84
Fiesta Corn Flan / 158
Finger Lakes Grape Bread / 103
Firecracker Salsa / 27

Fish
for complete listing see page 230
Florentine Roll with Shrimp Sauce / 242
Foamy Sauce / 260
Foiled Scallops / 241
For Sardine Lovers Only / 45
Francoise's Seafood Sauce / 243
French Coconut-Battered Shrimp / 42

French Toast
for complete listing see page 98
French Toast Pockets / 124
Fresh Apple Cake / 289
Fresh Cream of Broccoli Soup / 63
Freshest Blueberry Pie / 267
Frosted Honeydew / 249
Frosted Strawberry Squares / 261
Frozen Toffee Surprise / 251

Fruit
    Double Encore / 284
    Frosted Honeydew / 249
    Pavlova / 256
    Tally Ho Trifle / 255
    Velvet Fruit Dip / 28

Fruit Cake
    Holiday Jewels / 298
Fruit on a Cloud / 268
Fruity Cranberry Relish / 95
Garden Carbonara / 138

Garlic
    Gift of Garlic Pizza / 140
Gateau au Chocolate / 286
Gazpacho / 56
German Green Beans / 155
Gift of Garlic Pizza / 140
Glazed Apple Cookies / 299
Glazed Kielbasa / 38
Golden Autumn Timbales / 166
Gone-in-a-Flash Taco Dip / 26
Grab-bag Tortellini Salad / 71

Graham Glories / 309
Grand Finale / 252
Grapes
    Finger Lakes Grape Bread / 103
Greek Lamb / 202
Greek Tomato Salad / 85
Green Beans
    German Green Beans / 155
    Roast Beef Nicoise / 77
    Summer Night Chicken Salad / 75
    Winter Sunshine Salad / 89
Gregoire's Favorite Chicken / 220
Grilled Beef Kabobs / 180
Grilled Foods
    Grilled Zucchini with Basil
        Butter / 147
    Infamous Patio Kabobs / 200
    Lake George Lamb / 198
    Lamb Chops with Fresh Rose-
        mary / 201
    Marinated Butterflied Leg of
        Lamb / 199
    Mustard Flank Steak / 180
    Patio Chicken / 219
    Seafood al Fresco / 237
    Skewered Swordfish / 233
    Spring Lamb / 198
    Summer Grilled Chicken / 224
    Zesty Grilled Swordfish / 244
Grilled Jumbo Shrimp / 244
Grilled Nantucket Swordfish / 231
Grilled Pesto Chicken / 226
Grilled Pork Tenderloin / 186
Grilled Zucchini with Basil Butter / 147
Hacienda Sauce / 207
"Hail, Caesar!" / 82
Ham
for complete listing see page 178
    Swiss Brunch / 120
Ham Asparagus Tetrazzini / 188
Ham Strudel / 118
Harvest Soup with Brandy Cream / 55
Hawaiian Bread / 102
Hazelnut Heaven Sundae / 257

Hazelnut Mushroom Bisque / 59
Hearty Sicilian Soup / 68
Hell-of-a-Halibut / 231
Herbed Brie en Croute / 34
Holiday Jewels / 298
Hot Fiesta Dip / 26
Hot Florentine Dip / 21
Hunan Eggplant / 154
Ice Cream
    Cherry-Peach Flambe / 260
    Creamsicle Pie / 265
    Frozen Toffee Surprise / 251
    PBIF Pie / 271
    Peach Melba Ice Cream Pie / 272
    Hazelnut Heaven Sundae / 257
Incredulada Enchilada / 144
Indonesian Spiced Beef / 184
Infamous Patio Kabobs / 200
Irish Soda Bread / 106
Irresistible Pisa Dip / 25
Island Pie / 270
Kabobs
    Grilled Beef Kabobs / 180
    Infamous Patio Kabobs / 200
    Seafood al Fresco / 237
    Skewered Swordfish / 233
    Spiedis / 192
Kennebunkport Lobster / 232
Kielbasa
    Glazed Kielbasa / 38
    Mom's Lentil Soup / 57
Korean Beef / 185
Lake George Lamb / 198
Lamb
for complete listing see page 178
Lamb Chops with Fresh Rosemary / 201
Lasagne
    Low Cholesterol Turkey Lasagne / 136
    Noodles Ontario / 135
Lasagne del Mar / 240
Lasagne Rollatine / 137
Lebanese Nut Cookies / 296
Lemon
    Sassy Lemon Curd / 259

Luscious Lemon Mousse / 250
Lemon Barbecue Marinade / 205
Lemon Bubble Bread / 108
Lemon Charlotte / 285
Lemon Refresher / 92
Lemon Sangria / 46
Lemon Tea Punch / 47
Lentil Antipasto / 79
Lentils
    Mom's Lentil Soup / 57
Les Petits Choux / 29
Lime Butter / 208
Limelight Pie / 268
Limes
    Crispy Broccoli with Zesty Lime
        Dip / 29
*Linguine with Brie and Fresh Tomato
    Sauce* / 133
Lo Mein / 190
Lots o' Chocolate Drops / 311
Low Cholesterol Turkey Lasagne / 136
Luscious Lemon Mousse / 250
Macadamia Shortbread / 310
Male Chauvinist Punch / 50
Mandarin Romaine / 82
Maple Walnut Cake / 276
Marinated Butterflied Leg of Lamb / 199
Marmalade Monte Cristo / 123
    Marvelous Mustard Mousse / 96
Matzo Kugel / 118
Meat
for complete listing see page 178
Medieval Apple Fritters / 107
*Melt In Your Mouth Walnut
    Cookies* / 312
Memorable Marinade / 204
Meringue
    Fruit on a Cloud / 268
    Mocha Cloud / 269
    Pavlova / 256
    Strawberry Starlights / 308
Mincemeat
    Apple-Mince Torte / 274
Mint Chocolate Mousse Cake / 283

Mocha Cloud / 269
Mocha Magic / 259
Mom's Lentil Soup / 57
Morning Glory Salad / 85
Most-Asked-For Onion Casserole / 165
Mousse
  Luscious Lemon Mousse / 250
  Marvelous Mustard Mousse / 96
  Mint Chocolate Mousse Cake / 283
  Pots de Creme Parisienne / 254
  Pumpkin Mousse / 249
  Sumptuous Chocolate Mousse / 251
  The Chocolate Chill / 258
Muddy Mushrooms / 159
Muffins
for complete listing see page 98
Mushroom Supreme / 160
Mushrooms
  Baked Steak / 179
  Hazelnut Mushroom Bisque / 59
  Muddy Mushrooms / 159
  Windemere Mushrooms / 38
Mussels
  Naples Mussels / 44
Mustard
  Artichokes Dijon / 32
  Bella's Special Chicken / 214
  Creamy Mustard Dressing / 94
  Dilly Dijon Sauce / 203
  Marvelous Mustard Mousse / 96
  Roast Veal Dijon / 195
  Tangy Dijon Dressing / 94
  Upper Crust Marinade / 205
  Poulet a la Moutarde / 223
Mustard Flank Steak / 180
Mustard Street Sauce / 206
My Bleu Heaven Sauce / 208
Nachos Supreme / 36
Nana's Sugar Cookies / 313
Naples Mussels / 44
No Stress Chocolate Souffle / 252
Noodles
see also pasta
Noodles Ontario / 135

Nut Horn Crescents / 312
Oatmeal
  Caramel Delights / 302
  P. B. O. Colossals / 296
  Quaker Cake / 277
  The Ultimate Toffee Cookie / 297
Oktoberfest Rolt Kraut / 168
Ol' South Gumbo / 238
Old-Fashioned Currant Tarts / 273
Onion Cheese Strata / 119
Onions
  Cream of Vidalia Onion Soup / 61
  Most-Asked-For Onion Casserole / 165
  Vidalia Tomato Bake / 164
Open House Golden Punch / 49
Orange Brandy Chews / 314
Orange Coq Au Vin / 221
Orange Noodle Pudding / 128
Orange Roughy with Tomato and
    Onion / 239
Orange Waffles / 125
Oranges
  Creamsicle Pie / 265
  Mandarin Romaine / 82
  Pots de Creme Parisienne / 254
  Sponge Cake with Orange Sauce / 288
  Taster's Choice Zucchini Bread / 104
Oysters
  Smoked Oyster Spread / 45
P. B. O. Colossals / 296
Pancakes
for complete listing see page 98
Par Excellence / 254
Park Avenue Punch / 48
Party Poulet / 21
Pasta
for complete listing see page 130
  Grab-bag Tortellini Salad / 71
  Ham Asparagus Tetrazzini / 188
  Lo Mein / 190
  Orange Noodle Pudding / 128
  Sausage Tortellini Soup / 62
  Seafood Saffron Linguine / 236
  Spicy Shrimp Pasta / 233

Pasta Carbonara / 139
Pasta Verde / 131
Patio Chicken / 219
Pavlova / 256
PBIF Pie / 271
Peachy Cream Pie / 272
Peach Melba Ice Cream Pie / 272
Peaches
  A Peach of a Blueberry Pie / 264
  Cherry-Peach Flambe / 260
  Spiced Peaches / 126
Peanut Butter
  Babe Ruth Bars / 300
  Brown-eyed Susans / 302
  P. B. O. Colossals / 296
  Par Excellence / 254
  PBIF Pie / 271
  Peanutties / 295
  Whirligigs / 310
Peanutties / 295
Pears Burgundy / 127
Peas
  Crunchy Calico Peas / 159
  Red, White and Green Salad / 81
  Winter Sunshine Salad / 89
Pecan Tassies / 294
Pecans
  Chicken with Pecan Stuffing / 213
Pepper Sausage Ragout / 191
Pepperoni
  Irresistible Pisa Dip / 25
Pesto
  Grilled Pesto Chicken / 226
Pesto Cheesecake / 22
Phyllo
  Black Tie Chicken / 212
  Ham Strudel / 118
Pie
for complete listing see page 248
Pineapple
  Aloha Pie / 263
  Baked Aloha / 127
  Hawaiian Bread / 102

Pizza
for complete listing see page 130
    Breakfast Pizza / 114
Pizza Primavera / 31
Pizza with Pizzazz / 142
*Plantation Deep Dish Apple
    Crunch / 262*
Polynesian Crabmeat Bites / 39
Pop-A-Cheese Stack / 32
Popeye's Spinach Salad / 78
Poppyseed Lemon Bread / 102
Pork
for complete listing see page 178
    Pork Loin Roast with Peach
    Sauce / 191
Pot Stickers / 37
Potatoes
for complete listing see page 146
    Company's Coming Potatoes / 171
    Roast Beef Nicoise / 77
    Roasted New Potatoes with Garlic and
    Rosemary / 172
    Saucy Scalloped Potatoes / 173
    "Seconds, Please" Hash Browns / 174
    Spring Potato Salad / 87
    Swiss Potato Soup / 67
Potatoes El Greco / 87
Potatoes Monterey / 172
Potluck Beans / 170
Pots de Creme Parisienne / 254
Poulet a la Moutarde / 223
Poultry
for complete listing see page 210
Prairie Sauce / 204
Pucker-Up Lemon Kisses / 294
Pumpkin
    Golden Autumn Timbales / 166
    Thanksgiving Cake / 275
Pumpkin Mousse / 249
Punch
for complete listing see page 20
Quaker Cake / 277
Quiche

Strasbourg Quiche / 121
Raisin Puffs / 293
Raisin Scones / 106
Raspberry Glace Pie / 262
Raspberries
    Berried Chicken / 212
    Chocolate Raspberry Torte / 281
    Luscious Lemon Mousse / 250
    Peach Melba Ice Cream Pie / 272
    Tally Ho Trifle / 255
    The Chocolate Chill / 258
Raspberry Chocolate Supremes / 314
Raspberry Creme Poulet / 224
Raspberry Endive Salad / 83
Red, White and Green Salad / 81
Regal Cheesecake / 291
Rice
for complete listing see page 146
    Clubhouse Chicken Salad / 74
    Consomme Rice / 175
    Elegant Wild Rice / 175
    Spinach Rice Crunch / 162
    Summer Rice Salad / 78
    Wild Rice with Pecans / 176
Roast Beef Nicoise / 77
Roast Rack of Lamb / 201
Roast Veal Dijon / 195
*Roasted New Potatoes with Garlic and
    Rosemary / 172*
Rochester Wings / 39
Rocky Road Brownies / 315
Rolls
for complete listing see page 98
Roquefort Soup / 60
Rum
    Berry Wassail / 52
    Cranberry Bow Daiquiri / 48
Salad Dressings
for complete listing see page 70
Salads
for complete listing see page 70
Salmon
    Creamy Salmon Soup / 64
Salmon Filet Amandine / 239

Salsa
    Firecracker Salsa / 27
Sardines
    For Sardine Lovers Only / 45
Sassy Lemon Curd / 259
Saturday Night Scallops / 241
Sauces
for complete listing see page 178
    Chocolate Rum Torte / 282
    Cornish Hens with Purple Plum
    Sauce / 222
    Foamy Sauce / 260
    Francoise's Seafood Sauce / 243
    Grilled Pesto Chicken / 226
    Hazelnut Heaven Sundae / 257
    Lemon Charlotte / 285
    Mocha Magic / 259
    Pork Loin Roast with Peach
    Sauce / 191
    Sassy Lemon Curd / 259
    Scallops Jezebel / 40
    Sponge Cake with Orange Sauce / 288
    Stuffed Filet of Beef / 181
Saucy Lamb Shanks / 202
Saucy Scalloped Potatoes / 173
Sauerkraut
    Apple-Kraut Pork Chops / 186
    Ham and Sauerkraut Puff / 116
Sausage
    Back Country Cookout / 190
Sausage Tortellini Soup / 62
Say Cheese...Zucchini / 148
Scallop Chowder / 62
Scallops
for complete listing see page 230
    Seafarer's Pantry / 65
Scallops Jezebel / 40
Scones
    Raisin Scones / 106
Seafarer's Pantry / 65
Seafood
for complete listing see page 230
Seafood al Fresco / 237
Seafood Saffron Linguine / 236

Second Helping Tea / 51
"Seconds, Please" Hash Browns / 174
Sensational Scallop Saute / 236
   Sesame Linguine / 132
Sherbet
   Creamsicle Pie / 265
   Frosted Honeydew / 249
Shrimp
for complete listing see page 230
   Apres Ski Shrimp / 43
   Back Country Cookout / 190
   French Coconut-Battered Shrimp / 42
   Seafarer's Pantry / 65
   Spicy Baked Shrimp / 42
   True Cajun Jambalaya / 187
   Yum's the Word Chicken / 225
Shrimp Casserole / 235
Shrimp Curry / 235
Shrimp in Dill Cream / 40
Shrimp in Velvet Sauce / 245
Shrimp Orleans / 41
Shrimp Salad with Raspberry Dressing / 72
Skewered Swordfish / 233
Slim Chicken / 228
Sloppy Joe Dip / 27
Smoked Oyster Spread / 45
Snow Pea Stir-Fry / 150
Snowlight Eggnog / 50
Souffle
   Blintz Souffle / 114
   Carrot Souffle / 153
   Feather-Light Cheese Souffle / 117
   No Stress Chocolate Souffle / 252
Soups
for complete listing see page 54
Sour Cream Pancakes / 124
South-of-the-Border Enchiladas / 142
Spiced Peaches / 126
Spiced Yogurt Pound Cake / 275
Spicy Baked Shrimp / 42
Spicy Shrimp Pasta / 233
Spiedis / 192
Spinach

Coye Point Salad / 80
Florentine Roll with Shrimp
   Sauce / 242
Hot Florentine Dip / 21
Popeye's Spinach Salad / 78
Superlative Spinach Salad / 86
Veal Bolognese / 196
Spinach Rice Crunch / 162
Spinach-Artichoke Bake / 161
Sponge Cake with Orange Sauce / 288
Spring Lamb / 198
Spring Potato Salad / 87
Squash
see also Zucchini
   Golden Autumn Timbales / 166
   Harvest Soup with Brandy Cream / 55
   Thyme for Butternut Squash / 167
Strasbourg Quiche / 121
Strawberries
   Frosted Strawberry Squares / 261
Strawberry Creme / 128
Strawberry Ginger Bliss / 290
Strawberry Starlights / 308
Stuffed Filet of Beef / 181
Sugar and Spiced Nuts / 317
Summer Grilled Chicken / 224
Summer Night Chicken Salad / 75
Summer Rice Salad / 78
Summer Sunset Pasta / 132
Sumptuous Chocolate Mousse / 251
Sun-sational Slush / 51
Sunday Night Frittata / 120
Sunny Broccoli Salad / 80
Superlative Spinach Salad / 86
Swedish Tosca Cake / 287
Sweet and Sour Beans / 169
Sweet Potato Medley / 174
Swiss Brunch / 120
Swiss Potato Soup / 67
Swordfish
for complete listing see page 230
Szechwan Beef Marinade / 207
Taj Mahal Chicken / 227
Tally Ho Trifle / 255

Tangy Dijon Dressing / 94
Taster's Choice Zucchini Bread / 104
Tavern Beef Soup / 66
Tea
   Lemon Tea Punch / 47
   Second Helping Tea / 51
Tex's Bloody Mary Mix / 46
Thanksgiving Cake / 275
The Chocolate Chill / 258
The Ultimate Toffee Cookie / 297
Three Cheese Fettucini / 134
Thyme for Butternut Squash / 167
Toffee
   Butterscotch Heavenly Delight / 253
   Frozen Toffee Surprise / 251
   The Ultimate Toffee Cookie / 297
Tomato Chicken Enchiladas / 143
Tomatoes
   Bistro Tomato Soup / 64
   Cajun Cream of Tomato Soup / 57
   Chicken Italiano / 211
   Curried Tomato Bisque / 60
   Dijon Baked Tomatoes / 163
   Firecracker Salsa / 27
   Greek Tomato Salad / 85
   Grilled Pesto Chicken / 226
   Linguine with Brie and Fresh Tomato
      Sauce / 133
   Summer Sunset Pasta / 132
   Vegetable Vinaigrette / 90
   Vidalia Tomato Bake / 164
Tomatoes Stuffed with Dilled
   Vegetables / 163
Tortilla Tucks / 30
True Cajun Jambalaya / 187
Truffles for Your Valentine / 318
Tzimmes / 168
Upper Crust Marinade / 205
Veal
for complete listing see page 178
Veal Bolognese / 196
Veal Forestiere / 195
Veal Pistachio / 194
Veal Tarragon / 193

Vegetable Stuffed Flounder / 234
Vegetable Vinaigrette / 90
Vegetables
for complete listing see page 146
   Artichokes Dijon / 32
   Garden Carbonara / 138
   Pizza Primavera / 31
   Sunday Night Frittata / 120
   Vegetables Marinara / 169
Velvet Fruit Dip / 28
Vermont Salad Dressing / 93
Vidalia Tomato Bake / 164
Vineyard Chicken Salad / 74
Vodka
   Sun-sational Slush / 51
   Tex's Bloody Mary Mix / 46
Walnuts
   Fancy Fudge / 317
   Maple Walnut Cake / 276
   Melt In Your Mouth Walnut
      Cookies / 312
   Nut Horn Crescents / 312
   Sugar and Spiced Nuts / 317
   Wonderful Walnut Torte / 292
Wassail
   Berry Wassail / 52
What's-the-Secret Salad / 91
Whimsy Cakes / 290
Whirligigs / 310
Whiskey
   Male Chauvinist Punch / 50
   Park Avenue Punch / 48
   Snowlight Eggnog / 50
White Satin / 28
Wild Rice with Pecans / 176
Windemere Mushrooms / 38
Wines
for complete listing see page 319
   Arrivederci Veal / 197
   Bristol Mulled Wine / 52
   Chicken Tarragon / 215
   Estofado / 183
   Grilled Pork Tenderloin / 186
   Hazelnut Mushroom Bisque / 59

Lemon Sangria / 46
Memorable Marinade / 204
Open House Golden Punch / 49
Orange Coq Au Vin / 221
Pears Burgundy / 127
Pepper Sausage Ragout / 191
Poulet a la Moutarde / 223
Seafood Saffron Linguine / 236
Stuffed Filet of Beef / 181
Veal Bolognese / 196
Veal Pistachio / 194
Veal Tarragon / 193
Winter Apple Pie / 263
Winter Sunshine Salad / 89
Wonderful Walnut Torte / 292
Wonton Chicken Salad / 76
Wontons
   Pot Stickers / 37
   The Emperor's Wontons / 36
Yams
   Tzimmes / 168
Yes-You-Can-Grill Pizza / 141
Yogurt
   Peach Melba Ice Cream Pie / 272
   Spiced Yogurt Pound Cake / 275
   Summer Rice Salad / 78
   Taj Mahal Chicken / 227
Yum's the Word Chicken / 225
Zesty Grilled Swordfish / 244
Zesty Zucchini / 151
Zorba's Flaming Shrimp / 246
Zucchini
   Blue Ribbon Chocolate Cake / 279
   Grilled Zucchini with Basil
      Butter / 147
   Patio Chicken / 219
   Say Cheese...Zucchini / 148
   Taster's Choice Zucchini Bread / 104
   Zesty Zucchini / 151